T0380795

WHERE WILL YOU BE WHEN YOU GET WHERE YOU ARE GOING?

Make a Personal Theo-metric Assessment!

2nd Edition

Jesse W. Addison

WESTBOW
PRESS®
A DIVISION OF THOMAS NELSON
& ZONDERVAN

WestBow Press books may be ordered through booksellers or by contacting:

WestBow Press
A Division of Thomas Nelson & Zondervan
1663 Liberty Drive
Bloomington, IN 47403
www.westbowpress.com
844-714-3454

All Scripture quotations are from the ESV® Bible (The Holy Bible, English Standard Version®), copyright © 2001 by Crossway, a publishing ministry of Good News Publishers. Used by permission. All rights reserved.

ISBN: 978-1-6642-9796-8 (sc)
ISBN: 978-1-6642-9795-1 (e)

Library of Congress Control Number: 2023907351

Print information available on the last page.

WestBow Press rev. date: 7/26/2023

A Special Dedication

To the Spirit of God, our Lord, Jesus Christ, and God the Father as one, thank You for making me aware of You and for loving me, undeserving as I am—I believe in Jesus Christ.

To Judy, my departed loving wife of our youth—a gift from God and mother of my two wonderful daughters—it's no question God wanted you back.

To Jennifer, my oldest who is successfully leading the way through uncharted waters in life, I admire your claim of faith in the Lord in a very strong and spirited way.

To Jamie, my youngest who is successfully exceeding high expectations without your mother being there for you at very important times, I admire your faith and strength in the Lord.

To each of my grandchildren, may these words from Grandpa Bill help you understand and embrace God's Word, claim Jesus Christ as your Lord and Savior, and give you comfort that God's Spirit is leading you daily.

To Christi, my current loving wife—a former widow serving the Lord and others—your partnership and support in helping to bring this effort out of me is sincerely appreciated.

To anyone inclined to hear that "still small voice" of the Spirit of God leading you in your vocational endeavors and life's other myriad ways you spend your time on earth. May this little book help you act through God's grace to help you believe, abide, and obey Jesus daily in every way imaginable.

Context

The Lord is not slow to fulfill his promise as some count slowness, but is patient toward you, not wishing that any should perish, but that all should reach repentance. But the day of the Lord will come like a thief, and then the heavens will pass away with a roar, and the heavenly bodies will be burned up and dissolved, and the earth and the works that are done on it will be exposed.

Since all these things are thus to be dissolved, what sort of people ought you to be in lives of holiness and godliness, waiting for and hastening the coming of the day of God, because of which the heavens will be set on fire and dissolved, and the heavenly bodies will melt as they burn! But according to his promise we are waiting for new heavens and a new earth in which righteousness dwells.

Therefore, beloved, since you are waiting for these, be diligent to be found by him without spot or blemish, and at peace.

—2 Peter 3:9–14 (ESV)

Acknowledgments

Two people really jolted me into some of my deepest personal thoughts by their profound statements. And they probably would not even recognize that what they said had any deliberate or intentional impact on me specifically. I never knew them personally, but they triggered the most extensive Spirit-led exercise in mind-mapping in my life thus far, for which I am grateful. This book registers the outcome of that experience.

Dr. Ralph C. Hook,[1] a past educator and business dean at the University of Hawaii (Manoa Shidler College of Business), is one of these people. Dr. Hook presented a lay-ministry sermon at Kailua Methodist Church on Oahu in the early 1970s titled "The Seven Ports of Life." He stated in his sermon that there are only "seven ways to spend time in our lives." Dr. Hook's compelling sermon stuck with me in a profound way. I quickly learned that his "buckets" for our time gave me the key portals for organizing all my thoughts to better manage my time. After I lived through the turbulent 1960s, Dr. Hook's seven special buckets for time eventually helped me develop a useful matrix to continuously self-examine my personal goals and performance and ultimately discover where I will be when I get where I am going. I kindheartedly honor Dr. Hook by labeling his portals with a mnemonic called "FISHERS." As I remember Dr. Hook indicated, that we all share these little buckets of time during our life, but only one holds any of our thoughts, deeds, beliefs, and faith that will outlive us—spiritual. Dr. Hook's seven ports of life are discussed in the chapter headed "Dimension Three of Five-Portals of Earthly Time" showing how we use these distinctive little buckets of time.

Also, sometime in the early 1980s, the late and popular country comedian Jerry Clower[2] offered this profound question: "Where will you be when you get where you are going?" That poignant question has taken on a special personal meaning for me. Rev. Dr. Robert S. Owens, Jr., senior pastor of the First Presbyterian Church of Honolulu, Hawaii, first drew my attention to this question in 1988 when he presented a sermon titled by the same question. Pastor Bob's message that day had more to do with how to focus on your vocation than your job or profession. But, being a former full-time hospital chaplain, this question commanded my attention at a deeper and more pastoral level. This question also commanded enormous attention for every patient who showed a sincere interest.

Correspondingly, with these two exemplary impressions in mind as I visited with patients, I found I was more relaxed when I addressed two related critical pastoral care questions. Firstly, how comfortable is your soul with the Lord Jesus Christ? And secondly, how can I help strengthen your relationship with Him? During these discussions, I have come to appreciate that it is more important to question, "Where am I going?" rather than "Where did I come from?"

Although I have never personally met Dr. Hook or Mr. Clower, their statements have been with me throughout the construction of my own specific ideas regarding not only where I am but also where I will spend eternity. Certainly, we are all destined to encounter the Spirit of God prior to meeting

Jesus face to face (or Satan if we are condemned to hell). Surely, we will be given a choice to make before we leave earth. When I visited patients who are in doubt about eternity while they are being treated for potential terminal infirmities, I never had to wait too long for an opportunity to engage their souls about where they will be when they get where they are going, even when their dominant thoughts may question, "Why do bad things happen to good people?"[3]

Contents

Preface

This book presents a refreshingly different vision of systematic Christian apologetics and eschatology; it is filled with scriptural touchstones, gun-barrel-straight sound reasoning, and intuitive graphical illustrations. While personal "faith" continues unchallenged with a firm grip on all believers, this book is intended to help you gain either new faith or stronger faith. Therefore, I not only share with you my own walk of faith but also how I came to embrace an inescapable mathematical graphical vision I branded as a "Theo-metric" approach to salvation. It relates well to situations in pastoral care and chaplaincy, life in general, and the lost predicament of human souls.

I rely on 3-D metrics to combine verbal/audio and visual/graphical approaches to learning where the universal language of mathematics works nicely to make the connection instinctive. By adding two additional dimensions, I visually demonstrate the only pathway to salvation. These last two dimensions dictate where you will be when you get where you are going. These last two dimensions are also critical in representing and assessing our faith in Jesus Christ, here and now, and for eternity.

So, allow me to walk you through a step-by-step building process that enables you to easily follow the dynamic forces at work as you build your own personal model. As your model begins to take shape, the structure comes into focus much like an image unfolding on a canvas for an artist. When complete, you will probably spontaneously recognize the "structured approach" touchstone that I embrace to connect and relate to Jesus Christ as my Lord and Savior. I am confident you will find some of your very own familiar touchstones in your model too. While the Spirit of God and Scripture are my anchor, some of my other personal touchstones arose from my experience in flying, mathematics, data systems, accounting, auditing, and management.

Your reading will lead you to a decision point where you will be offered a choice to accept, believe, abide, obey, and claim Jesus Christ as your Lord and Savior and how your daily affirmation of your choice will profit you eternally. When you first read about what I depict as our "lifeline" flowing through the "tension area" common to all of our lives, visualize you are on one of those modern winding monorail roller coasters traveling on a track in and through a cube space. I must warn you that the rail splits into two separate paths inside the cube. Be ready, it may come early or late along your way.

Also, be prepared to spend time searching your deepest levels of thought about your personal journey in life. Indeed, if you sincerely do this, you will have to search your soul like you never have before. I never thought Boolean logic could be applied to making a decision for Christ yet using "if-then-else-and-or" reasoning and the absolute nature of "zeroes and ones" in our decisions, we can attain much more absolute meaning than I ever thought possible. Five high-level figures transform from one straight vertical line to the full-blown 3-D model including two additional dimensions," connection" and "relationship." The best part comes at the completion of the final 5-D array. Enjoy the ride but watch out for the split in the track. Let God's Grace guide you by your faith.

Grace abounds,
Bill Addison

Introduction

I am enthusiastic about this little book because when I regularly communicated spiritual matters with hospital patients using my graphical Theo-metric model, it fulfilled a need that I could easily affirm in their eyes as they begin to overcome some of their spiritual constraints and start to connect and relate with the eternal Church triumphant. Tears confirmed the understanding that I sought to help patients find. I attest to no finer euphoric feeling anywhere; I hope this little book helps you find or enhance that feeling too—that is my greatest hope and joy.

You are about to encounter a new analytical approach to a simple time-tested faith based Christian grip on personal salvation where all people have just one individual soul. Allow me to introduce you to your own Theo-metric mathematical graphical 3-D model that can help you make a personal assessment of your soul's destination among all the major tensions in your life proceeding from the start of your beating heart and beyond its earthly retirement. Table 1 identifies three steps you will need to successfully navigate on the critical path of your own Theo-metric model.

Theo-metrics Defined

In making a precisely defined personal Theo-metric assessment follow these three steps:

1. **Adhere to a set of properties of a *particular communication path*,**

2. **Construct a definite abstract of the notion of *distance in a metric space*, and**

3. **Measure the *dynamics acting on your soul* that are attributed to God, Satan, and temporal earthly occupancy relative to our decisions, activities, and performance.**

Table 1. Theo-metrics Defined

There is a battle going on for our souls between spirit and flesh. The divine and the Devil want to take eternal possession of our souls for eternity in heaven or hell. If you are afraid of this emerging threat, then pretend you are dead and then live that way. The battle is raging, assess how you are doing today!

> So Jesus again said to them, "Truly, truly, I say to you, I am the door of the sheep. All who came before me are thieves and robbers, but the sheep did not listen to them. I am the door. If anyone enters by me, he will be saved and will go in and out and find pasture. The thief comes only to steal and kill and destroy. I came that they may have life and have it abundantly. I am the good shepherd. The good shepherd lays down his life for the sheep." (John 10:7–11 ESV).

Like sheep, all of us have strayed from the righteous path and wandered into the wilderness where substantial risk and danger often results in failure and where we become lost and astray. We are all like sheep.

So, when performing pastoral care duties as a Chaplain, I sometimes feared leaving a patient's hospital room and failing to share sufficient strength for the enrichment of his or her soul. When I did fail, I could sense it by getting a hollow, empty feeling. It is a horrible feeling. Thus, I always strived to contact a patient's soul before I even entered the room. When I am invited to preach, I preach the same way on the way up to the mountaintop with the souls of fellow worshippers. When I pray, I also try to lift up other souls in the name of Jesus Christ.

Hence, the single greatest question we all have is not strife among ourselves; it is one that is greater than we are. It boils down to this question, "Do you believe He is who He says He is?" As John wrote in chapter 3 of his gospel about Nicodemus, the Pharisee, a member of the Jewish ruling council, when he came to visit Jesus at night, we find out that Nicodemus had similar concern. He said,

> "Rabbi, we know that you are a teacher come from God, for no one can do these signs that you do unless God is with him." Jesus answered him, "Truly, truly, I say to you, unless one is born again he cannot see the kingdom of God." Nicodemus said to him, "How can a man be born when he is old? Can he enter a second time into his mother's womb and be born?" Jesus answered, "Truly, truly, I say to you, unless one is born of water and the Spirit, he cannot enter the kingdom of God. That which is born of the flesh is flesh, and that which is born of the Spirit is spirit. Do not marvel that I said to you, 'You must be born again.' The wind blows where it wishes, and you hear its sound, but you do not know where it comes from or where it goes. So, it is with everyone who is born of the Spirit."

> Nicodemus said to him, "How can these things be?" Jesus answered him, "Are you the teacher of Israel and yet you do not understand these things? Truly, truly, I say to you, we speak of what we know, and bear witness to what we have seen, but you do not receive our testimony. If I have told you earthly things and you do not believe, how can you believe if I tell you heavenly things? No one has ascended into heaven except he who descended from heaven, the Son of Man. And as Moses lifted up the serpent in the wilderness, so must the Son of Man be lifted up, that whoever believes in him may have eternal life.

> For God so loved the world, that he gave his only Son, that whoever believes in him should not perish but have eternal life. For God did not send his Son into the world to condemn the world, but in order that the world might be saved through him. Whoever believes in him is not condemned, but whoever does not believe is condemned already, because he has not believed in the name of the only Son of God. And this is the judgment: the light has come into the world, and people loved the darkness rather than the light because their works were evil. For everyone who does wicked things hates the light and does not come to the light, lest his works should be exposed. But whoever does what is true comes to the light, so that it may be clearly seen that his works have been carried out in God (John 3:2–21 ESV).

Just like when the people who are now married were single, there is a point in time when we remember when we got married on a certain day. There is also a particular point in time when we graduate from high school, college, or graduate programs. There is also a point in time when we became born again. If you have no recollection of such a point in time when your guilty heart melted with remorse into the hands of Jesus and your tongue confessed that Jesus Christ is Lord, then cry out. You need a petition to God's Holy Spirit to come into your life right now. There is only a limited time to lament. This is because our lifeline is like a never-ending rope with a knot in the middle. The knot represents our life on earth. But a larger part of the rope leads to the knot, which stretches from before the foundation of the world when our names were chosen to be placed into the Lamb's Book of Life. An even larger part of the rope leads away from the knot but in two directions to "where we will be when we get where we are going." While we are living in the knot of life on this temporal earth, the most important thing we can do is to place all the remaining end of our rope in the hands of the Lord, Jesus Christ, before we get out of the knot. We do not want to see any of our rope get into the wrong hands once we are released from the bounds of our earthly knot. The soul that is committed to Christ walks with Him now and eternally. Become born again yesterday. Come to Jesus. "Because, if you confess with your mouth that Jesus is Lord and believe in your heart that God raised him from the dead, you will be saved." (Romans 10:9 ESV).

While I was driving to the hospital one day, I found myself having a discussion with an internal "still, small voice" while listening to the book of Jonah from a dramatized version of the Bible that I keep on a thumb drive in my car radio. I got to a point where I just stopped the car in the parking lot and turned everything off and just listened carefully to the internal voice from the Spirit of God. The resulting dialogue followed a familiar pattern of a strategic business plan (i.e., vision, mission, strategies, goals, objectives, milestones, measures, outputs, outcomes, qualities, etc.); however, it was bigger than a feeble physical and/or elusive emotional business plan. It existed at God's spiritual level. It was the kind of experience that gives you an electric tingle throughout your whole body, rendering you motionless while the hair stands up on the back of your neck. It was like what some would describe as the feeling before lightning strikes. The subsequent dialogue went like this (Table 2):

"Father, Lord, and Spirit (or a possibly an angelic messenger), I'm probably going to see twenty or more patients in that hospital in front of me today, and most suffer with severe illness. My own health condition with three stents and a pacemaker is consistent with some of those who I will see. Why are we suffering? Why is that? Why are we really?"

Bill, you know the answer to that. I am surprised at you saying that.

"Lord, I know that I have been down the Roman Road. I know the steps of salvation, and I know I've been born again because I love you and I hate sin. But I want to go further for myself and those souls who I see, to give them real comfort, strength, and genuine peace and some eternal sense of heavenly quality."

Okay, Bill, listen up! Here are forty topics and associated Scripture passages to think about very carefully:

1. **You know that God's predestined chosen elect were placed in the Lamb's Book of Life before the foundation of the world** (Matthew 7:13-14, 21; 25:24-34; Luke 10:20; John 17:24; Ephesians 1:4; Revelation 13:8, 13–17; 17:4-8).

2. **You know that God authorized the creation of all things through His Son, Jesus Christ, by and through the power of the Holy Spirit** (Genesis 1:26-31, 2:7, 3:8; John 1:1–5).

3. In God's creation, He also included angels along with humans. He gave you the name of three angels in His Word—Gabriel, Michael, and Lucifer—and there are many thousands more that are unnamed (Revelation 12:4-9; 13:8; Psalm 148:5).

4. Both humans and angels were given free will (to abide or not to abide), one of two critical operative elements in His overall master plan (Exodus 35:22, 29; Joshua 24:15; Proverbs 6:19; John 8:31–36).

5. As you know, Lucifer was the most powerful angel of all the angels, but he contended with God until he finally rebelled to overthrow God (Isaiah 14:12–15; Ezekiel 28:13–19).

6. Lucifer's greed and pride became so strong that God removed him and his followers from heaven (Isaiah 14:12–15; Ezekiel 28:13–19; Luke 10:18; 2 Peter 2:4; Revelation 12:4-9).

7. The conflict is not over. Lucifer has a new name—Satan! All of Satan's followers are no longer angels either. They are his devils for whom the gloom of utter darkness has been reserved forever (Genesis 3:14; Job 38:33; 1 Peter 5:8-9; 2 Peter 2:17; Jude 1:13).

8. God's *vision* is to restore His kingdom to perfection for all eternity through His free grace, the other component of the two critical operative elements in His overall master plan (Mark 12:28–34; Ephesian 2:8-9).

9. God's *mission* is to conquer all evil for all eternity by proclaiming the gospel to the ends of the world (Mark 13:10).

10. God's *strategy* is to work through His free grace and the free will of each soul, which dictates that you choose to follow Jesus to fish for the souls of men (Mark 1:17).

11. God's *goal* is that all souls will be saved because the time is fulfilled, and the kingdom of God is at hand. Repent and believe in the gospel (Mark 1:17; 1 Timothy 2:1-5).

12. God's *objective* is to make sure all souls have an opportunity to be saved. Remember, "Whoever does the will of God, he is my brother, and sister, and mother" (Mark 3:31–35).

13. God's *milestones* are saving one soul at a time (Mark 9:38–41).

14. God's *measures* are saved souls. Altar calls are real; they count regardless of where the moment occurs (Matthew 10:32).

15. God's *outputs* are achieved after a soul's salvation (John 15:6).

16. God's *outcomes* are His delivered saints (Mark 9:33–37; John 3:15–21).

17. God's *qualities* are recognized when believers arrive at the *bema seat* of Christ where the crowns of life are presented (Mark 9:41; Ephesians 6:8–9; Matthew 25:34).

18. God's joy will come when those whom He has chosen will be loyal and faithful to Him only, not like that untrustworthy Lucifer (Luke 16:10–11; Revelation 17:14).

19. **The humans God created could have lived in his garden forever. But they fell into Satan's trap, and they were tempted and ate the forbidden fruit** (Genesis 3:1–7).

20. **All was well in God's garden at creation until Lucifer, now Satan, slithered in as a snake and deceived the people into thinking that if they ate the forbidden fruit God commanded them not to eat, they, too, could be like God, knowing the difference between good and evil** (Genesis 3:8–13).

21. **The humans in God's garden allowed Satan to deceive them into using their free will to ignore God and to follow him. The resulting death, illness, and sin on earth is connected with God's need for assurance of total quality in His perfect restored kingdom** (Genesis 3:14–19).

22. **At that moment death and all of its causes entered into them and was destined to enter into each of their descendants, both male and female, and yet they and all others still have a free will to make by God's grace—to claim His Son and live with Him in paradise or reject and/or blaspheme Him and His Holy Spirit and die a torturous, unending death with Satan in hell for all eternity** (Genesis 3:20–24).

23. **So, God's vision is that His chosen who use their free will to seek Him and be near Him in heaven will remain true worshippers and glorify Him and Him only forever** (Psalm 54:6; Mark 12:28–34).

24. **Then God will be able to count on the loyalty of His chosen because He will know they want to be there by their love. He will not allow anything false or evil to enter into His perfect kingdom** (Luke 16:13; John 14:21–24; 21:15–17).

25. **Here is the ultimate measure God makes. Remember, by God's free grace both angels and men were given free will to choose to follow God or Lucifer** (Romans 5:17).

26. **If God's earthly human creatures use their free will to choose life everlasting through the grace He sent with His Son, Jesus Christ, they will stay in his Book of Life; however, if they choose eternal death through the blasphemy of His Holy Spirit, they will be erased from His Book of Life, and they will be sent to the lake of fire with Satan and his devils** (Romans 5:12–21).

27. **The souls that have been chosen as the elect were predestined before the foundation of the world when their names were placed into the Lamb's Book of Life, and they will be lifted up and glorified in rapture and go with Him to heaven and wait for the Father's command to return in total victory** (Matthew 24:30–36; 1 Thessalonians 4:13–18; 1 Peter 2–9; Revelation 17:14).

28. **The end time is near. The days are numbered, and they cannot be lengthened or shortened by a single tittle** (Job 14:5–7).

29. But not even death can shield God's love from His elect when they claim Jesus for their salvation. Before their days are through, they are assured of redemption. Judgment is now (2 Corinthians 6:2; John 3:16–21)!

30. Once victory is complete in the Lord Jesus Christ, God's perfect heaven, the New Jerusalem, will descend to a new earth purified by fire (Revelation 3:12; 2 Peter 3).

31. Then God may be assured that all who are present have exercised their free will to be there by God's free grace (Philemon 14).

32. Unlike Lucifer and his kind, the saints in God's paradise can be counted on to be ever faithful, ever true (1 Timothy 1:12; Revelation 2:25).

33. Consequently death, sickness, pain, suffering, along with many other calamities and sin began immediately following humankind succumbing to temptation. All became separated from God and need reconciliation (Genesis 3:20–24).

34. Nothing has changed even with God's flood delivered in the time of Noah and God's perfect laws given to Moses in the wilderness (Genesis 7:10; Genesis 17:1-27; Exodus 20:3–17).

35. Lovingly God sent His only Son to earth to bring hapless humankind salvation and eternal life by His grace through faith in Jesus Christ to each mortal (John 10:10; John 14:6; Ephesian 2:8-9).

36. Mankind continues to fail to obey God's laws and the greatest commandment issued by God's Son, Jesus Christ, and the Great Commission—to make disciples of all nations, baptizing them in the name of the Father and of the Son and of the Holy Spirit, teaching them to observe all that I have commanded you (Psalm 68:35; Matthew 22:36–40; 28:19–20; 2 Thessalonians 1:7–10).

37. Therefore, temptation, sin, and grief prevail on earth and will prevail until death, and sin is defeated at the sound of the last trumpet when Jesus Christ returns in all His glory (1 Corinthians 15:26; Revelation 21:2; 22:20).

38. He will not be alone. Those who are chosen to be caught up in the rapture and meet Him in the clouds will be with Him at the last battle on the earth—Armageddon (John 6:37, 39, 40; 1 Thessalonians 4:13–18; Jude 1:14-15).

39. God set forth in Christ as a plan for the fullness of time to unite all things in Him, things in heaven and things on earth according for His purpose and the mystery of His will (Ephesians 1:4–14; 2:1–10; 3:9–10).

40. Death will be the last enemy to be destroyed. His pure kingdom will be restored (1 Corinthians 15:26).

Table 2. God's Eternal Plan from Scriptures

So, tell every patient you meet that illness is not anything more than a symptom of their temporal life in a dying and decaying world that chose to be like Satan, who tried to become like God. Their illnesses and sins are indispensable apparatuses and essential components of God's strategic plan to purge His kingdom of all evil for all time.

I urge you to bring their focus on illness as a symptom of eternal death and encourage them to make their free choice for their salvation through God's Son, Jesus Christ, who overcame death on the cross for all of them forever. Encourage them to trust God's master plan and surrender any shred of pride and greed for a hopelessly decaying world. God must know He can trust them for a long, long time—for eternity. God's free grace and their free will to choose salvation through faith in God's Son, Jesus Christ, are essential for His plan to be perfectly consummated.

"Okay, I get it. I am to convey to them that it is all about God's free grace and our faith in Jesus Christ and it is our free choice to accept, believe, and confess that He is our only Lord and Savior. Thanks."

Right, now just go in there and go to work, Bill, and keep Figure 1 below in mind. Imagine that this may have been what Scripture says Jesus scribbled in the dirt at the attempted stoning of the adulterous woman.

God did not even spare His own Son but offered Him up for us all. How will He not also with Him grant us everything? Paul writes,

What then shall we say to these things? If God is for us, who can be against us? He who did not spare his own Son but gave him up for us all, how will he not also with him graciously give us all things? Who shall bring any charge against God's elect? It is God who justifies. Who is to condemn? Christ Jesus is the one who died—more than that, who was raised—who is at the right hand of God, who indeed is interceding for us. Who shall separate us from the love of Christ? Shall tribulation, or distress, or persecution, or famine, or nakedness, or danger, or sword? As it is written, "For your sake we are being killed all the day long; we are regarded as sheep to be slaughtered." No, in all these things we are more than conquerors through him who loved us. For I am sure that neither death nor life, nor angels nor rulers, nor things present nor things to come, nor powers, nor height nor depth, nor anything else in all creation, will be able to separate us from the love of God in Christ Jesus our Lord (Romans 8:31–39 ESV).

So, borrowing from the term *theodicy*, I concur that God's goodness and omnipotence must be viewed in the existence of evil for this age. That condition may be observed by using a comparison of creation to a big test track where we are the prototypes with many modifications pending. Take a lap around the circuit track in Figure 1 for illustrative purposes.

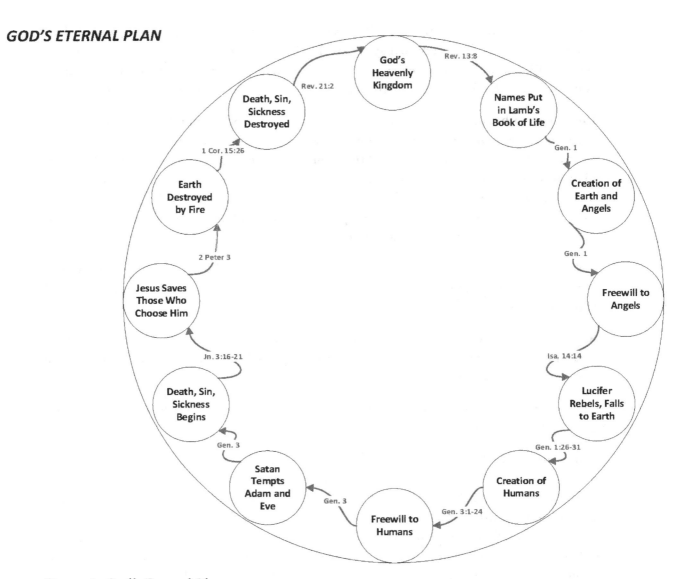

Figure 1. God's Eternal Plan

By beginning clockwise from the top of Figure 1, it appears that God's eternal plan must be: (1) to restore His perfectly pure kingdom through a strategy of delivering His amazing free grace to us by His Son, Jesus Christ, for our salvation; (2) to enable us through the power of the Holy Spirit to exercise our free will to believe Jesus is who He says He is; and (3) to do what He says. Correspondingly, when we get a *vision* like this on how to do something, it is then we can do it. So, my vision follows in 3-D mathematical graphic form for all of life's *good, bad,* and *ugly* components. But it also has two additional *connection* and *relationship* components for a total of five dimensions. Therefore, get a vision too. If my vision helps you, great. If not, get your own and kindly share it with me.

A Pastoral Prayer

Our heavenly Father, we know what Jesus did for us by dying on the cross. We know He is alive at this moment and sits at Your right hand in heaven. We believe that His blood was shed for the forgiveness of our sins. We confess that we are all sinners in a lost and helpless world. We cannot go to heaven by our own works no matter what we do. Through Your free grace, we put our faith in your Son, Jesus Christ, to take us across to the final side of our lifeline to Your perfect eternal kingdom. Help us to see more clearly the reality of our complete eternal lifeline with You. Open our eyes to the glory and honor of the life of service—the life of regeneration, justification, sanctification, glorification, and blessing. Focus our spiritual vision to help us know for certain where we will be when we get where we are going (by believing in Your Son, Jesus Christ). Open our hearts to the presence of Your Holy Spirit so that we can know You have called us to a life of obedience, and we are to share the good news with all. We yield our minds and our imaginations to an understanding of Your larger purpose and vision for our total lives and restoration of Your perfect kingdom. Help us to love, follow and obey Him, who came not to be served but to serve. Teach us to find our greatest joy in the way we make a life of faithfulness in Jesus Christ and give continuous thanks for what He did for us as our Savior by enabling us to be born again. We offer our prayer in the name of Jesus, who said, "But it shall not be so among you. But whoever would be great among you must be your servant, and whoever would be first among you must be slave of all. For even the Son of Man came not to be served but to serve, and to give his life as a ransom for many." (Mark 10:43–45 ESV). Amen.

This book presents a picture of what it is to be born again at a particular point in time. When I surrendered this earthly temporal world and claimed Jesus Christ for my salvation in God's perfect eternal kingdom, the circumstances were alarming, and although not fully developed at the time, it was fully regenerating. I am anxious for that day when I will be fully glorified; "What a day that will be!" Read the convicting and stirring words of the gospel hymn by that name composed by Jim Hill at the biographical link or elsewhere.[4]

What a Hospital Chaplain Really Hears

Here are some physical, emotional, and spiritual conditions that represent examples that patients bring to the hospital.

Overwhelming Physical Conditions

Upon visiting a man recovering from alcohol abuse for the sixth time after multiple unproductive rehabilitation programs, he stated he was suicidal. His father, who had been a close loved one, had died recently, and his mother had also passed away while he was in the hospital. These losses along with other physical infirmities left him hopeless and visibly despondent. After I listened for quite some time, I stated that as a volunteer chaplain, I promote holding on to a minimum of three foundations for hope in overcoming all dependencies—physical well-being, emotional stability, and spiritual assurance. I stated, "Like a good stack of pancakes, you should have at least three, but the spiritual pancake on top has all the good stuff like butter, syrup, fruit, powdered sugar, cinnamon, nuts and whipped cream." I asked about his top pancake. He said he did not have one. I said, "Do you want one?"

Tears immediately followed, which answered my question. I told him that although I had been a chaplain for quite some time, I was just a volunteer now, which meant I was dedicated to be here for him as well as others I meet. He asked, "How do you do that?"

I said, "I don't. The Spirit of God does that. I am just the carrier pigeon." I encourage you, and others I meet to open your heart to be receptive to the action by God's Spirit. I do what I do by letting you put all the pieces together yourself. As I shared with him a summary high-level overview of the contents in this book, he began to build for himself his own model, which I refer to as Theo-metrics.

I explained that Theo-metrics is nothing more than a mathematical graphical 3-D tool for making a self-appraisal for determining where you will be when you get where you are going. You get the assurance of peace for your physical (body), emotional (mind), and spiritual (soul) realms in the meantime.

At times like these, I often share with certain patients my thoughts on the term *theodicy*. It brings to light how our soul is the *prize* between God and Satan. Some tend to believe that our spirits or inner-selves have something to do with spiritual. Our spirits—high or low, inward or outward—are an emotional state of elation or depression. However, our soul is bigger than that simply because it goes on beyond us into eternity. It is an eternal possession in spiritual warfare. Our soul is either in Holy Communion with God, or it's not. It is not an emotional disposition of our outlook or state of mind. The soul is all about our love and permanent personal relationship with the Lord Jesus Christ. Don't let anybody serve you a short stack of pancakes. Demand a full serving and enjoy the good stuff with your pancakes.

In all levels of society, I get confirmation that our personas consist of three levels of being—physical (body), emotional (mind), and spiritual (soul). Only one will outlive the mortal body and mind. That is spiritual and that is where the soul resides. We all need three pancakes. If we are one pancake short of a full stack, then we suffer with a severe feeling of hollowness just like the feeling we get when we are starving. We need to seek another pancake when we need one. Exert full internal control.

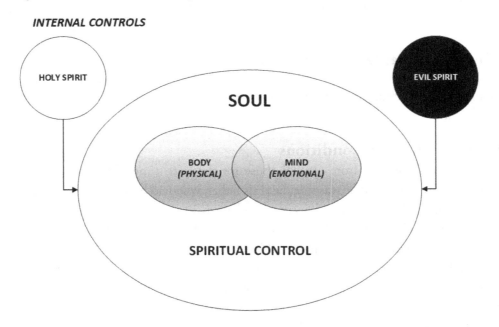

Figure 2. Internal Controls

As you proceed, pretend this is an instruction manual for assembling something. At some point I am confident you will get that "ah-ha" moment that this patient got. When the above patient arrived at that point, he said, "I needed another pancake! That is what is missing." We spent about an hour putting together a complete Theo-metric spiritual assessment for this patient. He now knows where he will be when he gets where he is going. He came to accept and love Jesus Christ as his Lord and Savior that day. He is now born again, and he gained a peace that surpasses all understanding. "And the peace of God, which surpasses all understanding, will guard your hearts and your minds in Christ Jesus." (Philippians 4:7 ESV).

Physicians can do some good for our physical needs, but they may not provide any relief for our emotional or spiritual well-being. If they do, it is probably an exception rather than the rule.

Psychologists or sociologists can do some good for our emotional needs, but they may not provide any relief for our physical or spiritual well-being. If they do, it is probably an exception rather than the rule.

Clergy can do some good for our spiritual needs, but they may not provide any relief for our physical or emotional well-being. If they do, it is probably an exception rather than the rule, even though I have witnessed numerous miraculous healings of patients that cannot be explained in human terms. Recall that John and Paul say the Spirit of God goes where the Spirit wants (John 3:8; 1 Corinthians 2:11)

Spiritual well-being has to come from outside our normal realm of physical and emotional paraphernalia and it has to come from God. All clergy can do is encourage us with ideas like those presented here to seek Jesus and pray for the Spirit of God to come into our lives. Then when it does, the spiritual "good stuff" melts and permeates deep down into our souls, and our entire stack of pancakes will be improved along with our physical and emotional well-being.

As you read further, you, too, will be able to build your own personal version of the Theo-metrics model and plot your personal location in the 3-D matrix. All the necessary components will be provided as you continue to read.

Overwhelming Emotional Conditions

During another visit with a middle-aged woman hospital patient, I heard far more about emotional issues and needs than I did about her current physical condition. Little was initially volunteered about her spiritual needs. As I listened, I learned that she really had more concern about the emotional things impacting her life than her illnesses. So when I heard about the emotional conditions at length, I asked if she was getting spiritual support from her church. Her answer revealed that she had not been attending church and that she did not consider herself a religious person. She explained that her husband of twenty-three years was mentally and physically abusive and that she stopped going to church because he got upset when she attended services. She stated that she also feared for her own safety and the safety of her children. I referred her to a case manager for support and encouraged her to find support from God's Spirit and His Word as well as through prayer and a church of her choice when appropriate. I asked her if she had a personal relationship with Jesus, and she stated that she did not know and that she could not understand how He could love her because of perceived low self-esteem resulting from living in an abusive environment. I reassured her that Jesus loves each of us and that He did not measure things valued by this world as we all are tempted to do. He loves us and ignores all that. He longs for a personal relationship with us more than anything else. Eye contact was instant, and tears of relief began to flow like a leaky faucet. I provided a tissue, and as she dried her eyes, I pulled a little diagram out of my Bible and told her, "I want to give you something that will last you for a lifetime, and it will give you strength if you allow it to work inside your mind and let it touch your heart and soul."

She said, "Okay." I then told her she needed to think of only one children's toy jack and its three axes while I handed her the below diagram on the three dimensions of life. It is fully described in greater depth in the following chapters.

ETERNAL MODEL

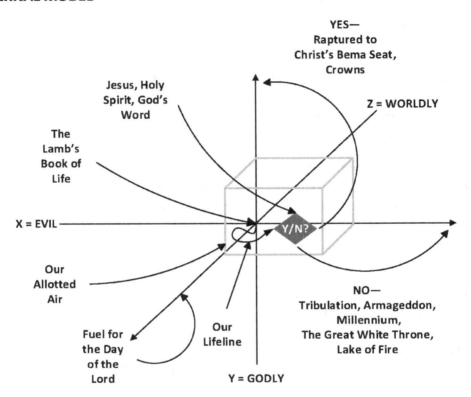

Figure 3. God's Eternal Model

As I waited for her to study the above figure, I asked her, "What is represented by the little curved line inside the cube titled 'Our Lifeline'?"

As she studied the little drawing, she spoke the words, "That's me!" and more tears started to flow.

I asked her, "How close do you think Jesus is now?"

She cried more tears, but this time they were tears of joy. She was ahead of me once she grasped the concept of her lifeline and her tension area on the little sheet of paper. I never caught up to her. She was born again! She finished my analogy for me and she kept the little sheet of paper for safekeeping inside the Bible I provided.

I included this patient's story in this book because it is my hope that you, too, will find a loving relationship with Jesus in your crooked little lifeline as it travels through your own tension area. I hope you will let the little figure and others to come safely lead you to "where you will be when you get where you are going." My prayer with this patient included thoughts and petitions that she would be able to feel the presence of Jesus for the rest of her life, claiming Him every day of her life here on earth and trusting Him to lead her safely home with Him. Where does your lifeline go? Please press on.

By the way, this simple model is also related to the controls in a cartesian 3-D diagram. These same mathematical controls can also be applied to our spiritual journey and help us get to where we want to be when we get to where we are going. No works are required, just receptiveness to God's free grace through the Spirit of God to love and desire a personal relationship with Christ Jesus. Nothing more is needed than just a wish to let Jesus intercede for us for all our sins. It all starts with a free will and the desire. In the last invitation in the Word of God, it says, "The Spirit and the Bride say, 'Come.' And let the one who hears say, 'Come.' And let the one who is thirsty come; let the one who desires take the water of life without price" (Revelation 22:17 ESV).

A wish is all it takes to make your lifeline turn back to God. He will be there to meet you when you do. We get to meet Him for nothing we *do* in life. The best example of a wish like this is as follows:

> One of the criminals who were hanged railed at him, saying, "Are you not the Christ? Save yourself and us!" But the other rebuked him, saying, "Do you not fear God, since you are under the same sentence of condemnation? And we indeed justly, for we are receiving the due reward of our deeds; but this man has done nothing wrong." And he said, "Jesus, remember me when you come into your kingdom." And he said to him, "Truly, I say to you, today you will be with me in Paradise." (Luke 23:39–43 ESV).

That criminal on the cross with Jesus was born again right there in public just as he approached the end of his mortal lifeline. He never paid his tithes, took the Lord's supper, was baptized, heard a church bell, or read the New Testament. He couldn't tell the difference between a bagpipe and a pipe organ or the difference between a cow bell and a church bell. He didn't have any interest in the color of the carpet or the size of the chandelier. He just *wished* to go with Jesus. And Jesus said, "Today you will be with me in paradise." His judgment was over. He made the right choice before his time on earth was over.

Jesus has a big flock. There is no way for the human mind to extend arms around it. "And I have other sheep that are not of this fold. I must bring them also, and they will listen to my voice. So there will be one flock, one shepherd" (John 10:16 ESV).

Overwhelming Spiritual Conditions
Two other patient visits come to mind that highlight those patients' spiritual conditions at the time.

We All Pray to the Same God?
During a patient encounter with a man and his wife of a faith group other than my own, I related how I had prayed for him in the chapel that morning before I met them. After I discovered his physical needs, I shared with them that I routinely came into the hospital and departed the hospital via the chapel to pray for the needs of all patients, particularly those with whom I met. I also told him that I would pray for him again later in the day as I departed for home. His response was one of thankfulness and appreciation; however, he added, "That is good. We all pray to the same god."

I thought for a minute while I parsed his words. I then stated, "You know, in my study of world religions I am led to believe that only in Christianity does God have a Son and no other religions profess that except Christianity. That is a major difference in the gods that are in place for each devotee."

He stated, "That is observant. I will give that some thought." I also reassured him that I would be lifting him up in Christian prayer separately. I thanked him and his wife for their time and departed just as his physician was entering the room. I did pray for that patient in the chapel twice that day as I routinely did for all patients. I prayed not just for his physical healing but also for his spiritual growth. Patients of other faith groups do not worship gods with a son and do not have love and forgiveness from God as core tenants in their beliefs. Only Christianity affords these rich values. Our top spiritual pancake needs to be credible and authentic to nourish our souls. There is no eternally sustaining substitute.

No Forgiveness Available?

Another patient initiated a call for a chaplain's visit while he was experiencing severe complications related to his nervous system because of long-term alcohol abuse. As we spoke together for several hours, I mostly listened and assisted where possible. I also shared with him that I had prayed for him before I arrived at his bedside. Since he initiated the call, I was unaware of important personal information. I asked him about his age and faith group and discovered that he was a middle-aged male who had practiced his faith for more than thirty years. He was very well versed in not only his faith but other faiths too.

We spent a lot of time talking about his faith. He shared most of his beliefs with me, and he was very concerned that alcohol consumption was not permitted. His journey with alcohol was lengthy, and he was worried that his relationship with his faith was in severe jeopardy and would result in punishment because he could not stop his addiction. I complimented him on his awareness of a need for a spiritual anchor.

After I served him an order of my special pancakes, I said, "It is obvious you have a third spiritual pancake in your stack besides the ones for emotional and physical needs." He acknowledged that it was definitely there, and he expressed a need to explore other faiths because of some dissatisfaction over not getting sufficient short- and long-term help to overcome his alcohol problem. He showed a spiritual hunger for more.

He stated that his relationships with his faith group leaders only went as far as them saying that they would pray and be there for him, but they did not go beyond that point or offer any lasting help. He asked me how he could fill the void. I told him that without Jesus Christ, the top pancake was missing in action. I told him my own Christian faith would not let me eliminate Jesus Christ in my approach in providing spiritual care. I indicated that I felt patients needed Him in their corner for continuous help in fighting off the unrelenting temptations of Satan. I asked him to think of a personal relationship with Jesus as eternal.

He quickly assumed that I am a supporter of twelve-step programs, and he dismissed them as ineffective.[5] I said, "I feel that they have many good points, but they are available from many sources, spiritual (i.e., Celebrate Recovery), secular (i.e., AA), or both." Before I could go further, he said that he had come to a point where in lieu of a twelve-step program, he relied on only two things to help him combat his addiction, which included confining his thoughts to aggression and his own personal convictions. However, those have not held up very well. I told him that oddly enough, those were standard approaches but that there were more things to consider. I told him, "You may want to consider having an ombudsman in your corner twenty-four hours a day and seven days a week. That overseer comes when you first ask yourself the question, 'Where will I be when I get where I am going?'"

He said, "I really did not think about my problem in those large-scale terms. I worry about just day-to-day conflict."

I told him, "I escape the day-to-day limitations by pushing out the walls of my personal surroundings or tension area as far as I can until I can think outside of it. I take it to a point where I focus on continuously walking on a hot cherry pie fresh out of the oven that has a thin crust with holes and weak spots all over it. I make sure that I visualize that should I fall through the crust at any moment, the only thing holding me up out of the hot bubbly lake of fire below is the hands of my Lord, Jesus Christ. He is always there for me. He never sleeps. He never misses, and He does not need a net to catch me."

He said, "But I don't have that, and I don't have any hope of getting that in my faith group." He said that his study of world religions revealed that they all had the same god.

Like my statement with the previous patient, I asked him to pause for just a minute, and I said, "My study of non-Christian world religions reveals that god has no son; however, my Bible tells me that Jesus Christ is the one and only Son of God, so religions other than Christianity cannot worship the same god."

He said, "You have a good point. I need to think about that." He continued, "I do believe in Jesus Christ, but I am inclined to think that he is a prophet and that he did not die but was lifted up."

I said, "I have a different take on that too. Unlike you, I believe that He did die, and it was for all my sins and the sins of the entire world. He arose from the dead and ascended too. When I confess all of my sins to Him (as best as I remember them or as they come to mind) and repent for those sins, I have faith He will forgive me. I am a sinner, and I cannot avoid sinning in my life; however, because I have a Comforter in the Holy Spirit, I know that Jesus will wash away all my sins and make them as white as snow through the power of His very own blood, which was shed for me on the cross at Calvary."

I added, "Through the power of His Word and the continuous conviction of the Holy Spirit, He is always in my corner. He has been there since before the foundation of the world when my name was written into the Lamb's Book of Life. I know I can reach up and stretch out my hand and tag Him to step into the ring for me and take on the evils of alcohol or any other sinful addiction that I may have. I know He will win too because when He comes back, all the things in this temporal world will become fuel. They will burn and melt and raise the molten fluid level in the lake of fire. All our temporal works will melt from that intense heat."

He said, "So alcohol, drugs, nicotine, sex, homosexuality, laziness, gluttony will get consumed too."

I said, "Yup."

A big contemplative pause followed, and then he said, "I don't have Jesus in my corner or His forgiveness."

I said, "May I pray with you in Jesus' name?"

He said, "Yup."

We prayed together for the Lord Jesus Christ to melt his heart and for him to put his trust in Him regarding all of his needs, letting temporal things go away through the power of the Holy Spirit. I shared with him that I would be continuing to pray for him in the chapel as I went home and as the Lord brought him to mind in the days to come. And I did, even now as the words are applied to this page and as I reread them from time to time.

The previously outlined patient is no longer alone. He has help to conquer his addiction, and he believes that Jesus is who He says He is. He also knows where he will be when he gets where he is going. He came to Jesus to confess, be forgiven, and be born again. Today he is!

We All Need a Picture of Life

Scriptures contain numerous visuals like the stairway to heaven described by Jacob in Genesis, the potter's wheel, and broken jar in Jeremiah, the wheel within a wheel in Ezekiel, the plumb line in Amos, and the big fish in Jonah. The Bible itself is described as a double-edge sword in Hebrews. These visual examples help us understand the magnitude and scope of God's awesome power, and it would be more difficult to understand without them. Without having any direct personal visual experience like those, I have settled on a personal "mind-mapping 3-D graphical matrix." Of the many forms of learning, none have been more insightful to me than mathematical graphical expressions. All other forms stand on their own merit, but when we *let* something in mathematics, we give permission to our minds to hold on to something in a graphical visual form that has personal meaning within the realm of our existence. The term *let* is used at least fifteen times to describe how God put the universe in place. Likewise, when we use the term *let*, it opens a gateway of logic and reason where we can gain an understanding of broad new relationships that are useful in understanding our immediate everyday living and serve as a basis to help us operate more confidently and securely.

As a former aviator, I relied on many mathematical matrixes for almost everything that made a flight successful. I found myself often depicting everything from the approach pattern for an airfield to intricate aerobatic maneuvers in graphical 3-D arrays and all in a mathematical context. Math is at the heart of navigational instruments, the artificial horizon, and balanced flight displays, etc. The phrase "A picture is worth a thousand words" has high value for my way of thinking. Have you ever wondered why so many pilots talk with their hands? I can imagine how today's advanced submariners can even communicate in similar ways below the surface. It is an accounting for speed and climb or decent through control of power, pitch, roll, and yaw. Rules like altitude is controlled by throttle power, speed is controlled by pitch with the elevator; all controls require instantaneous human responses, and they are all rooted in math. These can be mind-boggling without a graphical reference, especially when both may be needed simultaneously. Many other aeronautical and nautical examples exist, many that are complex. While I was learning to fly in Cessna 150s in college, my female instructor had a very visual manner for teaching spin recoveries. She once asked me to concentrate on a spinning warehouse on the ground as we descended in my first spin. She said, "Make the plane stop turning by stepping on the opposite rudder pedal until it stops. Then hold it steady with both pedals." I did as she said. Then she said, "Now as we regain cruise airspeed, find the sky and the clouds by lifting the nose with the elevator by pulling back on the yoke." I did that too. Finally, she said, "Now hold this altitude with the throttle and cruise airspeed with the nose." Cool, I did that as well. Rules are good.

I said, "Can we do that again?"

She said, "Yup, I'm glad you asked." I had no trouble remembering her visual references for spin recoveries after that. She had many other visuals for everything aeronautical. She was a real smooth pro. It was there that I first gained confidence and a real appreciation for performance in 3-D environments. What an exciting challenge.

Why Do We Need to Know This Stuff?

Many former high school math students I taught regularly yearned for practical examples of how complicated equations and relationships apply to real life. Their favorite question was, "Why do we need to know this stuff?" A classroom discussion of arithmetic progressions produced one such question while I was teaching high school algebra one day. I responded, "Have you or your parents ever driven down a street at the posted speed limit and the lights turned green as you approached the intersections? Enough said, go figure! Someday soon you may be able to make a living and put some food on the table by knowing and using this stuff. Someone may ask you to fly airplanes too. So do you now also want to explore geometric progressions and harmonic progressions?" The classroom fell silent.

In this discourse I continue to rely on some of the same simple practical examples in mathematical graphical 3-D form to help all of us visualize and apply God's Word to our life—with a lot of help from the Spirit of God. Accordingly, the foremost mathematical absolutes that constantly come to mind are: (1) that we only have one entrance into this world and (2) that we will exit to only one of two destinations—heaven or hell.

> There was a rich man who was clothed in purple and fine linen and who feasted sumptuously every day. And at his gate was laid a poor man named Lazarus, covered with sores, who desired to be fed with what fell from the rich man's table. Moreover, even the dogs came and licked his sores. The poor man died and was carried by the angels to Abraham's side. The rich man also died and was buried, and in Hades, being in torment, he lifted up his eyes and saw Abraham far off and Lazarus at his side. And he called out, "Father Abraham, have mercy on me, and send Lazarus to dip the end of his finger in water and cool my tongue, for I am in anguish in this flame." But Abraham said, "Child, remember that you in your lifetime received your good things, and Lazarus in like manner bad things; but now he is comforted here, and you are in anguish." (Luke 16:19–25 ESV).

So as I peer through the unique Theo-metric or mathematical graphical eyepiece described here, I am reassured that I am working with solid practical examples derived from Scripture passages like those previously quoted. But there is more. What about my choices?

Why Metrics?

The question, "Why not metrics?" would be a better approach. If you have ever taken a vocational interest inventory exam (i.e., Kuder, Strong, etc.), you know how effective the use of metrics can be. In those cases these tests use bottom-up processes to present summary results from what appears to the examinee as disparate yes/no choices to detailed questions. To attain the highly valuable summary information for assessment as well as planning and development of the careers for the examinee, a metrics methodology is utilized. I benefitted greatly from taking both exams when I entered college. Looking back, I fulfilled separate careers in the top three summary areas of interests indicated in my results. In the scenario proffered here, the same metrics methodology is applied; however, we will use a top-down process. This methodology is just as useful, and if your own personal assessment is authentic, you will get credible results here as well. Yet, your results will last a tad bit longer than a career. Try eternity.

The matrix model described in the following pages enhances my vision and personal understanding, reinforces my faith, and rests on the foundation of the truth in Scripture. My pastor tells me that members are always asking him to use more visuals in his sermons. I remember him using a free-standing door and frame and a woman at a potter's wheel during his deliveries on separate occasions. Very effective! So I do not fear any repercussions from theologians who may label what has been done here with grandiose religious words. The sum of this work is no more than just a word and image picture or illustration like so many sermons delivered every Sunday morning. I only fear God if I have failed to do everything herein in accordance with His Word and His will as best I can. And so I intend to expand the previous examples into a complete picture showing where we will be when we get where we are going. Now let's begin to flesh out our spiritual pancakes!

Thesis Demarcated

Thus, my thesis for this work encompasses four separate but related areas that include:

1. **Our lives extending from a point where our names were entered in the Lamb's Book of Life *before* the foundation of the world,**

2. **Our conception and our birth,**

3. **Our journey through our temporal lives as an "air breather" to a point where we eventually meet God's Son, Jesus Christ, face-to-face when we die or when He returns to rapture His saints, and**

4. **Our realistic expectations that we should have upon our ultimate occupation of His perfect heavenly kingdom for eternity as revealed in Scripture.**

Table 3. Thesis Demarcated

In this context the term *eschatology* is blown away about temporal thinking of just the end time here on earth. In God's strategic plan we must have a rearview mirror of His and our distant past, a face mirror for now, and a long-range mirrored telescope (i.e., Hubble or Webb type) to look ahead; we must employ many omni-type thoughts. Your brand of *apologetics* may need to be stretched a bit as well. This is big stuff.

Therefore, within that context, we should try to think like God as best we can about the two operative elements of God's free grace and our free will as they play out in God's eternal plan. Their decisive point of union between the two results in our being born again, and it also enables God to be assured that we can be trusted. This union enables God to be assured that there will be *no evil* in His perfect kingdom, the New Jerusalem. When we choose to be with Him just as He chose us, a perfect relationship based on complete mutual love and trust is consummated for eternity.

Allow me to ponder Isaiah's vision of the haystack and just imagine the lion and the ox eating straw together. I am confident that Leo, the lion, may be equipped with new dentures to manage that straw. The wolf likewise could have teeth like the lamb to graze in the green pastures. The serpent will have no need to harm the child with fangs (Isaiah 11:6–9; 65:25). And in all probability, fish in the River of Life may be possibly caught but not kept. "Catch and release" will be the honor code unbroken forever. Whenever we get hungry, you can just grab your favorite pod of fruit from the orchards that line the riverbanks of that awesome River of Life, which flows from the throne of God. That is where that never-ending yield of fruit is produced every thirty days. Vegetarians, you have the right idea regarding the way to subsist. Since nothing dies in heaven, it is likely that there will be no meat to eat; just fruits and veggies will be served in eternity. What a day that will be!

But while each of our lifelines are confined to our individual tension areas in this life, we do well to remember that we are walking on that thin crust (like a hot cherry pie) with holes and weak spots that will not support us and prevent us from falling into the lake of fire in Hades. Should we drift over one of these dangerous eternal pitfalls, only the hands of Jesus Christ can catch us and lift us up to the safety of His loving arms.[6] We will all eventually venture out over one of these soft spots or holes during our journey in our personal tension area. At those times especially (and always), it is extremely important to nurture our relationship with our Lord, Jesus Christ. It is essential when these unexpected surprises take place. Our souls depend on it.

First, let's explore how we got into this condition. What physical, emotional, and spiritual environmental limits control our lives as we know them? What roles do the following seven limitations have on us?

Life's Limitations

These physical, emotional, and spiritual limits on our lives will be thoroughly fleshed out in detail within the scope of Theo-metrics modeling:

1. **Bad things do happen to good people, all people (none are good)**

2. **God of the Holy Trinity**

3. **Satan and the condition of sin in our life**

4. **Our temporal earthly environment**

5. **Time before we were conceived**

6. **Time while we are living**

7. **Time after we die**

Table 4. Life's Limitations

To get my arms around all of that, I identify five dimensions of life to illustrate our personal 3-D mind map. The five dimensions are employed in a Theo-metric mathematical graphical model in such a way that will enable you to make your own personal assessment of your soul, adjust if necessary and gain a solid footing for eternity. Employing 3-D artwork will quickly reveal three of these directional dimensions (i.e., Cartesian coordinate system of X [width], Y [height], and Z [depth] axis, etc.). While three-dimensional artwork can also quickly give you a unique clue about the amazing realm of tension in which we all live, the fourth and fifth dimensions of life are a lot more difficult to portray in art. Difficulties arise when you attempt to draw a spatial image of any of our connections (fourth dimension) and relationships (fifth dimension). This is especially true for your relationship with God, the threats from Satan, and your own temporal earthly environment. Feel the tension yet?

Spatial Communications!

Okay, let us digress. You know that two-dimensional artistic and visual impressions can divulge realistic three-dimensional shapes and spaces for many common applications that you experience every day without even noticing. But depth is difficult to capture on a flat surface, and a skillful artist is needed to depict conditions that are true to life by using depth of field with various artistic shading techniques. Hold a hand over one eye, and you can see what I mean. Knowing basic concepts of how two-dimensional art can accomplish these depth perception tasks helps us all communicate spatially.

Video Games

Video games have evolved from flat two-dimensional art objects like "Pac-Man" and "Frogger" to advanced three-dimensional illustrations that are much more intense and can command and control realistic interior drama through both connections and relationships.

Television in 3-D

Televisions are now produced to broadcast three-dimensional content. Electronic headset gaming in virtual reality worlds takes these three-dimensional devices to the limits of the game developers' imagination. Scene after scene of artistic characters and vivid geography interact in stereoscopic 3-D effect, sometimes with widespread scope with full head tracking of movement (think IMAX). Watch for use of this technology in education, communication, medicine, and many other practical commercial applications in the future. Ever explore Tableau software and anotamage imaging table?

Geographical Positioning Systems (GPS)

Today's GPS already takes advantage of three-dimensional artwork to help us find more realistic physical destinations. Sometimes it even helps golfers find the green and the hole.

Computer-Aided Design (CAD)/Computer-Assisted Manufacturing (CAM)

Modern CAD system output can be quickly translated from a design engineer's workstation into fully integrated CAM equipment that directs robots like lathes and other electronically controlled industrial equipment to produce products that roll off assembly lines and into our workplace, homes, and garages with minimal human involvement. Good idea to know some math if you are planning to put food on the table for your family by working in this demanding setting.

3-D Dental, Cardiovascular, and Other Health X-Rays

Next time you are at your dentist or your cardiologist, chances are you will get a new type of X-ray. It will be digitized, and the image of your teeth or your heart will be available in 3-D on a computer screen. The doctor can even rotate the image in all directions to diagnose your condition more thoroughly so that he or she can help save those pearly whites or pinpoint a lethal blockage in your heart. Greater comfort and safety are provided by the more informative 3-D images that are now available.

Other Special Equipment

In the previously outlined instances, numerous products begin with a vision of the inner structure of an intricate mechanism like a petroleum blowout preventer for drilling rigs or deep-water drilling platforms and then get fleshed out with essential engineering support architecture. The technology is also applied to major items like shipbuilding as well. Boats and submarines can be printed in one piece with 3-D printers.

Artificial body parts like knees or hips can get their start with an accurate three-dimensional engineering drawing of whatever a designer can visualize. Similarly, it took the transformation of a vision of a gigantic modern wind turbine to get it from the drawing board or screen to the wind farms in the fields or sea coasts where it produces clean electricity.

Further, many smaller pieces of equipment, specialized parts, and dedicated tools can currently be printed from technical drawings on a 3-D resin printer that can deliver a working plastic model in color. These printers can now replicate functional objects, including integrated moving parts like engines with pistons and connecting rods. These new printers can scan an object like an adjustable wrench into a 3-D image, which can then be sent to a special resin-based printer that will yield a working object that is nearly identical even down to the colors.[7] One of these 3-D printers was recently sent to the International Space Station to make spare parts while in orbit. Many smaller items in libraries and museums can be scanned for patrons to receive and examine at home. I intend to print out four-inch clear resin cubes containing my Theo-metric mathematical, graphical models to coincide with the release of this book. They will make nice desk paper weights for the gal or guy who thinks he or she has everything.

I firmly believe that 3-D printer applications will be found in even greater abundance and sophistication in the future. For example, seamless automobile bodies and large complex components are on the horizon for 3-D printers. "Six-axis" industrial lathes[8] now use CAD/CAM controlled procedures to seamlessly cut metal stock along X, Y, and Z axis while controlling A, B, and C bidirectional rotation. Your aluminum laptop computer case was likely tooled by one of these lathes. Tools like that make imaginary 3-D pinball machines with 3-D flipper control buttons come to mind. It is also important to grasp that each A, B, C rotational component of the respective X, Y, Z axis can have positive or negative spin or none.

What Is a Tesseract?

As usual, there is always more. Research the term *tesseract* on the Web or elsewhere. Here you can go beyond 3-D, all the way to 4-D and elsewhere to visually inspect the properties of objects of higher dimensions. Moving models of a tesseract, or a four-dimensional hypercube, will enable you to observe interesting 4-D modeling concepts.

Theo-metric Vision

Going beyond 3-D and 4-D takes a little "art" to enhance that science. Both artists and engineers normally must begin with some kind of a vision. They then try to make that image meaningful to others by means of common everyday examples to illustrate or convey their ideas, usually moving from the simple macros to the complex micro detail of their minds to reveal their vision. However, our individual collective lives are much more complex than any automated assembly line process. We need a 5-D personal mind map to help visualize our complete eternal journey. So here we go. Let's begin by raising the curtain to reveal a full five-dimensional illustration of "where we will be when we get where we are going" one dimension at time. Let the ***letting*** begin.

Good Characteristics of Life
I love simplicity, so I start by keeping my Theo-metric vision as simple as I can. I ***let*** a single vertical line (Y-axis) represent the first dimension of all that is ***good*** from our triune God.

Bad Characteristics of Life
To represent the second dimension of all that is ***bad*** and belongs to Satan, who is diametrically opposed to God and all that is good, I ***let*** another intersecting single perpendicular line (X-axis). Incidentally I find it interesting that these two lines form a cross.

Ugly Characteristics of Life
And to represent the third dimension of everything else that is ***ugly*** in this temporal world, I ***let*** another intersecting transverse single line (Z-axis) that conveys the depth we are seeking.

Connection Characteristics of Life
Now with our 3-D array firmly in place (the X, Y, and Z components are now looking much like individual toy jacks), we can set artificial limits or ***connections*** that build visible boundaries for something, or someone trapped on earth between the dynamic forces of each dimension. These outer boundaries form a cube or tension area that expresses the fourth dimension for our need to connect (as in gravity). Think of an upper corner room on the outer frame of a multistory house before the drywall and siding are applied.

Relationship Characteristics of Life
Finally the fifth dimension is our individual lifeline that desperately needs to have a total ***relationship*** with God, Jesus, and the Holy Spirit. This lifeline actually begins even before conception and birth. It began when our names were placed in the Lamb's Book of Life before the foundation of the world. It then passes through the "airbreather's" cube previously outlined, which is called our tension area. Our individual lifelines also end up going somewhere after death into eternity in heaven or hell. Unfortunately, our pathetic human chronological measuring instruments are miserably insufficient to meter out any meaningful expression of how much time that represents. Only God knows.

Subsequently these five-dimensions now complete my Theo-metric mathematical graphic 3-D model, which includes a single curved lifeline for our individual time: (1) prior to conception and birth, (2) during life, and (3) after death. Each of us has a *lifeline* that will travel through our personal *tension area* of life. This Theo-metric picture is made in the same manner as an artist who begins with a few lines on a blank canvas. In fleshing out my thoughts, I discovered I needed additional tools to bring all these images together and make **connections** and form ***relationships***. So, I decided to rely on my existing knowledge, skills, and abilities by using mathematics, graphics and matrixes. I found several basic algebra, geometry, trigonometry, and calculus books that gave me threads of information for fleshing out the context of my picture. After that, it seemed as though everything else started to fall into place each time I picked up my study Bible. The Scripture passages became more alive for me, and verse after verse exploded with new connections and relationships onto my mental Theo-metric mathematical graphical 5-D canvas. My vision improved!

What about the Attributes of the Five Dimensions of Life?

Yes, each of the five dimensions of life have their own root/primitive level attributes. Seven for each of the five dimensions should be sufficient for our model. But we need to keep in mind that three dimensions are directional and two are relational which dictates using a 5-D matrix.

35 High-Level Attributes Require a Dimensional Accounting

Although the following 2-D table does an excellent job of inventorying thirty-five root/primitive-level combined attributes for all five dimensions, it also by itself demonstrates the inherent weakness in only making a flat assessment. It cannot visually portray an image of all of the thirty-five attributes we encounter in life. What jumps off the page is that it forfeits the integral triangulation advantage exploited in a 3-D assessment.

2-D Personal Assessment Table		Life's Five Dimensions				
		Three "Directional" Dimensions			Two "Relational" Dimensions	
		#1	#2	#3	#4	#5
		<u>GODLY</u>	<u>SATANIC</u>	<u>EARTHLY</u>	<u>CONNECTION</u>	<u>RELATIONSHIP</u>
Life's 35 Attributes	#1	*Love*	*Sloth*	*Family*	*Lifeline*	*Dependency*
	#2	*Hope*	*Lust*	*Interpersonal*	*Timeline*	*Alliance*
	#3	*Faith*	*Anger*	*Specialty*	*Want to*	*Affinity*
	#4	*Truth*	*Pride*	*Health*	*Relate to*	*Kinship*
	#5	*Purity*	*Envy*	*Education*	*Free grace*	*Consanguinity*
	#6	*Honor*	*Greed*	*Recreation*	*Free will*	*Mutuality*
	#7	*Justice*	*Gluttony*	*Spiritual*	*Free Choice*	*Involvement*

Table 5. 2-D Personal Assessment Table

A 2-D Personal Assessment Will Not Compute; 3-D is Essential

You can see that the previous table is devoid of mental depth perception, and it contains insensible and illogical indications, making it impossible to profile and optimize interactivity between the attributes. A sound indexing strategy is not possible. Insist on making an all-encompassing and more comprehensive 3-D personal assessment to gain a fuller understanding of where you will be when you get where you are going. Demand knowing which direction your lifeline is headed. Get ready. This is the fun part.

Five Dimensions of Life's Personal Picture

Now that we have decomposed life into five dimensions, let us flesh out each dimension, making room for seven attributes for each. Relying on a few concrete terms that are fully documented in our universal language of mathematics, we will ensure tighter focus on the soul and where it is going for eternity. From here, my goal is to facilitate keeping my head on a swivel to help me profile what is presented to me in my individual 3-D personal picture or lifeline as well as to predict possible emerging issues that may impact my lifeline. We need continuous personal assessments for all five dimensions in life, but as suggested by the previous table, we also need to include the seven root/primitive-level attributes of each dimension to optimize our vision and get a clear picture of what we are doing to ourselves. Clearly, 3-D triangulation methodology shatters the value of 2-D depictions. Research the term "3-D triangulation" for some mind-popping graphic image examples.

First Dimension Is for God (Y-Axis—Height)

So again, beginning from the top, usually reference to anything as being one or two dimensional is less than complimentary. And I am confident of this one thing, putting any space payload into orbit or into deep space based on only a one-dimensional model is a recipe for disaster. I would not want to be part of that kind space travel. However, when the character of God is represented as the anchor of a model, the first dimension, feeble human simulation must surrender to the fact that any model cannot convey the context of God being omnipresent, omniscient, omnipotent, omni-righteous, omnidirectional, or omni-everything. God has everything covered, including all frail human models, and the attributes of God are always **good**. These high-level attributes are love, hope, faith, truth, purity, honor, and justice given out of God's free grace.

Second Dimension Is for Satan (X-Axis—Width)

Similarly flat two-dimensional graphics do very little to provide sufficient perspective or vision into anything as important as the soul either. A second dimension has minimal impact on clarity. Reliance on a 2-D product leaves a lot to be desired. Imagine mountain climbing using only two-dimensional information—up and down and right and left without accounting for the in and out bluffs and crags on the mountain. Maybe two-dimensions could accurately apply to a fake arcade vertical climbing wall, but it has little practical application in real life. That aside, two dimensions nicely represents the opposing relationship between Satan and God. Satan is always pulling in the opposite direction of God, so when God moves up, Satan moves down, and when God moves right, Satan moves left. These forces are always opposing, and the attributes of Satan are always **bad**. These high-level attributes are sloth, lust, anger, pride, envy, greed, and gluttony that Satan uses to tempt us constantly.

Third Dimension Is for Earth (Z-Axis—Depth)

Three dimensions are where depth perspective becomes important to our vision, and we can see the **ugly** with greater clarity. While the artist, architect, or engineer uses a third dimension, it can become very worthwhile in making their work highly deliverable and more meaningful, but we must hold all this earthly stuff at arm's length. Have you ever seen a child play with two-dimensional blocks or jacks? The real world does not face us adults in two dimensions either. Thank God for giving us cognizance of three dimensions in His world and His universe. I cannot imagine living on a flat 2-D world.

However, a 3-D view introduces additional tension into our pictures as well as our lives. It creates boundaries for a room housing all the tension where we reside while our hearts are beating and we're breathing air. This 3-D view enables the fourth-dimension framework that is produced because of the dynamic interaction between the three opposing forces within well-defined boundaries. The attributes of this temporal earth are always **ugly** because all but one will not last. They are family, interpersonal, specialty, health, education, recreation, and spiritual.

Fourth Dimension is for Connections (to Our Tension Area)

Hence, a good three-dimensional design is worthless unless there is a **connection** to real life within specified limits with a fourth dimension. We are a connectional people, but there are boundaries like age, physicality, mentality, and many other factors. All of these limits are depicted by a cube within the positive quadrant of my Theo-metric mathematical graphical model, where an arbitrary unit of one is plotted along each 3-D axes (X, Y, and Z) and connected to form a cube. Observe that everyone has one of these customized cubes that contains his or her personal lifeline (Figure 3).

One might have asked Michelangelo why he painted one of the ceiling squares of the well-known Sistine Chapel like he did, showing man attempting to connect to God. Apparently, Michelangelo thought we should have connections too. Like Michelangelo's famous painting with man reaching for the hand of God, it is indicative that many of us reach out for God in a similar way. But every way we try to connect with God, we fail except for one—the path that leads us via Jesus Christ. We can only reach God one way, but this requires another more insightful dimension, the fifth dimension and our need for relationship! Like gravity connects us to earth temporarily, the seven attributes of our **connection** dimension tie us to our tension area. They require us to keep our heads on swivels for achieving that permanent eternal **connection** we are seeking. These attributes include our lifeline, timeline, want-to (desire), relate-to (relations), free grace, free will, and free choice.

Fifth Dimension is for Relationships (for Our Safe Harbor)

The fifth dimension of **relationships** infiltrates all parts of our lives, bringing us joy as well as pain and suffering. It is woven into our fabric, and the gate is wide. But a relationship with God is different. The gate is narrow and can only be achieved by the Spirit of God empowering us to come to Jesus Christ as our Savior by God's free grace through our free will and our faith. Without this critical relationship with Jesus, pain and suffering erodes and decays all other relations in our lives. Just like family, God longs for our relationship with Him, so He sent us His Son, Jesus Christ, to bridge the gap between us and the Almighty. Oh, how helpful it would be if Michelangelo had painted Jesus into his famous painting. God's presence and His calling are too deep for meager words, but the power of visuals, such as the one in the Sistine Chapel, reveal a need for relationship that could not be improved on with a thousand words or even a million words. One visit to the virtual tour of the Sistine Chapel[9] will provide sufficient conviction.

Imagine how Chinese finger prisons capture two fingers that are placed inside with one on each end. As you attempt to pull your fingers out, the prison gets tighter. When we demonstrate the desire to pull on Jesus, His grip gets tighter, and we attain not only connection but **relationship** with Him and His Father. Jesus is the only bridge for that. Trust and love the relationship. It is the strongest the world has ever known. It is the only bridge that can get us where we will be when we get where we are going. The seven attributes of **relationships** are dependency, alliance, affinity, kinship, consanguinity, mutuality, and involvement.

Faith is at the heart of our relationship with God. It begins with our unity with Him in one body, one Spirit, and one LORD, and it includes the following words from Peter:

> His divine power has granted to us all things that pertain to life and godliness, through the knowledge of him who called us to his own glory and excellence, by which he has granted to us his precious and very great promises, so that through them you may become partakers of the divine nature, having escaped from the corruption that is in the world because of sinful desire. For this very reason, make every effort to supplement your faith with virtue, and virtue with knowledge, and knowledge with self-control, and self-control with steadfastness, and steadfastness with godliness, and godliness with brotherly affection, and brotherly affection with love. For if these qualities are yours and are increasing, they keep you from being ineffective or unfruitful in the knowledge of our Lord Jesus Christ. For whoever lacks these qualities is so nearsighted that he is blind, having forgotten that he was cleansed from his former sins. Therefore, brothers, be all the more diligent to confirm your calling and election, for if you practice these qualities, you will never fall. For in this way there will be richly provided for you an entrance into the eternal kingdom of our Lord and Savior Jesus Christ (2 Peter 1:3–11 ESV).

Further, just as the revolution in 3-D architecture, construction, mechanical design, and industrial manufacturing has made vast improvements that were only possible through the mining of technical information and reliance on graphical modeling and simulation software, Theo-metric images can through faith: (1) bring us closer to God, (2) help understand and remember the truths of Scripture, (3) be a primary way God gives us hope and encouragement, and (4) provide a powerful tool for evangelism.[10]

Likewise, our study of God's Word in a matrix context using all five dimensions of life can be greatly beneficial when fully attributed. For example, Jesus taught us to pray in the Lord's Prayer, but it is more than a prayer. It also holds the elements necessary for God's eternal strategic plan. It contains all five-dimensions of life necessary to relate our laments to God, specifically: (1) His Father in His eternal heavenly kingdom (**good**), (2) the need to avoid the evil one and his flaming abode (**bad**), (3) the temporal earthly environment where we currently subsist and reside (**ugly**), (4) a bond through the leading from His Holy Spirit (**connection**), and (5) His desire for a loving bond (**relationship**) as proven by what Jesus Himself did on the cross, assuring us eternity with Him.

Besides, Paul's tightly written 5-D discourse in his letter to the Colossians also reveals the same all-inclusive perspective. "For you have died, and your life is hidden with Christ in God" (Colossians 3:3 ESV).

When we are regenerated and die to this world, we gain life to the fullest reward possible by His gift of free grace through our free will and faith in Jesus Christ.

Thus, the purpose behind my five-dimensional Theo-metric mathematical graphical 3-D model is to satisfy my desire to do a simulated flyby, a walk-through, or work-around of my entire life to observe or examine what is going on as I move through life continuously and age. Accordingly, as an observer, these images help me achieve enhanced insight. They promise support for being able to make a personal Theo-metric assessment in seeking a stronger bond with God through Jesus Christ as the Spirit of God leads me. You can too. The changes you make will bend your lifeline too.

Incidentally the graphical image that intrigues me the most is the one Jesus wrote on the ground at the accusation and attempted execution of the woman caught in adultery (John 7:53–8:11). Knowing the supremacy of Christ, a mere mortal can't even imagine what He was drawing or writing in the sand. Perhaps He wrote of the sins common to them all, for the Bible says He knows what is in the heart of man (John 2:25). Perhaps the trial for adultery in the Old Testament involving dust from the floor of the tabernacle mixed with holy water was on His mind (Numbers 5:11–31). However, I cannot help but wonder if it had any resemblance to my little Theo-metric 3-D model. That would be encouraging—perhaps so, perhaps not. After all, Paul informs us about the centrality of Christ as follows: "He is the image of the invisible God, the firstborn of all creation. For by him all things were created, in heaven and on earth, visible and invisible, whether thrones or dominions or rulers or authorities—all things were created through him and for him" (Colossians 1:15–16 ESV).

Ready, Set, Go…Run the Race

Once I recognized that my picture or mind map, like all graphics, needed a minimum of five dimensions to enable me to observe my lifeline with fuller depth perception, it did not take long for me to discover that a basic three-dimensional array of lines that intersect is where I had to start. Take, for example, one individual children's toy jack. I found that image allowed me to hang root/primitive-level attributes and other ideas all over one of them to address the fourth dimension (**connection**) and the fifth dimension (**relationship**).

One single jack is at the heart of the virtual nature of Theo-metrics and making a personal and practical 3-D assessment of where you will be when you get where you are going. The three axes (X, Y, and Z) of each jack allow connections to be arrayed all over them in matrix fashion to represent key relationships in life.

Paul likes directional metaphors like breadth, length, height, and depth too. These little toy jacks come to mind as I read about his illustrations.

> For this reason I bow my knees before the Father, from whom every family in heaven and on earth is named, that according to the riches of his glory he may grant you to be strengthened with power through his Spirit in your inner being, so that Christ may dwell in your hearts through faith—that you, being rooted and grounded in love, may have strength to comprehend with all the saints what is the **breadth** and **length** and **height** and **depth**, and to know the **love of Christ** that surpasses knowledge, that you may be **filled with all the fullness of God** (Ephesians 3:14–19 ESV).

Likewise, Paul also used dimensional words that are aligned with discovering these dynamics at work on our lifeline. Look closely below for the three Theo-metric axes of life for the things that can hang on the **good** (Y), **bad** (X), and **ugly** (Z) axes. Also, see how they dynamically interact to **connect** and **relate** to Jesus through the power of the Holy Spirit.

If then you have been raised with Christ, seek the things that are **above**, where Christ is, seated at the right hand of God. Set your minds on things that are above, not on things that are on **earth**. For you have died, and your life is hidden with Christ in God. When Christ who is your life appears, then you also will appear with him in glory. Put to **death** therefore what is earthly in you: sexual immorality, impurity, passion, evil desire, and covetousness, which is idolatry. On account of these the wrath of God is coming. In these you too once walked, when you were living in them. But now you must put them all away: anger, wrath, malice, slander, and obscene talk from your mouth. Do not lie to one another, seeing that you have put off the old self with its practices and have put on the new self, which is being renewed in knowledge after the image of its creator. Here there is not Greek and Jew, circumcised and uncircumcised, barbarian, Scythian, slave, free; but Christ is all, and in all. Put on then, as God's chosen ones, holy and beloved, compassionate hearts, kindness, humility, meekness, and patience, bearing with one another and, if one has a complaint against another, forgiving each other; as the Lord has forgiven you, so you also must forgive. And above all these put on love, which binds everything together in perfect harmony. And let the peace of Christ rule in your hearts, to which indeed you were called in one body. And be thankful. Let the word of Christ dwell in you richly, teaching and admonishing one another in all wisdom, singing psalms and hymns and spiritual songs, with thankfulness in your hearts to God. And whatever you do, in word or deed, **do everything in the name of the Lord Jesus**, giving thanks to **God the Father through him** (Colossians 3:1–17 ESV).

Ok, the hard part is over. So now examine your own personal tension area and start making your own personal Theo-metric assessment of your lifeline, you know it better than anyone. Succeeding chapters will lay down more detailed matrix modeling points to assist you with structure and help make personal considerations and decisions.

How Far Are We Going?

The distance you run depends on variables inside your tension area. While toy jacks became my initial high-level design concept for my Theo-metric model, I realized that one size wouldn't fit all. In attempting to optimize the utility of one of these simple toys, it became readily apparent that generally all environments that came to mind have three dimensions and our personal **connectional** limits and **relationships** can also change with time. These changes need to be assessed too. Furthermore, I contemplated that God must surely think in at least five dimensions and probably many other dimensions that we don't even know about. Subsequently while I was reflecting on the title of my seminary's weekly newsletter *Kairos and Chronos*, I found that I was urged to expand my thinking to include not only linear concepts that are expressed in chronological (*Chronos*) time but also nonlinear concepts while I was trying to think in God's (*Kairos*) time by using such thoughts found in Scripture as follows: "But do not overlook this one fact, beloved, that with the Lord one day is as a thousand years, and a thousand years as one day" (2 Peter 3:8 ESV).

The idea of God's ability to think about and act on everything before, during, and after the foundation of the world all at the same time for everything and everybody is mind-boggling to this sinner. God is really big, and we are really small. Consider this "For my thoughts are not your thoughts, neither are your ways my ways, declares the LORD" (Isaiah 55:8 ESV).

When God spoke to Amos using the image of a plumb line, He set that vertical reference for His people, Israel, to compare them to a wall built straight.

> This is what he showed me: behold, the Lord was standing beside a wall built with a plumb line, with a plumb line in his hand. And the LORD said to me, "Amos, what do you see?" And I said, "A plumb line." Then the Lord said, "Behold, I am setting a plumb line in the midst of my people Israel; I will never again pass by them." (Amos 7:7–8 ESV).

That standard obviously served more than just the ancient builders. It clearly represented God's standard for the performance of both kingdoms of Israel and Judah. Arbitrary construction was not part of God's plan. He provided a clear standard for the people of Israel and for us. Today builders like us enjoy knowing that Jesus Christ is our plumb line, where the covenants of law and grace meet through the power of the Holy Spirit. Jesus reminds us not to just abide but also to obey and to follow God's building codes daily (John 15). Thus, we must construct everything we do in recognition of God's perfect eternal plan and His perfect attributes.

We Are Going as Far as the Mind Can See

Although painfully inadequate, continue building your high-level model and *let* the following: (1) the customary Y-axis (height) for your vertical plumb line to represent the arm for God's law, His Word, and His Son's acts of grace in our lives through the presence of His Holy Spirit; (2) the customary horizontal X-axis (width) for the traits of Satan's carnal mindedness, which is diametrically opposed to the arm of God; and (3) the transverse Z-axis (depth) for the support that enables all of the temporal diversions that we face in our life on earth.

Now pick equal arbitrary units of one along each axis where all the connected coordinates form a cube. I call this cube the tension area in our lives. We all have one. Next, limit each axis to seven attributes at the broadest divisions of each high-level 3-D element (X, Y, and Z). It is here where we can now drill down into each one of these aspects to expose the primitive or root levels of meaning and assign specific detailed binary terms. Notice how we have now activated the power of matrices with this critical pivotal step. Notice when you multiply seven by seven by seven, you can ascertain that we are always confronted with at least 343 mini cubes of tension in our lives (Figure 4). This concept of decomposition for labeling or indexing the root levels of our tension areas is discussed in detail in later chapters.

A Theo-metric Cube Could Help Steer Us

A Theo-metric cube gathers everything together to make our personal assessment simple. Here is where we deliberately break down the **good**, **bad**, and **ugly** components of our tension area into 343 mini-tension areas. This is where valuable **connections** and **relationships** come into play.

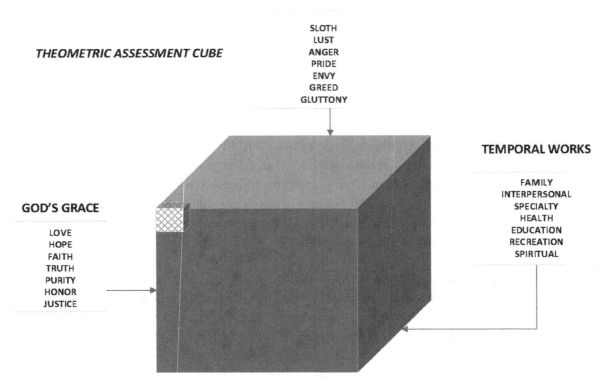

CARNAL MINDEDNESS

SLOTH
LUST
ANGER
PRIDE
ENVY
GREED
GLUTTONY

THEOMETRIC ASSESSMENT CUBE

TEMPORAL WORKS

FAMILY
INTERPERSONAL
SPECIALTY
HEALTH
EDUCATION
RECREATION
SPIRITUAL

GOD'S GRACE

LOVE
HOPE
FAITH
TRUTH
PURITY
HONOR
JUSTICE

7 X 7 X 7 = 343 MINI-TENSION AREAS TO EVALUATE

Figure 4. A Theo-metric Cube with 343 Mini-Tension Areas

Let us take a few samples:

#	X-axis	Y-axis	Z-axis	Tension Area
1	Sloth (1)	Love (1)	Family (1)	Child refusing to do chores
2	Greed (6)	Faith (3)	Interpersonal (2)	Political differences on gold standard
3	Lust (2)	Faith (3)	Recreation (6)	Entertainment content

Table 6. Theo-metric Samples of Mini-Tension Areas

Go ahead. Pick any mini cube at the intersection of X, Y, and Z, and you will have started your own personal Theo-metric appraisal. For example, if you start with mini-cube sample #1, you will find a condition that is less than desirable.

Find mini-cube sample #1 at the intersection of:

X=1 (**sloth**),

Y=1 (**love**), and

Z=1 (**family**).

In the case #1, we find that if we are lazy about loving family in a godly manner, we can suspect that it is a sign that improvement is needed. But using just that one sample is not the complete picture. There are 342 more mini cubes to go. So do not stop with just one mini cube. I bet you can't appraise just one (Table 6). Go ahead. Open up a 343-line spreadsheet and give yourself a "self-assigned personal score" for what is going on in each of your personal tension areas. Use a pivot table to trend your scores too. It will reveal where improvement is most needed.

Do you agree there is a lot more to this process than just assessing 343 potential tension areas in your life? There are major influences at work in those 343 areas.

Find mini-cube sample #2 at the intersection of:

X=6 (**greed**),

Y=3 (**faith**), and

Z=2 (**interpersonal**).

Given everything temporal is political, tell me how this mini-cube does not apply to politics. Consider how we now just unilaterally print more money without any linkage to the former 1971 Bretton Woods Accord[11] on adherence to a global gold standard. Therefore, how can separation of church and state not result in conflict over our funny money within the tension areas in our collective lives and still gain approval by God for our nation, state, county, or city? Like God's "plumb line," we obviously need to get back on the gold standard yesterday. Benchmarks like that are the foundations for accountability and credibility that uphold truth, purity, honor, justice, and other key attributes of God.

Lastly, find the mini-cube sample #3 at the intersection of:

X=2 (**lust**),

Y=3 (**faith**), and

Z=6 (**recreation**).

Explain how we can watch sinful acts in movies and videos or listen to the sin contained in the music that is promoted today with God's approval. I think you see what I mean.

Everything has God's scrutiny. We should also have an equal level of personal leadership and professional skepticism about everything else too. Accordingly, these 343 mini cubes hold all the tensions we experience in life. First, we all should process and recognize what is going on in all 343 mini cubes, some even in our sleep. We owe it to ourselves, to everybody else, and to God. Otherwise, we could be found asleep at the wheel. Second, if we feel remorse, even if we awaken with remorse that is a sign for needed change. It's time to do something about it. Third, repent and repair the connection if that is what is needed, or build a new connection. Then eliminate the grindstones and sin as gracefully as possible. Detach, as necessary.

I also found that I needed to depict our personal and interpersonal relationships in this graphical environment, especially relationships that would convey the impact of all the tension activity going on in the 5-D graphical X, Y, and Z matrix with all of its 343 little cubes of mini tension. So, from this point on, I will not only deliver points tied to each of these five dimensions but also present the connections and relationships involved. The little individual cubes in the larger cube are the basis for building your own individual Theo-metric mathematical graphical model. A full accounting involves a full assessment of each of the five dimensions individually, collectively, and continuously. Think of this mapping and drilling "process" in a way that is like a late-model automobile with computerized electronic engine control and power-train control modules. These "black box" brains in your late-model cars process millions of signals from hundreds of sensors each second and send corrective instructions back to the engine, transmission, or any of the car's vital systems. Aircraft have these systems as well. The matrix mapping in those systems is parallel with your model.

Let's include one last example by plotting the tension between Martha, Mary, and Jesus in Luke 10:39–42.

#	X-axis	Y-axis	Z-axis	Tension Area
1	Anger (3)	Justice (7)	Family (1)	Martha wants Mary to help her.
2	Pride (4)	Hope (2)	Spiritual (7)	Mary wants to listen to Jesus.
3	Jesus has **NO** sin (0)	Love (1)	Education (5)	Jesus teaches Mary.

Table 7. Sample Tension between Martha, Mary, and Jesus

Try out these samples on your own.

Find mini-cube sample #1 at the intersection of:

X=3 (**anger**),

Y=7 (**justice**), and

Z=1 (**family**)

Find mini-cube sample #2 at the intersection of:

X=4 (**pride**),

Y=2 (**hope**), and

Z=7 (**spiritual**)

Find mini-cube sample #3 at the intersection of:

X=0 (**Jesus has *no* sin**),

Y=1 (**love**), and

Z=5 (**education**)

How did you do? I realize this drill may have seemed like playing chess on a three-dimensional board in the dark. Don't worry. Alternatively, just pray for understanding, guidance, and strength and just forget about all of this matrix stuff if you want, as unlikely as that may be. It's like going into a corner to sit and *not* think about a white bear. Go ahead, try it. You just cannot do it.

When I preach, I gravitate to topical sermons. So, clergy reading this can find these 343 mini cubes a reliable source for spot-on sermon topics by reviewing each of these little boxes of tension. I guarantee it! Take mini-cube sample #1 and see how fast the tension between love, family, and sloth arises. Based on God's Word, and with a little help from your concordance, preach that topic. Hey, it can almost preach itself!

Some say it takes a minimum of twenty moves to solve a Rubik's Cube. When all is said and done, this Theo-metric cube only takes **one**. That move is to believe that Jesus Christ is your Lord and Savior and do what He says. Martha and Mary did even with their obvious tension.

Lifelines Are Made to Be Bent

Let's pause to deviate from this early hint of a conclusion for some more preliminary graphics that make the Theo-metric model fully complete and operational. The question that this graphical array posed to me was this: Where will my own lifeline be when I get where I am going for eternity? The Bible says that the only two options upon reaching the end of our lifeline on earth (at the boundaries of our tension area) are either heaven or hell. As a result, I added a fork in our lifeline inside the tension-area cube without giving it a specific set of 5-D coordinates. Because God enters into our tension area unannounced, it is the biggest variable we will ever experience. I concluded that the coordinates of that fork are really predetermined by God in His own *Kairos* time. His arrival and our response determine the destination and outcome of our journey. All of us will get to experience our own encounter with God the Father, our Lord, Jesus Christ, the Son, and the Spirit of God—all in a single Trinitarian *Chronos* event (i.e., Noah, Moses, Jonah, Samuel, Jeremiah, Paul, etc.). We know God will intervene whenever He desires; however, we also know our free will provides for a totally independent response to God's call and His free grace. Yet I'm equally confidant that God not only enabled but also already foreknew what that decision would be. Consider the call of the men named above and many other biblical characters who were called by God. They responded, even though some were reluctant. God is unrelenting. He will get His way. It is best not to fight it unless you want to experience the same thing that Jonah did. Just remember that big fish can be equipped with big jaws and sharp teeth. When God wants us, God will get us.

If you made it to this point, you are probably wondering what kind of guy would think of this stuff. Keep reading. This kind of drill calls for a little more intense mental exercise sometimes. Recall that the Spirit of God goes where the Spirit of God wants. It has been told that when Helen Keller[12] received the gift of language and heard about God, she said she already knew about Him, but she just did not know His name.

As soon as God's symbolic arrow strikes our lifeline like a bolt of lightning, *Kairos* and *Chronos* come together, and we must make the most important decision we will ever make at the fork in our lifeline (Figure 3). So, will I, as a sinner, accept, believe, love, and claim Jesus Christ as my Lord and Savior and put my faith in Him to forgive me for all my sins when I confess? If I say "No," I remain unforgiven and condemned as lost to burn in hell for eternity with the goats and the rich man. However, if I say, "Yes," I am assured by my perfect submission that I will be saved and be with Jesus in His kingdom of heaven forever. A yes response to God's call ensures that we are born again and that we will not die a second fiery and eternal death. Our names will remain in the Book of Life without God blotting them out by taking an eraser to them. The only thing we can **do** to cause God to take our names out of the Book of Life is to blaspheme or reject His call by the Holy Spirit to believe in His Son, Jesus Christ, our LORD, and Savior. No response from us at all is as bad as a no. When your lifeline comes out of the diamond symbol, have a yes answer ready. Our salvation is assured, and we are saved by His grace through our faith at the exact moment when we say, "Yes" (Figure 3). "But above all, my brothers, do not swear, either by heaven or by earth or by any other oath, but let your "yes" be yes and your "no" be no, so that you may not fall under condemnation" (James 5:12 ESV).

God Wants Us Back

I'm certain Judy, my first wife, submitted to Jesus long before she passed away and way before she began serving as a Stephen minister (a one-on-one caregiving ministry of bearing others burdens as the result of tragedies or crises like severe sicknesses)[13] to other breast cancer patients. At her funeral an elementary school friend of mine saw my grief and shared this profound thought: "Bill, God wanted her back." His words hit me like ten tons of bricks. Because of her relationship with Jesus, I instantly grasped his wisdom and realized that she belonged to Him, not me. She was only on temporary loan to me in this temporal earthly setting. Some of her contacts through her Stephen ministry later confirmed what I already knew. She not only loved the Lord with all her heart but encouraged others like them to do the same in their times of extreme need.

Spiritual truth is all about deep faith and a mature personal relationship with Jesus through the power of the Holy Spirit. Take a moment to study our dilemma by observing the truth in the Theo-metric mathematical graphic model (Figure 3). Put yourself on the lifeline and keep alert for the fork in the road. You will be glad you did.

The remainder of this little book decomposes each component into the root/primitive level for each high-level axis and demonstrates how our lifeline is bent by the dynamics of the connections and relationships we embrace for each axis.

Faith Is the Glue for Connection and Relationship to Jesus

"Great Is Our Faithfulness, O God, Our Father" is an all-time favorite hymn that stresses our need for a faithful relationship with God. Rev. Dr. Cleo J. LaRue[14] spoke of our right relationship with God in his sermon delivered at Mt. Zion Baptist Church in Austin, Texas, on February 4, 1996, where students from our local seminary were invited guests. Dr. LaRue did not disappoint. In his strong introduction, he related a solid case for faith in a powerful account of an old woman anguishing over her son's very high fever. The setting was described as far from town in a remote wooded area where no medical facilities existed. The channels of communication were described as very restricted, no personal car or private phone available. However, the woman's character was described as very determined and resourceful; through borrowing a neighbor's phone, her plea for a doctor finally met with success. But that was not all. Dr. LaRue also described the doctor's urgent need for ice for the boy; but the woman did not have an operating freezer or any other logistical support to get some. Dr. LaRue depicted the woman's high frustration in detail, but he also indicated that while she was in her deepest despair, she turned to God in prayer for help. Lastly, Dr. LaRue revealed how her prayer for ice was answered when a severe thunderstorm brought wind, rain, and hail into the scene. Ice was delivered on time; the feverish boy recovered. Like the ice in this story, faith is a gift of free grace from God.

As I listened to Dr. LaRue's story of this woman and her son that cold winter day, my mind was drawn to the faith of Abraham and the sacrifice of his son Isaac.

> When they came to the place of which God had told him, Abraham built the altar there and laid the wood in order and bound Isaac his son and laid him on the altar, on top of the wood. Then Abraham reached out his hand and took the knife to slaughter his son. But the angel of the Lord called to him from heaven and said, "Abraham, Abraham!" And he said, "Here I am." He said, "Do not lay your hand on the boy or do anything to him, for now I know that you fear God, seeing you have not withheld your son, your only son, from me." And Abraham lifted up his eyes and looked, and behold, behind him was a ram, caught in a thicket by his horns. And Abraham went and took the ram and offered it up as a burnt offering instead of his son. So Abraham called the name of that place, "The Lord will provide"; as it is said to this day, "On the mount of the Lord it shall be provided."

> And the angel of the Lord called to Abraham a second time from heaven and said, "By myself I have sworn, declares the Lord, because you have done this and have not withheld your son, your only son, I will surely bless you, and I will surely multiply your offspring as the stars of heaven and as the sand that is on the seashore. And your offspring shall possess the gate of his enemies, and in your offspring shall all the nations of the earth be blessed, because you have obeyed my voice." (Genesis 22:13-18 ESV).

Recently, while I was giving proper subjective consideration to our framework for salvation about the above context diagram (Figure 3), I gained assurance that my own personal Theo-metric vision appears to be sufficiently complete. I began to answer my own questions about where I would be when I get where I am going. Knowing God is sovereign, omnipotent, omnipresent, omniscient, omni-righteous, omnidirectional, and omni-everything, I understand He already knows our deepest thoughts and what response you and I will make. Daily recognition, remorse, repentance, and confession is a necessary given for all of us. We need to stay up on prayer. Then we begin to serve God out of our grateful response for what He has already done for us. Up until that point of commitment (recall the diamond "<>" symbol on our lifeline) to a relationship with Christ, our works are not counted for good. In other words, we cannot work our way to heaven; however, rewards await all saints for abiding in the Great Commandment and helping attain the Lord's Great Commission. Jesus is the reason for everything!

Role of Religious Denominations?

Often patients ask me, "What denomination are you?" before I even get through the door to a hospital room. I tell them, "First I am a Christian, but my public worship is in a Baptist house of God." As indispensable as denominations are for individual and corporate worship, education, and visibly advancing God's will through cooperation in the mission field, it may not surprise you that I have not found any one particular true Christian denominational faith group significantly more vital than another in the final outcome for our individual response to God's call and the salvation of our soul. They are collectively part of the church's foundational rock vested in Peter.[15] While the below denominations provide a highly useful and effective cooperative purpose, our personal faith in Jesus must come first. Personal faith is the glue for all of us to connect and relate to Jesus Christ in daily Holy Communion. The knowledge and acceptance of organized Christian denominations, while very essential and supportive, is not absolutely necessary to effect a real change on the heart and life of self and others. Real change in our heart and soul is dictated by the magnitude of God's free grace through our personal faith and free will. However, denominations like those below vastly improve exposure for Christ in the world and they are critically needed and worthy of support.

Family Tree of Religious Denominations

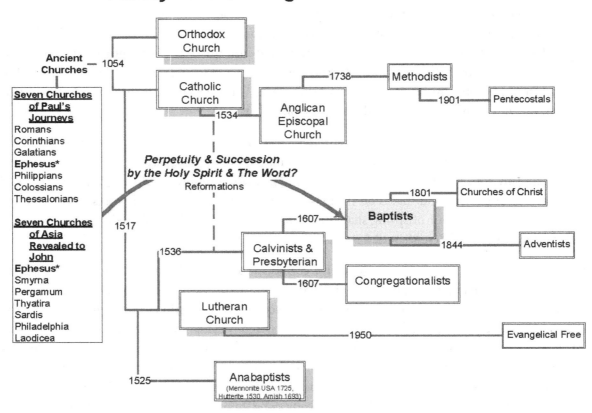

Figure 5. Family Tree of Religious Denominations

While the above image reflects the growth of the early Christian churches through today, I believe there is an underlying guarantee of perpetuity and succession enabled through the power of the Holy Spirit. Some Baptists like me and many from other church bodies trust that binding to hold together all congregations of all baptized believers since the time of Christ (Figure 5) and for that I give my deepest thanks. Each denominational path collectively marks a solid path to the church triumphant. Many churches, regardless of denomination, have suffered much for Christ then and even now (i.e., Christian Coptic Church of Egypt which predates all modern churches). My prayers include strength and perseverance for these persecuted Christian churches and their followers; I pray they may be witnesses for others in their strife. May God speed in their recovery and may He enhance their growth from other global, national, state, and local missions through strong denominational and/or cooperative program support. Accordingly, I pray, each individual church, independent or otherwise, at the "grass roots" would strive to become at least a "Two-bit" church by giving 25 percent of their annual budget for mission outreach programs.

Important, too, are the theological divisions in 1534–1536 attributed to followers of the Armenians and Reformers:

- **Armenians (not just grace alone)**
  - Jacobus Arminius (Anglicans)
  - Simon Episcopes (Episcopalians)
  - John Wesley (Methodists)
- **Reformers (grace alone)**
  - Martin Luther (Lutherans)
  - John Calvin (Presbyterians)
  - Ulrich Zwingli (Swiss Reformer)

Table 8. Reformers

This kind of diversity of thought promotes the growth of Christ for the ears that are more attuned to the subtleties in alignment to the faith; faith is faith that is expressed best as an authentic "yes" or "no." From the time that the one criminal on the cross who died alongside Jesus recognized his sins, felt remorse, acknowledged Jesus, believed, confessed, repented, confirmed, and went to be with the Lord until today, we need to give a collective thanks for those that have followed his example of simple faith. And even those who regard perpetuity and succession as an inextricable link to the early apostles and disciples, the first step of salvation is through the free grace of God enabled by the power of the Holy Spirit. So let the Spirit of God and the Word of God guide you in your walk of faith. Except for the minimal "work" involved in enunciating the word "Yes," I gravitate 99.999 percent to "grace alone" thinking by the Reformers previously listed above. It is grace that does the doing, not faith. Giving comes from the grace of God, faith is the receiving. Redemption comes not by willing and doing, but by faith in Jesus Christ as Lord and Savior. Recall from Paul, "For by grace you have been saved through faith. And this is not your own doing; it is the gift of God" (Ephesians 2:8 ESV).

So, perpetuity assumes that some Christian faith groups (i.e., Baptists, etc.) have existed since the time of Christ.[16] And, succession argues that these churches actually existed in an unbroken chain since the time of Christ by the Holy Spirit and God's Word.[17] When taken together, or separately, it appears to me that there is still a lot of room for all church bodies to rally around this idea of perpetuity and succession without a whole lot of conflict with scripture or other faith groups.

Per Jesus Himself, the Bible says about God's free grace leading us to the kingdom of heaven,

And Jesus answered him, "Blessed are you, Simon Bar-Jonah! For flesh and blood has not revealed this to you, but my Father who is in heaven. And I tell you, you are Peter, and on this rock I will build my church, and the gates of hell shall not prevail against it. I will give you the keys of the kingdom of heaven, and whatever you bind on earth shall be bound in heaven, and whatever you loose on earth shall be loosed in heaven." (Matthew 16:17–19 ESV).

Consider a person in an isolated area who happens upon a copy of the Holy Bible in a language he or she could read and understand, and that person then arrives at salvation separately from any outside human help. Recollect from John that the Spirit of God goes where the Spirit of God wants. It is that Spirit of God that our Lord intended to direct and perpetuate the gospel message, His teachings, and all of Scripture until He returns. Control by God's Spirit does not single out a particular individual, congregation, or denomination as having total control over the succession of the church across many generations. Therefore, I strongly encourage, embrace, and promote all traditional Christian denominational ministries, including Web evangelism projects (i.e., "I Stand Sunday" recently televised in Houston) and many enthusiastic evangelical publications. Without missionary outreach and humanitarian church programs, the progress toward accomplishment of the Great Commission would be significantly diminished. I once was blessed to chair a Service and Outreach Commission where the church's stated goal was to share 25% of the financial talents of the church within and outside the local community. Of all churches I have been associated with in the past 65 years, I believe that church exhibited what it takes to lead the way by attaining over 20% of their total budget with a six-digit figure going to support 20 organizations that minister to those in need. They were proud to be known as a church striving to become a "Two-bit Church." It appears that a minimum level of church performance in service and outreach should be 10% of tithes received. The Great Commission is not about in-reach; it's about outreach.

So my response to patients' well founded deeply religious concerns for a particular faith group has to be one that will cut to the chase bypassing denominational fences. I place a higher emphasis on ecumenical evangelism. I admire the succinct question reportedly asked to people on the street, regardless of faith group, by the late evangelist Frank Jenner of George Street in Sydney, Australia: "If you died tonight, are you certain that your soul will go to heaven?"[18] In the rooms of a hospital I have to be just as vigorous as Frank Jenner as I *fish* for souls for Christ in a "spiritual" watershed of "streams" flowing to the eternal "church triumphant." When I use a fly rod, my presentation of the carrot on that stick must be done in an active, attractive way and not with passivity. Yet, it also needs to be unencumbered by partitioned "religious" clusters of "ponds" found within the present "church militant" harbored and anchored on earth. If possible, best to remember that Jesus Christ is the head of the church, both militant and triumphant, and the church universal does not reside in a wooden, steel, or brick box, but it is in **us**, for we are His temple. Paul writes in chapter six of his first letter to the Corinthians, asking, "Or do you not know that your body is a temple of the Holy Spirit within you, whom you have from God? You are not your own . . ."

So, I pray the Spirit of God is leading me in ministry endeavors like it led Frank Jenner, as I try to serve others and our Lord, Jesus Christ, our one and only Savior, as mandated by His Holy Scripture in His Great Commission.

Now the eleven disciples went to Galilee, to the mountain to which Jesus had directed them. And when they saw him they worshiped him, but some doubted. And Jesus came and said to them, "All authority in heaven and on earth has been given to me. Go therefore and make disciples of all nations, baptizing them in the name of the Father and of the Son and of the Holy Spirit, teaching them to observe all that I have commanded you. And behold, I am with you always, to the end of the age." (Matthew 28:16–20 ESV).

Your Turn

So, by examining the details of all the individual components of your Theo-metric mathematical model outlined above, you can now establish a solid foundation for building and personalizing your own model; the model applies to everyone.

Starting to feel the tension yet? Got your relationship with Jesus? I've got mine. I'm glad I won't be in this temporal tension area forever! The gospel hymn, "I'm Go-in' Up" by Mary McDonald[19] provides good insight into my personal blessed assurance. Also, "I'll Fly Away" by Albert E. Brumley[20] inspires me in the same way. It has been called the most recorded gospel song.

Dimension One of Five—Portals of Godly Time

Dimension one of our mind map, when decomposed, represents seven portals or attributes of God's character on a vertical Y-axis (Figure 3). It is everything **good** that impacts our lives. Because of these crucial attributes, we can surrender everything on this earth, giving it up, praising God for what He has done for us through the sacrifice of His Son, Jesus Christ, for all of us to enjoy eternal life with Him in our heavenly home. These authoritative truths are confirmed by God throughout the Bible, the infallible Word of God. When we acknowledge God's grace from the Holy Spirit and accept Jesus Christ as our Lord and Savior, we are born again until mortal death and then graduate to life eternal with the church triumphant. It is through these attributes we find the desire to believe, love, trust, and obey Him.

> Make a joyful noise to the LORD, all the earth; break forth into joyous song and sing praises! Sing praises to the LORD with the lyre, with the lyre and the sound of melody! With trumpets and the sound of the horn make a joyful noise before the King, the LORD! Let the sea roar, and all that fills it; the world and those who dwell in it! Let the rivers clap their hands; let the hills sing for joy together before the LORD, for he comes to judge the earth. He will judge the world with righteousness, and the peoples with equity (Psalm 98:4-9).

God

God the Father almighty is the Godhead of His Son, Jesus Christ, and of the Holy Spirit. The three are one in three persons, the blessed Trinity. YHWH, Jehovah God is omniscient, omnipotent, omnipresent, omnidirectional, and omni-righteous. He is omni-everything—everything except a false god. No other God exists. He is sovereign and eternal. He has a purpose and a plan that spans: (1) the time of His former perfect kingdom, (2) the redemption of His elect through Jesus Christ, and (3) while also ranging to the time of His assured perfect kingdom after evil is destroyed for all eternity. He is the only God with a Son, Jesus Christ. No other god has a Son sent to earth to sacrificially die on our behalf for our sins and provide salvation to those who put their total love, hope, trust, and faith in Him. When we follow Jesus, we give God the glory He is due and satisfy His primary objective; not to lose any of His elect, not one to the evil one.

For godly time opportunities in life, our signal light is always **green** for **good** when we believe in His Son, Jesus Christ, through the power of the Holy Spirit. Conventional traffic lights contain a red stoplight, an amber caution light, and a green go light that appear independent of one another to safely control traffic. God is good and holds out everything that goes upward. These godly signals will lead us safely through all the earthly intersections we enter. It is the good that no pagan god can ever counterfeit. Dr. Mark Peters, D.D.S., has devoted an entire book regarding things that are *up*, and his fourth chapter deals with getting ourselves trained *up* for what is ahead.[21] Good idea!

Good training should include official doctrinal papers held out by denominations of the Reformed faith. They are great resources for reference and reflection on key points of faith while promoting growth and strengthening belief (i.e., The Scots Confession;[22] The Second Helvetic Confession;[23] The Westminster Confession of Faith;[24] and The Baptist Faith and Message 2000[25] (*this confession progressed from the former Baptist Confession of Faith of 1689/Second London Confession of 1689 that modeled the Westminster Confession of Faith*). Although statements in these papers are replete with ample footnotes connecting to God's Word, the documents do not supersede the Bible; but a review of these documents and others like The Apostles' Creed, will take you where you will find help to focus on Scripture holistically and gain assurance of your faith from many leaders of the faith. Then again, don't forget faith has to be built on Holy Scriptures, nothing less than the Bible.

For example, the God of Christians is the one true and only living and creator God that is unsurpassed in love, power, spirit, authority, sovereignty, dominion, wisdom, judgment, fairness, holiness, graciousness, forgiveness, eternalness, and goodness. The unity of God is expressed in three persons as God the Father, God the Son, and God the Holy Spirit; all triune attributes are distinct yet all in one. God knows all things for all times and all decisions that apply to the past, present, and the future. When I ponder that, then I realize God knows all the thoughts and deeds of all generations, all at the same time. The psalmist also says He knows all our tears. Wow!

Although I particularly like that God's knowledge extends to everything, including the future decisions of His free creatures, I also know that He cannot be constrained by the limits of human thinking and our attempt to put Him in a human box. God knows all, and He knows all the time. The psalmist writes,

> O Lord, you have searched me and known me! You know when I sit down and when I rise up; you discern my thoughts from afar. You search out my path and my lying down and are acquainted with all my ways. Even before a word is on my tongue, behold, O Lord, you know it altogether. You hem me in, behind and before, and lay your hand upon me. Such knowledge is too wonderful for me; it is high; I cannot attain it. Where shall I go from your Spirit? Or where shall I flee from your presence? If I ascend to heaven, you are there! If I make my bed in Sheol, you are there! If I take the wings of the morning and dwell in the uttermost parts of the sea, even there your hand shall lead me, and your right hand shall hold me. If I say, "Surely the darkness shall cover me, and the light about me be night," even the darkness is not dark to you; the night is bright as the day, for darkness is as light with you. For you formed my inward parts; you knitted me together in my mother's womb. I praise you, for I am fearfully and wonderfully made. Wonderful are your works; my soul knows it very well. My frame was not hidden from you, when I was being made in secret, intricately woven in the depths of the earth. Your eyes saw my unformed substance; in your book were written, every one of them, the days that were formed for me, when as yet there was none of them. How precious to me are your thoughts, O God! How vast is the sum of them! If I would count them, they are more than the sand. I awake, and I am still with you. Oh that you would slay the wicked, O God! O men of blood, depart from me! They speak against you with malicious intent; your enemies take your name in vain. Do I not hate those who hate you, O Lord? And do I not loathe those who rise up against you? I hate them with complete hatred; I count them my enemies. Search me, O God,

and know my heart! Try me and know my thoughts! And see if there be any grievous way in me and lead me in the way everlasting! (Psalm 139 ESV).

Take a moment to ponder a knot-shaped object of only one substance developed with intractable geometry; these continuous 3-D pretzel shaped knots also assist me in gaining some additional understanding of what could represent the connection and/or relationship between the separate Persons of God the Father, Jesus Christ the Son, and the Spirit of God pertaining to the Holy Trinity, which is also of just one substance. A three-leaf clover or the three states of water will suffice if you can't find a 3-D knot. While my understanding of the three-in-one relationship between God the Father, Jesus Christ the Son, and the Spirit of God is helped by reference to appropriate clever images, they are all feeble by comparison to our real God. Eventually faith will soon be sight. We will see Him face-to-face, and all understanding will be real. At that point we will likely need new hymnbooks beginning with the "Hallelujah Chorus"[26] or perhaps we will need all new hymns that will at least embody being in His presence rather than waiting in a way station like we are now.

God is so big, and we are so small. I find the connectivity of the Trinity intriguing and wonderfully unimaginable. Like the intractable geometry reference used above, another simple and useful illustration of the Trinity by Dr. Francis Brown illustrates the jurisdiction of the Y-axis by using a 3-D isometric projection and gives a better overall understanding.[27] Search the web for: "Concept diagram of the Holy Trinity" to see applicable drawings of Dr. Brown's illustration.

We do well to remember that for each of the powerful forces of the Holy Trinity, there are opposing forces from Satan's version of the trinity—Satan, the Antichrist, and the evil spirit. These evil components are constantly waging war with the Holy Trinity. Here is where conflict begins and eventually ends. Wherever conflict appears, it is due to the clash of these forces. We are clearly in the middle, caught in the crossfire, and the earth is the battlefield. Don't forget your password to get back to friendly lines if you have reason to go outside the wire perimeter of the Trinity— "Jesus lives!"

Don't stop now. Keep going. You are almost at eternal safety, peace, and rest. But first, let's study our theater of war more thoroughly. Look for the **green** terrain first. Its attributes are all **good**. The next chapter, Dimension Two of Five—Portals of Sinful Time, will address the attributes of the enemy, all of which are **bad**. The chapter that follows that, Dimension Three of Five—Portals of Earthly Time, will address the attributes of our earthly battlefield; they are all **ugly**.

God, the Father

Chapter nine of Nehemiah reveals many of the known attributes of God, the Father, as illustrated by terms like Leader, Protector, Regulator, Commander, Supporter, Sustainer, Deliverer, Sentinel, Provider, Purifier, Instructor, Forgiver, and Grantor of love, hope, faith, truth, purity, honor, justice, grace, and mercy to His people Israel as He led them out of Egypt and into the Promised Land. God, the Father continues to be trustworthy today to all His elect who affirm that He is God and place their trust and faith in His Word.

Further, chapters thirty-six through forty-one of Job and the fortieth chapter of Isaiah directly address the omniscience, omnipotence, and omnipresence of God. Scripture readings like these stretch our human understanding of God's majesty to the limit. I AM WHO I AM is God's own personal explanation of His majesty that he described to Moses in the third chapter of Exodus; no human word (or model) is adequate to convey God. God is the manifestation of His own glory.God, the Father, is the living God, who speaks uniquely through Jesus Christ, the Word made flesh, through the Holy Spirit, and through the Holy Scriptures. "He who has ears to hear, let him hear." (Matthew 11:15 ESV).

Jesus Christ, the Son of God

Jesus Christ is the only mediator and intercessor between God and man, and He oversees everything that is anything; for which He is the only heir. He overcame death on a cross for our sins yet saw no corruption. He is the head and Savior of His Church who will judge the world. John makes that clear when he writes,

> In the beginning was the Word, and the Word was with God, and the Word was God. He was in the beginning with God. All things were made through him, and without him was not any thing made that was made. In him was life, and the life was the light of men. The light shines in the darkness, and the darkness has not overcome it . . . And the Word became flesh and dwelt among us, and we have seen his glory, glory as of the only Son from the Father, full of grace and truth . . . No one has ever seen God; the only God, who is at the Father's side, he has made him known (John 1:1–5, 14, 18 ESV).

For this reason, nothing else is to be worshipped or invoked. Jesus Christ is the only looking glass we need to secure our faith through the power of the Holy Spirit; He persuades us to believe and obey. Everything was created by and through Jesus Christ. Jesus Christ is Lord! He is more than this world can satisfy. Psalm 95 says, "For he is our God, and we are the people of his pasture, and the sheep of his hand. Today if you hear his voice do not harden your hearts . . ."

But recollect this: We cannot have the **wow** without the **woe**. Peter comes to mind when he denied Jesus three times. But he did not stay in that sin. He was remorseful. He repented and wept bitterly. When after Jesus arose and caught Peter in the act of fishing for fish instead of the souls of men, Peter then left his net and moved on to do great things for the same Lord he denied. Just like Peter, Christ has washed away our sins with His death on the cross. When I reach into my pocket for change, I notice a little cross that I carry that always reminds me Christ has already paid for my sins. Praise God Almighty. Jesus Christ is the Messiah, believe, trust, and obey Him. According to the Gospel of John, Jesus is the door for the repentant that are saved; go in today, He is waiting inside for all who will enter. Per chapter three of John's Revelation, John also says Jesus is knocking on that door, don't wait until you see Him riding a white horse as described later in chapter nineteen of John's Revelation. By then the door will be shut forever.

Holy Spirit, the Spirit of God

The Holy Spirit, through prompting and revelation, helps people **see** and experience Jesus Christ as Savior. There cannot be an experience of Christ as Savior without an experience of the Holy Spirit.[28] We need to listen for the still small voice of the Spirit of God for recognizing sin, conviction of our sins, confession, and repentance. The Holy Spirit illuminates the truth and delivers understanding to enable us to laud Christ as our Savior. At that specific point, we are sealed by baptism into the Body of Christ as a new person to serve at God's will wherever called. We are born again.

The presence of the Holy Spirit in my life is real. How do I know? I once heard faith fully explained as, "When I know that I hate sin, I know I have been driven to that point." So, I know it is so because when it is so, it is so; so be it! Also, I don't even want to think about rejecting or blaspheming the Holy Spirit—the only unforgivable sin. I pray that there will never be a situation when I could ever do that. I truly fear God's eraser possibly blotting out my name from the Lamb's Book of Life. I have no greater fear.

> Have mercy on me, O God, according to your steadfast love; according to your abundant mercy blot out my transgressions. Wash me thoroughly from my iniquity, and cleanse me from my sin! For I know my transgressions, and my sin is ever before me. Against you, you only, have I sinned and done what is evil in your sight, so that you may be justified in your words and blameless in your judgment. Behold, I was brought forth in iniquity, and in sin did my mother conceive me. Behold, you delight in truth in the inward being, and you teach me wisdom in the secret heart. Purge me with hyssop, and I shall be clean; wash me, and I shall be whiter than snow. Let me hear joy and gladness; let the bones that you have broken rejoice. Hide your face from my sins, and blot out all my iniquities. Create in me a clean heart, O God, and renew a right spirit within me. Cast me not away from your presence, and take not your Holy Spirit from me. Restore to me the joy of your salvation, and uphold me with a willing spirit. Then I will teach transgressors your ways, and sinners will return to you. Deliver me from blood guiltiness, O God, O God of my salvation, and my tongue will sing aloud of your righteousness. O Lord, open my lips, and my mouth will declare your praise. For you will not delight in sacrifice, or I would give it; you will not be pleased with a burnt offering. The sacrifices of God are a broken spirit; a broken and contrite heart, O God, you will not despise. Do good to Zion in your good pleasure; build up the walls of Jerusalem; then will you delight in right sacrifices, in burnt offerings and whole burnt offerings; then bulls will be offered on your altar (Psalm 51:1-19 ESV).

The Spirit of God being equal in power and glory together with the Father and the Son, is to be believed, loved, obeyed, and worshipped and never resisted. We need to seek the Spirit of God in all that we do. It is the inward indwelling, illumination, and inspiration of the Holy Spirit that believers unite with Christ and not anything of the flesh and blood within us. By ourselves, we cannot think well without the guidance of the Holy Spirit. We who do not deserved grace are without hope unless the Spirit of God works in and through us.

Yes, "Change my heart, oh God, make it ever true; change my heart, oh God, may I be like you."[29]

Word of God

God's Word announces His love for the world and His yearning that all will be saved, the objective of God's plan to restore His pure kingdom. Therefore, I will sign every page of God's Word, the Holy Bible. I believe and trust it is the only authoritative, infallible, and inspired Word of God. I have faith that the Bible is pure, true, tested, and trustworthy; it dictates that I strive to obey its teachings. "In the beginning was the Word, and the Word was with God, and the Word was God" (John 1:1 ESV). "And the Word became flesh and dwelt among us, and we have seen his glory, glory as of the only Son from the Father, full of grace and truth" (John 1:14 ESV).

Here are some interesting and convincing facts from Jason and Ron Carlson about the Bible that recently appeared in greater detail. The Bible:

- Contains 66 books.

- Was written by 40 different authors.

- Was written over 1500 years.

- Was written in 3 different languages.

- Was written on 3 different continents.

- Was written with no historical errors or contradictions.

The entire Bible, from Genesis to Revelation, bears the mark of Divine inspiration.[30]

Separately, but related, five Latin phrases emerged out of the Protestant Reformation that strike me as having infinite merit, even today. In Latin, *sola* means *alone* or only, and the corresponding phrases are as follows:

- *Sola fide* means "by faith alone."

- *Sola Scriptura* means "by Scripture alone."

- *Solus Christus* means "through Christ alone."

- *Sola gratia* means "by grace alone."

- *Soli Deo gloria* means "glory to God alone."[31]

God's Holy Scriptures clearly teach us to define, defend, and obey our beliefs against cultural confusion that is hostile to the very notion of truth. Your defensive perimeter should contain each sola. God reveals Himself and His plan through Scriptures; they are a testimony to Christ, and they are not to be altered. His Word will not fail; God does what He promises.

While you are developing your own personal Theo-metric assessment, anchor your evaluation in the teachings of the Holy Bible and all its Scriptures. They are perfect and true! My confidence in my own salvation is embedded in the term *regeneration*, which starts with rebirth from the power and grace of God as revealed by His Holy Spirit and His Word. "For the Word of God is living and active, sharper than any two-edged sword, piercing to the division of soul and of spirit, of joints and of marrow, and discerning the thoughts and intentions of the heart" (Hebrews 4:12 ESV).

Attributes of a God Focus, Axis Y

At this point, begin to diligently separate the seven attributes of God into divisions of more detail. As presented earlier, the seven attributes of God are obtainable along our axis-Y focus. By God's infinite grace, there are no less than the following seven characteristic portals or attributes than what we now see through His Word:

1. Love

2. Hope

3. Faith

4. Truth

5. Purity

6. Honor

7. Justice

However, let's not forget what Paul writes to the Corinthians, "For now we see in a mirror dimly, but then face to face; now I know in part, but then I will know fully just as I also have been fully known" (1 Corinthians 13:12 ESV).

Hopefully, the fleshed-out Theo-metric 3-D model we are building will give us a broader understanding by visually intensifying the attributes of God against the seven attributes of the other two directional dimensions of Satan and earth that follow. It is important to remember that each attribute of each of the two other dimensional axes is never capable of being equal to the ones on the Y-axis! Like all matrix models, this model is for illustrating and gaining a fuller understanding of what is at play in our lives and how each component dynamically interacts on the other without contaminating one another (Figure 3).

1-Love

God's love is *agape* (godly love) love, not *phileo* and/or *storge* (brotherly love) or *eros* (erotic or passionate love) love. By contrast to the last two, God's love is pure love. It never fails. It is exemplified by the gospel of John 3:16 (ESV), which says, "For God so loved the world that he gave his only Son, that whoever believes in him shall not perish but have eternal life."

Here is a sample of the notoriety that has been given to the above well-known verse by Dr. Jerry Vines and others he mentions:

"John 3:16, perhaps the best-known verse in the Bible, is also perhaps both the first verse we learn and the last one we forget. This one verse has brought multitudes to Christ."

Dr. Herschel Hobbs, a former president of the Southern Baptist Convention and chairman of the Baptist Faith and Message Committee (1963), called John 3:16 "the Gospel in superlatives (the highest quality or degree of comparison)."

Martin Luther, the great reformer, called it "the Bible in miniature."

Dr. A. T. Robertson, seminary professor of Greek at Southern Baptist Theological Seminary in the early 1900s, referred to it as "the Little Gospel."

Others have called it "the Mount Everest of Holy Scripture; the most exquisite flower in the Garden of Holy Scripture; and "the Gospel in a nutshell."[32]

But for love to be complete communion between God and us, we must demonstrate a holy response from the inside, not just an outward image for the benefit of others. For that we must go to John 3:17–21 which requires we **do** His will and **obey** Him with all our heart, strength, and might through the power of the Spirit of God. It is those things that will be recognized and rewarded at the *bema seat* of Christ at the gathering of the raptured church triumphant.

2-Hope

God's hope is for a restored kingdom that is purified of all iniquity and perfect in every way. The scope of His hope eternal is that all should come to believe that Jesus Christ is Lord and be saved. Joel 2:32 (ESV) says, "And it shall come to pass that everyone who calls on the name of the Lord shall be saved. For in Mount Zion and in Jerusalem there shall be those who escape, as the Lord has said, and among the survivors shall be those whom the Lord calls." Acts 2:21 (ESV) says "And it shall come to pass that everyone who calls upon the name of the Lord shall be saved." And Romans 10:9 (ESV) says, "Because, if you confess with your mouth that Jesus is Lord and believe in your heart that God raised him from the dead, you will be saved."

God's hope and desire is for eternal peace that is never voided by the likes of Lucifer. Our hope should be likewise.

3-Faith

Scripture reveals that God is certain and is always faithful and true. He wants us to be like Him. Consider the following passages:

> Know therefore that the Lord your God is God, the faithful God who keeps covenant and steadfast love with those who love him and keep his commandments, to a thousand generations (Deuteronomy 7:9 ESV).

> So faith comes from hearing, and hearing through the word of Christ (Romans 10:17 ESV).

> God is faithful, and he will not let you be tempted beyond your ability, but with the temptation he will also provide the way of escape, that you may be able to endure it (1 Corinthians 10:13 ESV).

> And without faith it is impossible to please him, for whoever would draw near to God must believe that he exists and that he rewards those who seek him (Hebrews 11:6 ESV).

God the Father is assured His final victory will be achieved by the work of His Holy Spirit and His Son, Jesus Christ on the day of His choosing. Holistically thinking, God is very likely content knowing that when all of us are finally released into His creation fitted with free will, the interface with His free grace will culminate with a separation process that He has planned from the beginning. His end plan is to restore His perfect kingdom in the New Jerusalem, and it awaits this amalgamated purification process. The eminent purification process will exercise our freedom of choice that will separate all the past, present, and future tenants of this physical earth into believers and unbelievers. NOW is the time to make your choice between being a believer and non-believer. When believers die, their souls immediately become citizens in heaven; however, the souls of nonbelievers are immediately destined for hell as Jesus explained in the parable of the rich man and the poor man. At the breakup of all of earth's tenants, God will find that those who chose to be faithful are the ones He chose when the Lamb's Book of Life was filled in with the names of the elect at the beginning of time before the foundation of the world. These predestined citizens of His New Jerusalem want to be there just like God wants us to be there. This appears to be the way He will whet His sword to achieve a perfect relationship that is eternally consummated with no possible impurities. Finally, Holy Communion between God and His chosen will be attained for all eternity. To be a partaker in His emerging pure kingdom, we must follow Jesus with complete faith now.

4-Truth

God's truth is in His Word. Attainment of God's truth is not an intellectual exercise. It is a blessing imparted to us by God. "A person cannot receive even one thing unless it is given him from heaven" (John 3:27 ESV).

No matter how clearly written God's Word may be, if the reader is blind, he cannot see, and if the hearer is deaf, he cannot hear. We must open our heart to see and to hear God's Word. God already knows what is there (and what is not there). "He determines the number of the stars; he gives to all of them their names. Great is our Lord, and abundant in power; his understanding is beyond measure" (Psalm 147:4–5 ESV). First John 3:20 (ESV) says, "For whenever our heart condemns us, God is greater than our heart, and he knows everything."

5-Purity

God's purity is perfect. Paul says that because we are created in the likeness of God, we are to live in righteousness and holiness. "And to put on the new self, created after the likeness of God in true righteousness and holiness" (Ephesians 4:24 ESV). Second Corinthians 6:4–10 (ESV) then says,

> As servants of God we commend ourselves in every way: by great endurance, in afflictions, hardships, calamities, beatings, imprisonments, riots, labors, sleepless nights, hunger; by purity, knowledge, patience, kindness, the Holy Spirit, genuine love; by truthful speech, and the power of God; with the weapons of righteousness for the right hand and for the left; through honor and dishonor, through slander and praise. We are treated as impostors, and yet are true; as unknown, and yet well known; as dying, and behold, we live; as punished, and yet not killed; as sorrowful, yet always rejoicing; as poor, yet making many rich; as having nothing, yet possessing everything.

It is written in Job 14:4 that pure cannot come from the impure. God's Spirit is pure, and it opposes the desires of the flesh. Paul conveys this to the Galatians in a comment about purity of Spirit in terms of good fruits.

> But I say, walk by the Spirit, and you will not gratify the desires of the flesh. For the desires of the flesh are against the Spirit, and the desires of the Spirit are against the flesh, for these are opposed to each other, to keep you from doing the things you want to do. But if you are led by the Spirit, you are not under the law. Now the works of the flesh are evident: sexual immorality, impurity, sensuality, idolatry, sorcery, enmity, strife, jealousy, fits of anger, rivalries, dissensions, divisions, envy, drunkenness, orgies, and things like these. I warn you, as I warned you before, that those who do such things will not inherit the kingdom of God. But the fruit of the Spirit is love, joy, peace, patience, kindness, goodness, faithfulness, gentleness, self-control; against

such things there is no law. And those who belong to Christ Jesus have crucified the flesh with its passions and desires. If we live by the Spirit, let us also keep in step with the Spirit. Let us not become conceited, provoking one another, envying one another (Galatians 5:16–26 ESV).

Malachi 3:6 assures us that God has always been pure from the beginning, is now and ever will be. Someday heaven and earth will be pure without end.

6-Honor

We all realize what honor among thieves looks like; it is the antithesis of honor displayed by God. God's honor is based on total love and righteousness that little children can spot a mile away and come running. Little children are attracted by these two things because it rightfully attracts admiration, reverence, attention, confidence, poise, resolution, devotion, and faithfulness. These little ones seek out goodness, worth, virtue, reliability, and nobleness. We need to act like little children too.

Jesus will sit on His *bema seat* and honor the faithful who do these things. Proverbs 22:4 (ESV) states, "The reward for humility and fear of the Lord is riches and honor and life."

7-Justice

God's justice is fair and based on His principles of righteousness and morality in all things.

The unfaithful non-believer will see something other than a reward on the Day of the Lord. Paul writes clearly on this in 1 Corinthians 6:9. They will *not* inherit the kingdom of God. His justice must be served; therefore, sin must be punished. Deuteronomy 32:4 (ESV) says, "The Rock, his work is perfect, for all his ways are justice. A god of faithfulness and without iniquity, just and upright is he." Isaiah 11:1–5 (ESV) then says,

> There shall come forth a shoot from the stump of Jesse, and a branch from his roots shall bear fruit. And the Spirit of the Lord shall rest upon him, the Spirit of wisdom and understanding, the Spirit of counsel and might, the Spirit of knowledge and the fear of the Lord. And his delight shall be in the fear of the Lord. He shall not judge by what his eyes see, or decide disputes by what his ears hear, but with righteousness he shall judge the poor, and decide with equity for the meek of the earth; and he shall strike the earth with the rod of his mouth, and with the breath of his lips he shall kill the wicked. Righteousness shall be the belt of his waist, and faithfulness the belt of his loins.

We can run, but we cannot hide or resist. We can, and we do, but to no avail. Ask Jonah when you meet him if he was able to outswim God's "big fish." Recall that when Jonah finally conceded to God's will, the people of Nineveh repented. We just need to listen and do what He says to do. Good things will happen.

Worship

Continuous, 24-7 Worship

There is no good time to not worship. Matthew 18:20 (ESV) states, "For where two or three are gathered in my name, there am I among them."

Principles of Effective Worship

To be effective, we should show up with: (1) clean linen (prayed up, fessed up), (2) things only for God and not others, (3) nothing against our brother, (4) the best we can offer, (5) no disobedience, (6) the desire to treat all holy things in a holy manner, (7) selflessness for glory for self, (8) transparency before the Holy Spirit, who is the conductor of worship, (9) prayer for our church and our services, and (10) obedience to God's voice when He speaks to us in worship.[33]

The Faithful

To the casual observer, "faith" and "works" seems to get cross-threaded by Paul and James. Paul speaks of being saved by grace through faith alone. But, James said, "Faith without works is dead!" So, is there controversy here between Paul and James? Consider the following:

> For we hold that one is justified by faith apart from works of the law (Romans 3:28 ESV).

> So faith comes from hearing and hearing through the word of Christ (Romans 10:17 ESV).

> What good is it, my brothers, if someone says he has faith but does not have works? Can that faith save him? If a brother or sister is poorly clothed and lacking in daily food, and one of you says to them, "Go in peace, be warmed and filled," without giving them the things needed for the body, what good is that? So also faith by itself, if it does not have works, is dead (James 2:14–17 ESV).

Any Controversy?

There is no controversy! Faith is demonstrated by the works of salvation beginning at our second birth. Test your faith. Have you exercised your faith? Have you shared the good news? If not, then you are not exercising your faith. It is dead. Our works result from salvation; they are not a prerequisite for salvation. Nevertheless, for all Christians, works follow regeneration and they are the basis for our rewards in heaven at the *bema seat* of Christ. Our olive wreath is already pre-sized and waiting for us in a box on a shelf along with our white robes and palm branches for our hands in addition to other untold rewards (Revelation 7:9 pertains).

Now Jesus said, "In the same way, let your light shine before others, so that they may see your good works and give glory to your Father who is in heaven" (Matthew 5:16 ESV).

What Works Are Good Works?

Temporal good works prior to our second birth are counted as nothing in the kingdom of heaven. However, once saved, we are to put on the armor of God and be a soldier of the cross.

> Finally, be strong in the Lord and in the strength of his might. Put on the whole armor of God, that you may be able to stand against the schemes of the devil. For we do not wrestle against flesh and blood, but against the rulers, against the authorities, against the cosmic powers over this present darkness, against the spiritual forces of evil in the heavenly places. Therefore take up the whole armor of God, that you may be able to withstand in the evil day, and having done all, to stand firm. Stand therefore, having fastened on the belt of truth, and having put

on the breastplate of righteousness, and, as shoes for your feet, having put on the readiness given by the gospel of peace. In all circumstances take up the shield of faith, with which you can extinguish all the flaming darts of the evil one; and take the helmet of salvation, and the sword of the Spirit, which is the word of God, praying at all times in the Spirit, with all prayer and supplication. To that end keep alert with all perseverance, making supplication for all the saints, and also for me, that words may be given to me in opening my mouth boldly to proclaim the mystery of the gospel, for which I am an ambassador in chains, that I may declare it boldly, as I ought to speak (Ephesians 6:10–20 ESV).

Prayer

Adoration and gratitude are to be expressed through faith and love without ceasing both privately and corporately (publicly), and it is required by those who appeal to Him in prayer to give thanks for the gift of grace from God and the indwelling of the Holy Spirit. A mindfulness of God's presence, love, direction, and grace may be experienced. I once heard that thinking "YH" while inhaling and "WH" while exhaling during each breath brings about a deepening of our relationship with "YHWH" our Father.

Healing is often evident when God's hand brings restoration without any credit being attributed to human action. Sometimes God's hand also heals more than the physical need, going beyond to emotional and spiritual needs, and the latter being the ultimate gift from God.

The whole Word of God is of use to direct us in prayer, but the special rule of direction is contained in the form of prayer that Christ taught His disciples, commonly called the Lord's Prayer. We are to draw near to God with all holy reverence and confidence as children to a father, able and ready to help us, and we should pray with and for others.[34] Chapter five of first Thessalonians prods us to "Never stop praying." Remember, there is coming a day per Paul's words in Philippians 2:10-11 (ESV), "so that at the name of Jesus every knee should bow, in heaven and on earth and under the earth, and every tongue confess that Jesus Christ is Lord, to the glory of God the Father."

Seven Prayer Types to Consider (P-C-G-I-F-T-S)

These prayer types are by no means indicative of all prayer. However, they are high-level types to consider in your prayer life. Meditate on each one and drill down to where no further division is possible, namely to the root or primitive level. That is where you will find God waiting for you. Don't keep Him waiting, go there continuously with an undivided and unhindered heart.

P—Praise

This one is obvious. We are totally dependent upon God. His steadfast love endures forever. He is pleased to hear our praise for all that He has done for us. He expects and requires us to: (1) be sincere in our praise, (2) acknowledge our need and evil condition in humility in His holy presence, and (3) trust His promise in His Word that He will hear our praises in prayer and song for the sake of Jesus Christ our Lord.[35] It's not the number of words from our mouth or the notes from the instruments in our hands but the sincerity of our heart.

C—Confess

Jesus taught us to confess our debts or trespasses toward others. He also taught us to forgive others of debts or trespasses toward us in the prayer He gave to His disciples to take to our ancestors in this day and to the little ones who will follow us in the future. We should pray the Lord's Prayer over and over, pausing to bring all debts or trespasses into mind and confess these failures to God, including the ones not remembered or even known.

G—Guidance

Jesus also taught us to seek God leading us to righteousness and holiness and away from temptation and evil as we walk the Christian walk. That "still, small voice" must be heard, and it should be obeyed. When God's guidance comes, we need to follow it moment by moment, never stopping. We need to know sin when we see it, feel anathema toward it, and seek to overcome it.

I—Intercession

When we move from petition and supplication to intercession, we are shifting our center of gravity from not just to our own needs but to the needs and concerns of others as well. Intercessory prayer is selfless prayer, even self-giving prayer.[36] Dietrich Bonhoeffer has said, "Intercessory prayer is the purifying bath into which the individual and the fellowship must enter every day."[37]

Chaplains see people who are in desperate need of intercessory prayer. People who are patients, those going through divorce or difficult marriages, needy children, the aged, prisoners, stressed workers, and especially every lost soul all need our intercessory prayer.

F—Forgiveness

Jesus included instruction to pray for forgiveness of confessed sin in the Lord's Prayer. By that instruction we recognize the act of forgiving and the state of being forgiven of sin or injuries. When we confess our sins, especially to others, we receive not only forgiveness but also healing. "For when I kept silent, my bones wasted away through my groaning all day long." (Psalm 32:3 ESV). Psalm 130:3–4 (ESV) then says, "If you, O LORD, should mark iniquities, O Lord, who could stand? But with you there is forgiveness, that you may be feared."

Daniel 9:9 (ESV) says, "To the Lord our God belong mercy and forgiveness, for we have rebelled against him." Then Matthew 5:23–24 (ESV) states, "So if you are offering your gift at the altar and there remember that your brother has something against you, leave your gift there before the altar and go. First be reconciled to your brother, and then come and offer your gift."

Ephesians 1:7 (ESV) says, "In him we have redemption through his blood, the forgiveness of our trespasses, according to the riches of his grace." James 5:16 (ESV) then says, "Therefore, confess your sins to one another and pray for one another, that you may be healed. The prayer of a righteous person has great power as it is working." First John 1:9 (ESV) finally says, "If we confess our sins, he is faithful and just to forgive us our sins and to cleanse us from all unrighteousness."

Confessing to others need not be a mechanical requirement that is essential to be forgiven. Obviously, it is impossible in many situations, such as the time when a death or physical separation of one party is involved. However, whenever possible and appropriate, enjoy the healing from letting go vertically with God but also horizontally with others whenever possible. If we keep things to ourselves, they fester and cause more problems. Like a festering boil, lance it and open up the wound(s). Feel the joy of healing that it brings.[38]

T—Thanksgiving

Prayerful thanks have so many places where it belongs and is needed. It is the act of rendering thanks or the expression of gratitude for favors or mercies. Before meals, rising and lying down, safe journey, healing, successful ventures, and so many more conditions in life are worthy of our thanks to God. Before our annual Thanksgiving dinner, my wife and I turn to Psalm 100:1-5 (ESV), which says,

> Make a joyful noise to the LORD, all the earth! Serve the LORD with gladness! Come into his presence with singing! Know that the LORD, he is God! It is he who made us, and we are his; we are his people, and the sheep of his pasture. Enter his gates with thanksgiving, and his courts with praise! Give thanks to him; bless his name! For the LORD is good; his steadfast love endures forever, and his faithfulness to all generations."

First Timothy 4:4 (ESV) says, "For everything created by God is good, and nothing is to be rejected if it is received with thanksgiving."

Publicly, since 1620 when Pilgrims from the *Mayflower* landed at Plymouth Rock and gathered in a simple observance to give thanks for a successful voyage and a promise of freedom from much and varied oppression, we continue the tradition to publicly observe Thanksgiving as a day to celebrate divine goodness. Today, many Thanksgiving observances across the United States, take place in more formal ways, but we still set apart the day, many times in recognized religious services, to acknowledge the goodness of God. Special thanks are also characteristically lifted up for freedom from misfortunes and for God's graciousness. Thanksgiving celebrations, large or small, formal, or informal, honor God and demonstrate our desire to uphold the relationship we have with Him in advance of His blessings.

S—Salvation

While no prayer or reciting other special words alone will result in receiving salvation, Biblical salvation is only by God's grace through faith in Jesus Christ. However, Matthew 6:13 (ESV) reads "And lead us not into temptation, but deliver us from evil." where Jesus taught us to sincerely and deeply pray about the need for salvation from the fires of hell. The redemption of man from the bondage of sin and liability to eternal death and the conferring on him of everlasting happiness is the power of Biblical salvation. This kind of salvation is only found in the top "spiritual" pancake spoken of earlier. "And Moses said to the people, 'Fear not, stand firm, and see the salvation of the LORD, which he will work for you today. For the Egyptians whom you see today, you shall never see again'" (Exodus 14:13 ESV). "For godly grief produces a repentance that leads to salvation without regret, whereas worldly grief produces death" (2 Corinthians 7:10 ESV).

Salvation cannot be earned, maintained, or sustained by good works. Our good works are outputs, and our changed behaviors are outcomes of our salvation. Salvation is received by grace alone, through faith alone, through Christ alone. God's grace works to bring about our salvation and there is no salvation apart from personal and individual faith in the Lord Jesus Christ. When we feel the need to pray about salvation, God's grace has already started to work on us.

Please take a minute to find the diamond-shaped symbol <> that graphically identifies the moment when salvation comes (Figure 3). Pray for your salvation as a plea for help. It is the most important petition you can make to God. Isaiah 58:9 (ESV) explains, "Then you shall call, and the Lord will answer; you shall cry, and he will say, 'Here I am.'" By His grace, He will deliver you just like He did for the Hebrews at the crossing of the Red Sea. That was a moment too, literally a moment for all time where He protected the linage of Jesus for the Hebrew people and ultimately for us in this current age.

Four key terms partition salvation into identifiable subdivisions when believers come to Christ which are as follows: (1) recognition of sin and regeneration of the heart by the Holy Spirit leading to conviction and repentance through faith in Jesus Christ, (2) justification of the believer by exoneration of sin and favor with God, (3) sanctification of the believer through being set apart for God's service by the power of the Holy Spirit, and (4) glorification of the believer at the termination of temporal service of the redeemed.

It appears that our free will clearly has a role in working to confirm and keep our salvation intact in concert with God's free grace in everything we do. "But I preferred to do nothing without your consent in order that your goodness might not be by compulsion but of your own accord" (Philemon 1:14 ESV).

It also appears that our obedience is the outward evidence of God's grace and our free will to believe. For example, if we believe that the catcher in a trapeze act will catch us when we are signaled to jump, then we demonstrate our faith by the evidence of letting go of the first bar where we started. "Whoever believes in the Son has eternal life; whoever does not obey the Son shall not see life, but the wrath of God remains on him" (John 3:36 ESV).

Next, seven objects for our prayers follow which may also coincide with the seven ways we spend our time (i.e., Does a family member need guidance with difficult situations?):

Seven Prayer Components to Consider (F-I-S-H-E-R-S)
Like the prayer types listed previously, these seven components are by no means indicative of all prayer available or needed. Again, they are high-level components to consider in your prayer life. They, too, are worthy of your meditation on each one. These same portals are the primary sources for tension in our lives as attributed to Dr. Ralph Hook in the acknowledgments and later in the chapter titled "Dimension Three of Five—Portals of Earthly Time." So drill down yet again to where no further dissection of each component is possible, the root or primitive level. Then go to the Lord in prayer. God is still waiting for you to arrive.

F—Family
Recognizing family acknowledges that we all had one mother. So, we are truly one big family. Family is the basic building block of human life. Intuitively, no other godly family relationship is possible. So, here, I identify the group comprising a husband and a wife and their dependent children, constituting a fundamental unit in the organization of society since Eve, our first mom, delivered Cain, Able, and Seth. Sometimes there is discontent in our family. Every time this discontent appears, it needs prayer consistent with God's commandments. Recall that two commandments address the sanctity of marriage and family. The fifth commandment dictates we honor our father and mother to preserve

the authority of parents, and the seventh commandment prohibits adultery to preserve the purity of marriage.

Legitimate family relations include marriage, children through blood, or by legal adoption. Marriage is God's intended covenant lifelong commitment between one man and one woman for fulfilling His need to procreate His human race. Family is God's instrument for moving souls from the Lamb's Book of Life into life on earth.

Prayer to strengthen our families is exactly the right thing to do in these times when there are attacks everywhere on the very moral fiber of our mortal families. But the spiritual family will prevail by being connected through Jesus Christ from east and west and north and south. Here too, prayers for that eternal family are vital as well.

I—Interpersonal

Once more, since we all had one mother, that makes us all brothers and sisters—cousins at least. Coming together is most obvious in places where we find crossroads like air, land, or sea terminals. Gatherings in conferences, meetings, entertainment venues, schools, churches, chapels or synagogues, highways, stations, or anywhere people gather applies here. These assemblies sustain communication and social interaction. The Christian's role is cooperation in these crossroad settings, while striving to uphold social order. Christians should: (1) seek to make the will of Christ supreme in society through peaceful opposition to sin and oppression where needed, (2) apply principles of righteousness, truth, and brotherly love and encourage others to do the same, (3) work with all who are of good will in any good cause, and (4) always act in the spirit of love without compromise, remaining loyal to Christ and His truth.

So, Christians need to intently pray for our community, cities, counties, states, and nations to strengthen against those who would bring harm and threaten basic freedoms we enjoy through the Constitution of the United States as well as the Bill of Rights (Romans 13 pertains).

S—Specialty

Lines between vocational and professional sometimes blur. Vocation is a calling. Profession is commitment. Sometimes the two can come together in harmony like in the case of a volunteer chaplain.

But here we are focused on a person's specialty and how he or she uses their talents to further the kingdom of God; all that we are and have, we owe to Him. Christians not only have a spiritual responsibility to the whole world, but also have a stakeholder role in the spread of the gospel. Christians are therefore under obligation to serve Him with their time, talents, and material possessions; and should recognize all these as entrusted to them to serve God and others.

Prayer is vital in meeting the demands of our stewardship responsibilities that go with any professional or skilled role supporting and serving society and its well-being.

H—Health

Health is one of the easiest portals of life to demonstrate the perfunctory breakdown structure being illustrated in our overall Theo-metric model. There are seven systems of the body, including: (1)

tissue, (2) nervous, (3) skeletal, (4) circulatory, (5) respiratory, (6) digestive, and (7) reproductive. Drilling down to greater levels of detail to decompose this component of prayer enables us to pray with enhanced lament and grief over the specific suffering and infliction associated with the physical infirmity of one or more systems.

My role as a chaplain is to try to lend strength to the believer and *lead* other people to Christ sometimes at the most difficult and significant times of their lives. Most times I just get out of the way of the Holy Spirit and only help as I am permitted. I feel like I am just a carrier pigeon armed only with what the Lord packs into my little message pouch. Chaplaincy is a "being there" form of ministry that is anchored in love. Paul teaches, "Love is patient and kind; love does not envy or boast; it is not arrogant or rude. It does not insist on its own way; it is not irritable or resentful; it does not rejoice at wrongdoing but rejoices with the truth. Love bears all things, believes all things, hopes all things, endures all things" (1 Corinthians 13:4–7 ESV).

E—Education
Contemporary education pours into our lives from all directions; but educational preparation for evangelism, missions, and Christian education is also needed to fulfil the higher calling of the Lord's Great Commission.

Think of the fourteen temporal (seven **ugly**) and carnal (seven **bad**) attributes or characteristics that are competing against Christian education. These dynamics are at work in our churches, schools, and everywhere. Pray to overcome all fourteen conflicts that are impeding the Lord's Great Commission and are opposed to God's (seven **good**) attributes.

Accordingly, support for strong Christian education is needed when making a comprehensive and personal Theo-metric assessment. Christians should: (1) work to make disciples of all nations, (2) be there for others to advocate the new birth of the human spirit by the indwelling of the Holy Spirit, (3) promote the teachings of Christ on the spiritual necessity of the regenerate life, and (4) have a lifestyle in harmony with the gospel of Christ.

New birth creates a thirst for knowledge and Christian education is necessary to a complete spiritual program for Christ's people. Pray that we discharge education to our young and old alike to enthusiastically build godly character, discipline, and faith throughout the free society we enjoy and in a spiritually hungry world.

R—Recreation
Even Jesus took time to recreate those things in Him that had become exhausted. He needed rest and recuperation. We do too. When we retreat and allow time to recreate those things in us that have become exhausted, we return revived and stronger to resume our tasks for glory to God and others as emphasized in Mark 6:31 (ESV) following the miraculous feeding of the five thousand. Pray rest for God's children is bountiful.

S—Spiritual
Spiritual and religious liberties are a hallmark of freedom in the United States of America. Persecutions of Christians and others are rampant everywhere in the world. Even here atheists seek to eliminate the rights of Christians to practice their faith.

While Church and state should be separate, the state owes every church the protection and full, equal freedom to pursue its spiritual ends. A free church in a free state is the Christian ideal, and this implies the right of free and unhindered access to God on the part of all people.

Prayer needs for spiritual and religious leaders and those who support them should be heard far and wide to glorify and sustain the work of the Lord.

The Prayer of Jesus Himself

The real Lord's Prayer by Jesus before He went to the cross reads,

> Father, the hour has come; glorify your Son that the Son may glorify you, since you have given him authority over all flesh, to give eternal life to all whom you have given him. And this is eternal life, that they know you the only true God, and Jesus Christ whom you have sent. I glorified you on earth, having accomplished the work that you gave me to do. And now, Father, glorify me in your own presence with the glory that I had with you before the world existed.

> I have manifested your name to the people whom you gave me out of the world. Yours they were, and you gave them to me, and they have kept your word. Now they know that everything that you have given me is from you. For I have given them the words that you gave me, and they have received them and have come to know in truth that I came from you; and they have believed that you sent me. I am praying for them. I am not praying for the world but for those whom you have given me, for they are yours. All mine are yours, and yours are mine, and I am glorified in them. And I am no longer in the world, but they are in the world, and I am coming to you. Holy Father, keep them in your name, which you have given me, that they may be one, even as we are one. While I was with them, I kept them in your name, which you have given me. I have guarded them, and not one of them has been lost except the son of destruction, that the Scripture might be fulfilled. But now I am coming to you, and these things I speak in the world, that they may have my joy fulfilled in themselves. I have given them your word, and the world has hated them because they are not of the world, just as I am not of the world. I do not ask that you take them out of the world, but that you keep them from the evil one. They are not of the world, just as I am not of the world. Sanctify them in the truth; your word is truth. As you sent me into the world, so I have sent them into the world. And for their sake I consecrate myself, that they also may be sanctified in truth.

> I do not ask for these only, but also for those who will believe in me through their word, that they may all be one, just as you, Father, are in me, and I in you, that they also may be in us, so that the world may believe that you have sent me. The glory that you have given me I have given to them, that they may be one even as we are one, I in them and you in me, that they may become perfectly one, so that the world may know that you sent me and loved them even as you loved me. Father, I desire that they also, whom you have given me, may be with me where I am, to see my glory that you have given me because you loved me before the foundation of the world. O righteous Father, even though the world does not know you, I know you, and these know that you have sent me. I made known to them your name, and I will continue to make it known, that the love with which you have loved me may be in them, and I in them (John 17:1-26 ESV).

Body of Believers

The body of believers cannot be limited by a human term or a moment of time when viewed holistically from Scripture. "And people will come from east and west, and from north and south, and recline at table in the kingdom of God." (Luke 13:29 ESV).

The Church

There is only one body of all Christian believers—the church Catholic, "the one church that is universal, scattered through all parts of the world, and extended unto all times and is not limited to any times or sociopolitical places."[39]

While the collective churches of the holy Christian church universal combine to make up the temporal church militant, it befits all Christians to ensure that focus remains steadfast toward the eternal church triumphant and that not one of Christ's followers are lost.

Common Risk for All Believers—Who Is Painting Who?

So, does any particular group of believers paint, color, or influence the church, or does the church paint, color, or influence the particular group? What motivates each group to be a little different? What is the group's objective? What are the risks of such activity? What is the value added?" Since nothing temporal will survive the purification of earth by fire at the end of the age, then who is painting, coloring, or influencing who? I conclude that if I am painted, colored, or influenced by the blood of the Lamb that I will be lifted up white as snow by the time the fire comes. Who persuades, inspires, and informs who? Who is holding the paintbrush? Does the believer paint the church, or does the church paint the believer? Or does the non-believer paint the church and/or the believer? In answering this question, it is important that we gather around John 10:16 and embrace the fact that there is only one Shepherd and one sheepfold in heaven. None are painted by anything earthly or temporal.

Edward Mote (1834)[40] penned the succinct words that follow, which were later composed into music by William B. Bradbury (1863) that indicate how I will be dressed when the trumpet sounds. My glasses, pacemaker, stents, watch, and wedding ring yield to gravity while I vacate *terra firma*.

1. My hope is built on nothing less than Jesus' blood and righteousness.

   I dare not trust the sweetest frame, but wholly lean on Jesus' name.

   Chorus: On Christ the solid rock I stand; all other ground is sinking sand,

   all other ground is sinking sand.

2. When Darkness veils his lovely face, I rest on his unchanging grace.

   In every high and stormy gale, my anchor holds within the veil.

3. His oath, his covenant, his blood supports me in the whelming flood.

   When all around my soul gives way, he then is all my hope and stay.

4. When He shall come with trumpet sound, O may I then in him be found!

   Dressed in his righteousness alone, faultless to stand before the throne.

The most reliable testimony for what the Holy Spirit has already done to renew your heart to enable you to believe in Jesus Christ comes through believer's water baptism by immersion to identify yourself with Him to others. The Lord's Supper is like it because when you partake of the bread and the cup, you are remembering Christ's death and His blood that was shed for the complete remission of your sins. But there is more.

Take the two criminals on the cross next to Jesus. One of them could have said in so many words, "I know You. You're the one that raised Lazarus from the dead the other day. You are the Son of God. You must be. I am just a sinner, and I deserve what I got. But You did not do anything to deserve this suffering. I know I cannot get off this cross by myself, so please take me with You when we go." He just had Jesus in his heart, and he claimed Him as his Lord and Savior. He knew where he wanted to be when he got where he was going, and he got it—that very day! Unfortunately, the other criminal did not! His mind and heart were hard like Pharaoh's heart, which was set on the values of this temporal, earthly abode. Like Pharaoh, he did not get even that. His soul is burning in the lake of fire with the rich man today. The first criminal is standing next to Abraham and Lazarus in paradise with Jesus, even without a water baptism and there was no time to break bread and drink the cup.

So, in heaven, there will be no streets and neighborhoods reserved for a particular denomination. No Presbyterian Parkway, no Baptist Boulevard, no Lutheran Lane, no Methodist Main Street, or anything else lauding something temporal. We will all be under the same Lordship of Jesus Christ; perhaps we should demonstrate and embrace that more nowadays as well. During my time as a seminary student, I anticipated a deliberate blended ecumenical environment. But I found that respective groups of students were encouraged (and required at times) to align themselves mostly by their faith groups and doctrine. I often contrasted that environment with large crusade services or military chapel services where an ecumenical spirit exists and operates much differently. Refer to the earlier discussion of the history of denominations (Figure 5).

The Bible says,

> But now you must put them all away: anger, wrath, malice, slander, and obscene talk from your mouth. Do not lie to one another, seeing that you have put off the old self with its practices and have put on the new self, which is being renewed in knowledge after the image of its creator. Here there is not Greek and Jew, circumcised and uncircumcised, barbarian, Scythian, slave, free; but Christ is all, and in all. Put on then, as God's chosen ones, holy and beloved, compassionate hearts, kindness, humility, meekness, and patience, bearing with one another and, if one has a complaint against another, forgiving each other; as the Lord has forgiven you, so you also must forgive. And above all these put on love, which binds everything together in perfect harmony. And let the peace of Christ rule in your hearts, to which indeed you were called in one body. And be thankful. Let the word of Christ dwell in you richly, teaching and admonishing one another in all wisdom, singing psalms and hymns and spiritual songs, with thankfulness in your hearts to God. And whatever you do, in word or deed, do everything in the name of the Lord Jesus, giving thanks to God the Father through him (Colossians 3:8–17 ESV).

Can you discern what if any denomination Paul is speaking of? No? Doesn't a wedding, chapel services at sea or in the field, or perhaps even a funeral service come to mind when we read Paul's words? An individual or group Theo-metric assessment in our denomination-based churches would go a long way in neutralizing some our differences and help us focus on nurturing the *souls* of all present to help them get where they will be when we get where we are going while forgetting about the color of the carpet or if the church house needs a bigger chandelier. Can Christians be more interconnected? I have no doubt about what militant evil force is behind the previously mentioned impeders that are tripping us up. If you have any doubt, turn to C. S. Lewis for some clues in his book *The Screwtape Letters*[41] as once recommended by Supreme Court Justice Antonin Scalia during an interview and recorded in a recent newspaper article.[42]

Time Is Ticking

Dr. Richard Carlson's book *Don't Sweat the Small Stuff . . . and all of it is small stuff*, recommends some simple ways to keep the little things from taking over our lives. His table of contents lists a hundred points to remember in this effort. These points are all about fixing our attention on what is important and on what will be important a hundred years from now. One of his points (#6) that fit this realm is to "remind yourself that when you die, your in-basket won't be empty."[43]

In his book *The Present*, Dr. Spencer Johnson writes that the secret to enjoying your work and life is to be in the present, learn from the past, and help create the future.[44] Theo-metrics addresses all three and is another tool to help realize your purpose. Johnson also writes about the "handwriting on the wall" regarding the changes we face in life in his book *Who Moved My Cheese? —An Amazing Way to Deal with Change in Your Work and Life*.[45] When read together, these two works are highly effective in helping one get through the current moment. When the moment involves a change, move with it. These two books were very meaningful in helping me cope with the change associated with the loss of my first wife to breast cancer. They reinforced my inner gyro to make a move to seminary and grow my faith. Theo-metrics will even take you a little further as well—to the point where you know where you will be when you get where you are going. If Theo-metrics helps you relax about your destination as much as these two books by Spencer Johnson helped me relax about the present and the changes it may dictate, then the model is doing what I hoped it would do. I sincerely thank Richard Carlson and Spencer Johnson for their inspiring works and their wide applications for everyone.

Behold, I Come Quickly

While providing care for my first wife at the end stage of her life, I tried to support her the best way I knew how. She had only brief moments of consciousness in the final days, and when she awakened that last morning, the most natural thing I could think of was to ask her if I could read her the devotion for the day in *The Upper Room*.[46] She smiled and said, "Yes, I would like that." The Scripture reading was from Psalm 18.

> For who is God, but the LORD? And who is a rock, except our God? —the God who equipped me with strength and made my way blameless. He made my feet like the feet of a deer and set me secure on the heights. He trains my hands for war, so that my arms can bend a bow of bronze. You have given me the shield of your salvation, and your right hand supported me, and your gentleness made me great. You gave a wide place for my steps under me, and my feet did not slip (Psalm 18:31–36 ESV).

The accompanying story was titled "Letting Go." Little did I know that later that day she would let go. The little story that day portrayed a talented trapeze act that centered on the point when the leap by one artist must be perfectly timed with the catcher in the middle. The artist doing the leaping must have the faith not only to make a timed leap, but to also let go of the first bar and be prepared to grab the waiting nail scared hands of the catcher who will take him or her across to the other side. I told my wife that I look at the catcher in the story as Jesus, He does not miss, and He does not need a net. He has such a firm grip we will probably be able to feel the sticky stuff from the athletic tape wrapped around His wrists. He will grab us out of thin air and deposit us safely on the other platform every time when we have the faith to believe He will. I also don't recall seeing any trapeze artist looking back at the platform where they started. Their focus is always on what is ahead, always watching and waiting for a perfect connection and a sure relationship with the catcher. Practicing our faith every day brings experience that the catcher is also watching and waiting for us. He will not let us down. That same day that she let go of the surly bounds of earth and went to go to be with the Lord. I have used this work by D. D. Emmons many times with patients since that day with one addition to the story. I always add a catcher to the act; the performer on the other swinging bar in the middle that grabs the one leaping from the first bar. His name is Jesus and He never misses, and He refuses to use a net. He will take you across to the other side every time; He will keep you lifted high above the fiery pit reserved for Satan and his devils. He will take you to where you will be when you get where you are going. Thank you, Mr. Emmons, for your excellent work. I have faith that my wife made it safely to the other side that day. She had the faith too, and I thank you for your encouragement in the faith for both of us.

This memory makes me recall some of her favorite Scriptures, including Psalm 46, Isaiah 40, and John 14. She particularly delighted in Isaiah 40:20–31, which says,

> He who is too impoverished for an offering chooses wood that will not rot; he seeks out a skillful craftsman to set up an idol that will not move. Do you not know? Do you not hear? Has it not been told you from the beginning? Have you not understood from the foundations of the earth? It is he who sits above the circle of the earth, and its inhabitants are like grasshoppers; who stretches out the heavens like a curtain, and spreads them like a tent to dwell in; who brings princes to nothing, and makes the rulers of the earth as emptiness. Scarcely are they planted, scarcely sown, scarcely has their stem taken root in the earth, when he blows on them, and they wither, and the tempest carries them off like stubble. To whom then will you compare me, that I should be like him? says the Holy One. Lift up your eyes on high and see: who created these? He who brings out their host by number, calling them all by name, by the greatness of his might, and because he is strong in power not one is missing. Why do you say, O Jacob, and speak, O Israel, "My way is hidden from the LORD, and my right is disregarded by my God"? Have you not known? Have you not heard? The LORD is the everlasting God, the Creator of the ends of the earth. He does not faint or grow weary; his understanding is unsearchable. He gives power to the faint, and to him who has no might he increases strength. Even youths shall faint and be weary, and young men shall fall exhausted; but they who wait for the LORD shall renew their strength; they shall mount up with wings like eagles; they shall run and not be weary; they shall walk and not faint (Isaiah 40:20–31 ESV).

Psalm 46 says,

God is our refuge and strength, a very present help in trouble. Therefore, we will not fear though the earth gives way, though the mountains be moved into the heart of the sea, though its waters roar and foam, though the mountains tremble at its swelling. There is a river whose streams make glad the city of God, the holy habitation of the Most High. God is in the midst of her; she shall not be moved; God will help her when morning dawns. The nations rage, the kingdoms totter; he utters his voice, the earth melts. The LORD of hosts is with us; the God of Jacob is our fortress. Come, behold the works of the LORD, how he has brought desolations on the earth. He makes wars cease to the end of the earth; he breaks the bow and shatters the spear; he burns the chariots with fire. "Be still, and know that I am God. I will be exalted among the nations, I will be exalted in the earth!" The LORD of hosts is with us; the God of Jacob is our fortress (Psalms 46:1-11 ESV).

John 14 anchored her favorites,

"Let not your hearts be troubled. Believe in God; believe also in me. In my Father's house are many rooms. If it were not so, would I have told you that I go to prepare a place for you? And if I go and prepare a place for you, I will come again and will take you to myself, that where I am you may be also. And you know the way to where I am going." Thomas said to him, "Lord, we do not know where you are going. How can we know the way?" Jesus said to him, "I am the way, and the truth, and the life. No one comes to the Father except through me. If you had known me, you would have known my Father also. From now on you do know him and have seen him." Philip said to him, "Lord, show us the Father, and it is enough for us." Jesus said to him, "Have I been with you so long, and you still do not know me, Philip? Whoever has seen me has seen the Father. How can you say, 'Show us the Father'? Do you not believe that I am in the Father and the Father is in me? The words that I say to you I do not speak on my own authority, but the Father who dwells in me does his works. Believe me that I am in the Father and the Father is in me, or else believe on account of the works themselves. "Truly, truly, I say to you, whoever believes in me will also do the works that I do; and greater works than these will he do, because I am going to the Father. Whatever you ask in my name, this I will do, that the Father may be glorified in the Son. If you ask me anything in my name, I will do it. "If you love me, you will keep my commandments. And I will ask the Father, and he will give you another Helper, to be with you forever, even the Spirit of truth, whom the world cannot receive, because it neither sees him nor knows him. You know him, for he dwells with you and will be in you. "I will not leave you as orphans; I will come to you. Yet a little while and the world will see me no more, but you will see me. Because I live, you also will live. In that day you will know that I am in my Father, and you in me, and I in you. Whoever has my commandments and keeps them, he it is who loves me. And he who loves me will be loved by my Father, and I will love him and manifest myself to him." Judas (not Iscariot) said to him, "Lord, how is it that you will manifest yourself to us, and not to the world?" Jesus answered him, "If anyone loves me, he will keep my word, and my Father will love him, and we will come to him and make our home with him. Whoever does not love me does not keep my words. And the word that you hear is not mine but the Father's who sent me. "These things I have spoken to you while I am still with you. But the Helper, the Holy Spirit, whom the Father will send in my name, he will teach you all things and bring to your remembrance all that I have said to you. Peace I leave with you; my peace I give to you. Not as the world gives do I give to you. Let not your hearts be troubled, neither let them be afraid. You heard me say to you, 'I am going away, and I will come to you.' If you loved me, you would have rejoiced, because I am going to the Father, for the Father is greater than I. And now I have told you before it takes place, so that when it does take place you may believe. I will no longer talk much with you, for the ruler of this world is coming. He has no claim on me, but I do as the Father has commanded me, so that the world may know that I love the Father. Rise, let us go from here (John 14:1-31 ESV).

I also remember her asking me, "What will you do when I am gone?" I said I would probably go back to seminary. "That's good!" was her response. That assuring voice still echoes in my head as it did that day. I hear it as I work on assignments late at night like now and with my every waking hour. It is a sweet, sweet sound of love in my ear.

Jesus Christ Is Lord

My condensed faith is "one Shepherd, one pasture" from John 10:16. So as a Christian, I acknowledge my Lord and Savior, Jesus Christ through the power of the Holy Spirit to believe in that Great Shepherd of the Sheep. I know where I will be when I get where I am going; but where will you be when you get where you are going? Are you ready? Do you have your vision clearly fixed on the one who can guarantee your eternity? Who is your Shepherd? Jesus Christ or Satan? Where is your eternal pasture? Heaven or hell? What Trinity is your guide? The Holy Trinity or satanic trinity? Where is your treasure? Heaven or earth?

Remember 2 Peter 3 reminds us that on the Day of the Lord the earth will melt, so trying to hold on to anything of *terra firma* and all that is on it is *not* recommended. The words of verse 6 of "Amazing Grace" echo in my ear every time I read 2 Peter 3. "The earth will soon *dissolve* like snow, the sun forbear to shine. But God who called me here below, shall be forever mine."[47]

The New Testament good news is that in the life, death, and resurrection of Jesus, the Christ, and the dominion of God met and conquered the dominion of Satan, whereupon salvation was made available to all.[48] Resist the tentacles of the satanic trinity in all its shapes and forms. Seek out, abide, and obey the Holy Trinity.

For those of us who are heaven-bound, Jesus has given us His Great Commission for us to carry out. It's our mission. So, it is critical for us to know how to lead someone to Christ.

Memory Scriptures for Leading Others to Christ

1. **Acknowledge your lost condition.**

    a. Isaiah 53:6 says, "All we like sheep have gone astray; we have turned—every one—to his own way; and the LORD has laid on him the iniquity of us all."

    b. Romans 3:23 says, "For all have sinned and fall short of the glory of God."

2. **Believe the gospel of Jesus Christ.**

a. John 3:36 says, "Whoever believes in the Son has eternal life; whoever does not obey the Son shall not see life, but the wrath of God remains on him."

b. John 5:24 says, "Truly, truly, I say to you, whoever hears my word and believes him who sent me has eternal life. He does not come into judgment but has passed from death to life."

c. Acts 16:30 says, "Then he brought them out and said, 'Sirs, what must I do to be saved?'"

d. Acts 16:31 says, "And they said, 'Believe in the Lord Jesus, and you will be saved, you and your household.'"

e. Romans 5:8 says, "But God shows his love for us in that while we were still sinners, Christ died for us."

3. **Repent for your sins.**

a. Isaiah 55:7 says, "Let the wicked forsake his way, and the unrighteous man his thoughts; let him return to the LORD, that he may have compassion on him, and to our God, for he will abundantly pardon."

b. Luke 13:3 says, "No, I tell you; but unless you repent, you will all likewise perish."

c. Romans 6:23 says, "For the wages of sin is death, but the free gift of God is eternal life in Christ Jesus our Lord."

d. Acts 17:30 says, "The times of ignorance God overlooked, but now he commands all people everywhere to repent."

e. Revelation 20:14 says, "Then Death and Hades were thrown into the lake of fire. This is the second death, the lake of fire."

4. **Receive Christ as your Savior.**

a. John 1:12 says, "But to all who did receive him, who believed in his name, he gave the right to become children of God."

b. John 3:16 says, "For God so loved the world, that he gave his only Son, that whoever believes in him should not perish but have eternal life."[49]

c. John 3:17 says, "For God did not send his Son into the world to condemn the world, but in order that the world might be saved through him."

d. John 3:18 says, "Whoever believes in him is not condemned, but whoever does not believe is condemned already, because he has not believed in the name of the only Son of God."

e. John 3:19 says, "And this is the judgment: the light has come into the world, and people loved the darkness rather than the light because their works were evil."

f. John 3:20 says, "For everyone who does wicked things hates the light and does not come to the light, lest his works should be exposed."

g. John 3:21 says, "But whoever does what is true comes to the light, so that it may be clearly seen that his works have been carried out in God."

h. First John 5:12 says, "Whoever has the Son has life; whoever does not have the Son of God does not have life."

i. First John 5:13 says, "I write these things to you who believe in the name of the Son of God that you may know that you have eternal life."

j. Revelation 3:20 says, "Behold, I stand at the door and knock. If anyone hears my voice and opens the door, I will come in to him and eat with him, and he with me."

5. **Confess Him as your Lord.**

a. Mark 8:34 says, "And calling the crowd to him with his disciples, he said to them, 'If anyone would come after me, let him deny himself and take up his cross and follow me.'"

b. Mark 8:35 says, "For whoever would save his life will lose it, but whoever loses his life for my sake and the Gospel's will save it."

c. Mark 8:36 says, "For what does it profit a man to gain the whole world and forfeit his soul?"

d. Mark 8:37 says, "For what can a man give in return for his soul?"

e. Mark 8:38 says, "For whoever is ashamed of me and of my words in this adulterous and sinful generation, of him will the Son of Man also be ashamed when he comes in the glory of his Father with the holy angels."

f. Romans 10:9 says, "Because, if you confess with your mouth that Jesus is Lord and believe in your heart that God raised him from the dead, you will be saved."

g. Romans 10:10 says, "For with the heart one believes and is justified, and with the mouth one confesses and is saved."

6. **Be Baptized into Christ.**

a. Mark 16:16 says, "Whoever believes and is baptized will be saved, but whoever does not believe will be condemned."

b. Acts 2:38 says, "And Peter said to them, 'Repent and be baptized every one of you in the name of Jesus Christ for the forgiveness of your sins, and you will receive the gift of the Holy Spirit.'"

7. **Grow steadfast until death or the rapture.**

   a. John 6:47-54 says, "Truly, truly, I say to you, whoever believes has eternal life. I am the bread of life. Your fathers ate the manna in the wilderness, and they died. This is the bread that comes down from heaven, so that one may eat of it and not die. I am the living bread that came down from heaven. If anyone eats of this bread, he will live forever. And the bread that I will give for the life of the world is my flesh." The Jews then disputed among themselves, saying, "How can this man give us his flesh to eat?" So Jesus said to them, "Truly, truly, I say to you, unless you eat the flesh of the Son of Man and drink his blood, you have no life in you. Whoever feeds on my flesh and drinks my blood has eternal life, and I will raise him up on the last day."

   b. Acts 2:47 says, "Praising God and having favor with all the people. And the Lord added to their number day by day those who were being saved."

   c. Colossians 1:13 says, "He has delivered us from the domain of darkness and transferred us to the kingdom of his beloved Son."

Table 9. How to Lead Someone to Christ

Know these Scriptures (Tape them to the bathroom mirror and memorize them while you are shaving or drying your hair. If you seal them in a one-gallon zipper-type plastic bag, you can hang them from the shower head with a string.) Do not leave home without them fixed to the back of your eyelids; then abide and obey them!

During the late 1800s, D. L Moody's ministry included many anecdotes to clarify points in his sermons. One such anecdote on the free gift of God for salvation in Jesus Christ goes like this:

A Sunday school teacher wished to show his class how free the gift of God is. He took a silver watch from his pocket and offered it to the eldest boy in the class.

"It's yours, if you will take it."

The little fellow sat and grinned at the teacher. He thought he was joking. The teacher offered it to the next boy, and said, "Take that watch; it's yours."

The little fellow though he would be laughed at if he held out his hand, and therefore he sat still. In the same way the teacher went nearly round the class; but not one of them would accept the proffered gift. At length he came to the smallest boy. When the watch was offered to the little fellow, he took it and put it into his pocket. All the class laughed at him.

"I am thankful, my boy," said the teacher, "that you believe my word. The watch is yours. Take good care of it and wind it every night."

The rest of the class looked on in amazement; and one of them said: "Teacher, you don't mean that the watch is his? You don't mean that he hasn't to give it back to you?"

"No," said the teacher, "he hasn't to give it back to me. It is his own now."

"Oh! If I had only known that, wouldn't I have taken it."[50]

I also find that a review of the seven binary (yes/no) logical steps leading to a decision for Jesus Christ and salvation for eternal life in heaven is meaningful to process-minded individuals like me. It may come as a bit of a shock that many (as in Moody's anecdote previously outlined) will end up lost when they find out where they will be when they get where they are going. Come to Jesus and get back on track. It is not too late to run the race that is set before us. Complete all the steps below leading to heaven. Just say yes to Jesus through the free grace of God and faith in Jesus Christ by the power of the Holy Spirit, who enabled your free will to make that eternal choice.

1. Hear

2. Believe

3. Remorse

4. Repent

5. Confess

6. Baptize

7. Obey by faith until death

If you are not born again, then try again! Don't just stand at the door and knock. Stand at the door and pound on it! It all comes down to this: "Do you **believe** Jesus is who He says He is? Do you **do** what He says?" Become a disciple, make disciples, and share the good news.

Are You Fully Equipped for What Is Next?

So far, our mind-map matrix is still relatively simple. However, when tension is applied to our lifeline, things usually get messy as we are about to see. Here are two rather subtle but sometimes not-so-subtle examples.

Universal Languages—Math and Music

Math and music are two universal languages that we all enjoy. Although I enjoy music, it does not enjoy me. Nor does anyone else who has ever heard me attempt to demonstrate any musical skills or lack thereof. However, math has been a language that I can speak and convey to others effectively. Once as a high school algebra teacher, it seems I was able to hold my own. And later while I was developing software and logistical schemes in joint military operations, I again found math to be friendly and especially useful.

The complete Theo-metric mathematical graphical 3-D array depicted by Paul's three dimensions of life in Colossians 3 leads to forming the boundaries that frame the tension area in our mortal lives. Notice the origin of our mortal lifeline is at the point where the three dimensions cross. However, the completion of our lifeline is a variable to us and is not so easy to identify on a 3-D canvas. But one binary thing is certain. We have a decision to make for Christ **before** we get to the end of our mortal lifeline. **Yes** for Christ leads to eternal life. **No** for Christ leads to eternal death. This binary message is clear in any language, even when communicated in zeroes and ones. By defaulting to the null set (∅) of no decision for Christ, you default to no. There are no ties in the game of life—only winners and losers and there is no overtime to break a tie. Do the precise language of math for Christ and decide yes. It will make unmistakable music to your ears.

God v. Science

Many are looking for reason and logic to find another softer way to view life. Many of their approaches clearly try to muddy up or deliberately obfuscate our vision of where we will be when we get where are going. Many do not think at all. They are rooted in a work ethic with or without a Christian basis. Debates surrounding problems science has with religion and vice versa have existed in one form or another for a long time. Some scientists say that God doesn't help people when they need help. So how can God be good and all-powerful if He can't or won't help people in their time of need? Some scientists say that since God made everything, then all sickness, immorality, hatred, ugliness, and death was made by God. Therefore, He also made Satan and evil, so God must be evil.

However, on the other side of the debate for God, Jesus, and the Holy Spirit, we sometimes hear with equally intuitive logic about such things as heat versus cold, light versus dark. They explain that you can have lots of heat, but we don't have anything called *cold*. There is no such thing as cold. Otherwise, we would be able to go colder than the lowest measurable degree. Cold is only a word we use to describe the absence of heat.

If you argue that there is a good God and a bad God, you are viewing the concept of God as something finite, something we can measure. Science cannot even explain that kind of a thought. Scientists use electricity and magnetism but have never seen much less fully understood either one. Even evolution has never been confirmed by human senses. So, since no one has ever observed the process of evolution at work and cannot even prove that this process is an ongoing endeavor, it must be a mere opinion. Like a preacher, a scientist must take many things on faith.

Logic does not supplant faith. It never will. Why would anyone want to believe any of that for salvation?[51] Both sides in these debates point to philosophical premises that are flawed from the start. The conclusions must also be flawed because they are working on the premise of duality. However, a quick review of God's master plan in the Introduction reveals a much superior scenario—to restore a pure kingdom through God's free grace and our free will. By the power of the Holy Spirit, Jesus is the *only* bridge that connects these two freebies. As demonstration of God's sovereignty, no sin is great enough to tear us apart from the love of God in Christ Jesus, our Lord. "For I am sure that neither death nor life, nor angels nor rulers, nor things present nor things to come, nor powers, nor height nor depth, nor anything else in all creation, will be able to separate us from the love of God in Christ Jesus our Lord." (Romans 8:38–39 ESV).

So, when I was first led by the Holy Spirit to hate sin, I then knew in faith, when it is so, it is so—so be it. God's total sovereignty over creation must be viewed in the context of that which is from His original pure kingdom to His eternal restored pure kingdom (Figure 1). Since God put our names in the Lamb's Book of Life before the foundation of the world, He wants us to choose Him in grateful response for His Son, Jesus Christ, who conquered sin by the shedding of His blood on the cross for us. It is what God has already done for us. For that reason, believe in Jesus. Believe that He is our personal Savior. Our God-inspired conviction leads us to recognition, remorse, repentance, confession, baptism, and faithful obedience during this life, which leads to eternal life in heaven. We must turn, or we will burn. ***Our judgment is now!***

Dimension Two of Five—Portals of Sinful Time

Dimension two of our mind map, when decomposed, represents the seven portals or attributes of Satan's character on a horizontal X-axis (Figure 3). It is everything **bad** that is in our lives.

When Adam and Eve fell from grace in the Garden of Eden when they succumbed to Satan by eating the forbidden fruit, they condemned all humankind to eternal death and the fires of hell. So, we who are alive are already condemned to the flames of hell unless chosen by God to receive His saving grace through the power of the Holy Spirit, which fosters the growth of faith in His Son, Jesus Christ. When this occurs, we are regenerated or born again, and with hope, we fall in love with God.[52] Otherwise, rejection of the Spirit of God leads to damnation, and we are doomed, blasphemous reprobates for eternity. We will never see glory in heaven. Consequently, hell is where we will be when we get where we are going unless we discover our sins, find remorse, repent, confess, and change our ways before Christ while in this life.

Psalm 92:5–9 says,

> How great are your works, O LORD! Your thoughts are very deep! The stupid man cannot know; the fool cannot understand this: that though the wicked sprout like grass and all evildoers flourish, they are doomed to destruction forever; but you, O LORD, are on high forever. For behold, your enemies, O LORD, for behold, your enemies shall perish; all evildoers shall be scattered.

So, be prepared to stop for **red**. Satan is **bad**. Evil demons lurk everywhere. Even though constantly tempted to do otherwise, our stoplight should always be **red** for Satan and his demons. When we surrender to Satan and we turn away from and reject the Holy Spirit, we commit the only unforgivable sin—blasphemy!

Satan

For satanic intrusions in life, the signal light is always **red** for **bad** when we are tempted to drift into the Devil's battlefield domain. Satan is the grand adversary of man. He is the Devil, Prince of Darkness, and the chief of the fallen angels. Satan is the chief spirit of evil and enemy of God. He is the tempter of mankind and the master of hell. He is known as Beelzebub, the Devil, Lucifer, Old Nick, the Prince of Darkness, and the Tempter. So, in continuing to study our area of tension on the battlefield, look for the **red** terrain next. It is all **bad**. The chapter titled Dimension Three of Five—Portals of Earthly Time will address the attributes of the temporal nature of the battlefield. Those are short-lived and therefore very ugly. But first, let's take a closer look at what the Bible says about Satan.

Satan's Fall

How long did it take for Satan to fall? "And he said to them, 'I saw Satan fall like lightning from heaven'" (Luke 10:18 ESV). Judgment for Satan and his followers was as quick as lightning.

Isaiah Reveals How Satan Fell from Heaven.

Satan's evil took charge in his heart.

> How you are fallen from heaven, O Day Star, son of Dawn! How you are cut down to the ground, you who laid the nations low! You said in your heart, "I will ascend to heaven; above the stars of God, I will set my throne on high; I will sit on the mount of assembly in the far reaches of the north; I will ascend above the heights of the clouds; I will make myself like the Most High" (Isaiah 14:12–14 ESV).

Satan's big mistake was made when he tried to ascend above the heights of the clouds and make himself like the Most High. Now his time is short.

Ezekiel Reveals How Satan Fell from Heaven.

Satan's pride overcame wisdom and discernment.

> Your heart was proud because of your beauty; you corrupted your wisdom for the sake of your splendour. I cast you to the ground; I exposed you before kings, to feast their eyes on you. By the multitude of your iniquities, in the unrighteousness of your trade you profaned your sanctuaries; so, I brought fire out from your midst; it consumed you, and I turned you to ashes on the earth in the sight of all who saw you (Ezekiel 28:17–18 ESV).

Satan's other mistakes include a proud and vain heart, resulting in God casting him to the ground. The clock is ticking. The perfect kingdom of God is coming, and it will be fully restored.[53]

John Reveals How Satan Fell from Heaven

A day is coming!

> Now war arose in heaven, Michael and his angels fighting against the dragon. And the dragon and his angels fought back, but he was defeated, and there was no longer any place for them in heaven. And the great dragon was thrown down, that ancient serpent, who is called the devil and Satan, the deceiver of the whole world—he was thrown down to the earth, and his angels were thrown down with him. And I heard a loud voice in heaven, saying, "Now the salvation and the power and the kingdom of our God and the authority of his Christ have come, for the accuser of our brothers has been thrown down, who accuses them day and night before our God. And they have conquered him by the blood of the Lamb and by the word of their testimony, for they loved not their lives even unto death. Therefore, rejoice, O heavens and you who dwell in them! But woe to you, O earth and sea, for the devil has come down to you in great wrath, because he knows that his time is short! (Revelation 12:7–12 ESV).

Jesus wins! While studying in seminary, I heard about this riveting account from one of two other students at the gym:

I took a break to shoot a few hoops with a classmate late one evening at the gym. As we played out, we noticed that the custodian was patiently waiting for us to finish so he could dust mop the gym floor. My classmate noticed that he was reading in his Bible and went over to where the old man was sitting to find out what he was reading. He asked the man, "What are you reading?" The old man looked up and happily stated, "The Revelation." Amazed, my classmate asked in a superior tone, "Do you know what it means?" The old man humbly said, "Yup, sure do." My classmate, a bright fellow, could not resist asking, "Well, what do you think it means?" The old man grinned and said, "Jesus wins!" We helped him with the floor and turned out the lights.

Satan's Kingdom

As previously outlined above, John states in Revelation 12:12 that the Devil has come down to earth and sea. As a result of Lucifer's fall, all mankind is under the earthly domain of Satan—darkness and sin—until Jesus Christ, the King of Kings, and Lord of Lords, returns in complete and final victory at the battle of Armageddon at the end of the age.

Satan's Eternal Damnation

Satan knows that his time is short, for he knows Scripture too. "The God of peace will soon crush Satan under your feet. The grace of our Lord Jesus Christ be with you" (Romans 16:20 ESV). The wrath of Satan will be contained and crushed.

Attributes of a Satan Focus, Axis X

Beginning in 4 AD and lasting through the Reformation, a few diligent clerics summarized the attributes of sin into a group called the seven deadly sins, which represent the fallen condition of humanity that can be acted out in many ways. They are not intended to replace the Ten Commandments, but they do describe the attributes of the underlying sin that must be present at the time of breaking one of God's commandments. Satan uses each one of these attributes against us.

The Bible also summarizes the attributes of sin in the Old Testament.

> There are six things that the LORD hates, seven that are an abomination to him: haughty eyes, a lying tongue, and hands that shed innocent blood, a heart that devises wicked plans, feet that make haste to run to evil, a false witness who breathes out lies, and one who sows discord among brothers (Proverbs 6:16–19 ESV).

And the New Testament says, "Now the works of the flesh are evident: sexual immorality, impurity, sensuality, idolatry, sorcery, enmity, strife, jealousy, fits of anger, rivalries, dissensions, divisions" (Galatians 5:19–20 ESV).

Paul embellishes his list above with similar firmness, "Or do you not know that the unrighteous will not inherit the kingdom of God? Do not be deceived: neither the sexually immoral, nor idolaters, nor adulterers, nor men who practice homosexuality, nor thieves, nor the greedy, nor drunkards, nor revilers, nor swindlers will inherit the kingdom of God." (1 Corinthians 6:9-10 ESV).

The road to hell is filled with all sorts of sins. Here is a closer look at a few of the deadly ones that are grouped according to tradition. They are the distinctive lanes along the roadway to eternal damnation. These seven summary terms below, make up the deadliest "demonic mnemonic" (S-L-A-P-E-G-G) on our battlefield; they are the drivers behind sin and violations of the God's Ten Commandments (Figure 4).

1. Sloth

2. Lust

3. Anger

4. Pride

5. Envy

6. Greed

7. Gluttony

Hatred for these sins indicate signs of being "Born Again."

1-Sloth

The Bible speaks of sloth in terms that also align with the evils of procrastination and laziness. We procrastinate when we choose to delay doing what needs to be done. If awareness is clear for what needs doing, just do it. Scripture commends industriousness (Proverbs 12:24; 13:4 ESV) and rebukes sloth and slackness (Proverbs 15:19; 18:9 ESV). Motivation is triggered by knowing that your work is for the Lord and not people. "Whatever you do, work at it with all your heart, as working for the Lord, not for human masters," (Colossians 3:23 ESV). Further, Matthew 5:23-25 ESV dictates that we should not delay reconciling with anyone we have offended; there is never any good time to stall, but this one is clearly marked thusly, "Do not let the sun go down while you are still angry" (Ephesians 4:26 ESV). Delay gives Satan an upper hand and presents him with additional "opportunity" (Ephesians 4:27 ESV).

Also, failure to share the gospel where needed becomes a missed opportunity to serve the Lord. Recall the parable of the banquet where the host dictated that his servant go out and invite people from far and wide, "Go out quickly to the streets and lanes of the city, and bring in the poor and crippled and blind and lame" (Luke 14:21 ESV). He who hesitates is lost just like the lost in this parable.

Subsequently, even though people have ears to hear and eyes to see are still deaf and blind to the gospel message of salvation. A big danger lurks in that audacity. Satan's most effective weapon is to promote the idea that we have plenty of time to come to Christ. Not so; James 4:13-14 urges us to move quickly to come to Christ. The parable of the rich fool who built larger barns illustrates this shortcoming very effectively, "You fool, this night your soul is required of you" (Luke 12:16-21 ESV). Being prepared for the Lord and His coming is also illustrated by the parable of the ten virgins awaiting the arrival of the bridegroom for the start of the wedding feast in Matthew 25:1-13. When the bridegroom arrived, five of the virgins were unprepared because they delayed, thinking they had plenty of time. It was too late, and the door was shut. Pure laziness can be counted on showing up on the road to destruction. In His parable of the talents, Jesus said, "But his master answered him, 'You wicked and slothful servant! You knew that I reap where I have not sown and gather where I scattered no seed?'" (Matthew 25:26 ESV).

A contribution from the Old Testament says, "The soul of the sluggard craves and gets nothing, while the soul of the diligent is richly supplied." (Proverbs 13:4 ESV).

To finish, Paul's epistles say, "Whatever you do, work heartily, as for the Lord and not for men," (Colossians 3:23 ESV) and "For even when we were with you, we would give you this command: If anyone is not willing to work, let him not eat." (2 Thessalonians 3:10 ESV).

2-Lust

The Bible offers no latitude to us on the evil attribute of lustfulness, even taking our intent into account. Beginning in the Books of Moses, "You shall not commit adultery" Exodus 20:14 (ESV) and again "You shall not covet your neighbor's house; you shall not covet your neighbor's wife, or his male servant, or his female servant, or his ox, or his donkey, or anything that is your neighbor's" Exodus 20:17 (ESV). The law is clear. So also, The Sermon on the Mount reveals how Jesus reconfirmed and extended the law on this subject, "But I say, anyone who even looks at a woman with lustful intent has already committed adultery with her in his heart" Matthew 5:28 (ESV).

Wisdom from Job 31:11-12 (ESV) provides a succinct summary on lust by stating, "For that would be a heinous crime; that would be an iniquity to be punished by the judges; for that would be a fire that consumes as far as Abaddon, and it would burn to the root all my increase."

A paradox exists between lust and selfishness and holy living and selflessness. Lust is a "me" thing and holy living is an "others" thing. It is all about having an "inner" or an "outer" focus. Jesus is our mentor. He gave it all to us so that we might come to be more like Him.

James' epistle says, "But each person is tempted when he is lured and enticed by his own desire. Then desire when it has conceived gives birth to sin, and sin when it is fully grown brings forth death" (James 1:14-15 ESV).

So, turn away quickly before consumed by guilt and shame; turn, don't burn.[54]

3-Anger

Scripture places high value on handling anger in a Godly way. But first, this attribute must be decomposed into two forms of anger. One is prideful; one is righteous. These two root levels allow us to get a tighter focus on the primitive nature behind the two different forms of this emotion. It all boils down to what motivates the anger. These two emotional driven forms of anger require different personal internal controls and skill for each; both should be practiced continuously. An inherent risk is involved in thinking that righteous indignation is okay because it may lead to judgment, which is a problem unto itself. So, let's look at all forms of control holistically (Genesis 18:25, 50:19, 20; Psalm 145:8, 9, 17; Proverbs 15:1, 29:11; Matthew 5:43-48, 7:6, 10:16; Ephesians 4:15-19, 25-32; 1 Corinthians 2:15-16, 10:31; Romans 3:13-14, 8:28-29, 12:18, 19, 21; James 1:2-4, 1:20; and 1 John 1:9 pertain). Here is one way to count to ten:

1. Accept responsibility rather than justify the anger.

2. Turn to the Word of God for how to handle anger in a godly manner and overcome it, preferably in advance.

3. Pinpoint the type of anger, prideful or righteous.

4. Define the boundaries of justice as in violence to self or others as a warning to alert us to move in the appropriate direction.

5. Focus on the problem and not the person.

6. See God as an active participant.

7. Move the condition from your head to your heart; but don't lose your head, nobody wants it.

8. Allow God's wrath for the evil to supersede your own wrath.

9. Return good for evil; convert anger to love.

10. Communicate a solution to the problem that is honest, up to date, aware of the role of Satan, and acted out before reacting.

Jesus also said in the Sermon on the Mount,

> You have heard that it was said to those of old, "You shall not murder; and whoever murders will be liable to judgment." But I say to you that everyone who is angry with his brother will be liable to judgment; whoever insults his brother will be liable to the council; and whoever says, "You fool!" will be liable to the hell of fire. So if you are offering your gift at the altar and there remember that your brother has something against you, leave your gift there before the altar and go. First be reconciled to your brother, and then come and offer your gift. Come to terms quickly with your accuser while you are going with him to court, lest your accuser hand you over to the judge, and the judge to the guard, and you be put in prison. Truly, I say to you, you will never get out until you have paid the last penny." (Matthew 5:21–26 ESV).

The idiom "Nose to the grindstone" also comes to mind. When anger happens, you can just take your nose off the grindstone. Don't press harder. It will only cost you more flesh and agonizing pain. Just move away from the source of the pain. Saloons, taverns, bars, and grindstone cowboys are the kind of combination where prideful anger is often played out impulsively. Just don't go into saloons or other similar stomping grounds in the first place. There is no secret to the behavior that resides and thrives there.

4-Pride

Like anger, pride needs to be considered in two lights; the Bible is replete on both. Self-righteousness is one where thoughts are far from God and the other is humbleness that is connected by a relationship with God involving a job done well for Him. Proverbs 8:13 declares that God hates the first because it is a hindrance to our seeking Him. 2 Corinthians 10:13 proclaims God loves the second because He knows our work done well in humility for Him glorifies Him. When self-righteous pride takes root, the proud lose track of the importance of God and other people in their life because their thoughts turn to things of this world instead of eternal life and eternity. By contrast, when humility takes root, the pride God sees that is for His glory and others gives Him pleasure. Psalm 10:4 explains it thusly, "In his pride the wicked does not seek him; in all his thoughts there is no room for God." This kind of haughty pride is the opposite of the spirit of humility that God seeks. The following verses illustrate how selfish pride is a stumbling block. "Pride goes before destruction, and a haughty spirit before a fall. It is better to be of a lowly spirit with the poor than to divide the spoil with the proud" (Proverbs 16:18-19 ESV). Isaiah 14:12-15 records how Satan was cast out of heaven because of self-righteous pride. Isaiah 14:22 says therefore, God will cast Satan into hell at the final judgment, for those who defy God, disaster awaits. Self-righteous pride has also kept many from coming to Jesus.

Jesus also explains what defiles a person when he said, "What comes out of a person is what defiles him. For from within, out of the heart of man, come evil thoughts, sexual immorality, theft, murder, adultery, coveting, wickedness, deceit, sensuality, envy, slander, pride, foolishness. All these evil things come from within, and they defile a person" (Mark 7:20–23 ESV).

5-Envy

Diametrically opposed to God's love is envy. Scripture is clear about both. It is easy to see how this attribute of Satan is at work continuously. Paul wrote about love in 1 Corinthians 13:4 in a way that leaves no doubt that it does not envy. Love cannot exist on personal desires at the expense of another. It is selfless versus selfish. Love abides by God's laws and seeks after them void of envy. Romans 10:13 reveals how love fulfills the law but envy opposes God's law on covetousness (Exodus 20:17; Deuteronomy 5:21). "Envy makes the bones rot." (Proverbs 14:30 ESV). When others are blessed, God celebrates.

On the day that Jesus was crucified, Pilot "knew that it was out of envy that they had delivered him up" (Matthew 27:18 ESV).

Phrases like "What's yours is mine, and I'm going to take it" or "What's mine is mine, and I'm going to keep it" personify envy and relate closely to greed, which is described next. I wonder if thoughts like *"What's mine is ours, and we can share it"* or better yet, *"What's mine is yours, and you can have it"* ever enters the mix for those that do not care about God or others.

6-Greed

Perhaps one of Satan's strongest attributes is to tempt us with earthly possessions. On riches, Jesus warned, "Do not lay up for yourselves treasures on earth, where moth and rust destroy and where thieves break in and steal . . ., You cannot serve God and money" (Matthew 6:19 and 24 ESV) and to "Take care, and be on your guard against all covetousness, for one's life does not consist in the abundance of his possessions" (Luke 12:15 ESV). The lure for more stuff is hard to resist and Satan knows it. Elsewhere, the Bible says, "The love of money is a root of all kinds of evil," (1 Timothy 6:9-10 ESV). Further, "For you may be sure of this, that everyone who is sexually immoral or impure, or who is covetous (that is, an idolater), has no inheritance in the kingdom of Christ and God" (Ephesians 5:5 ESV). So, "Keep your lives free from the love of money and be content with what you have, because God has said, 'I will never leave you; or forsake you.'" (Hebrews 13:5 ESV).

Look at the words of Jesus regarding the rich young man, "And behold, a man came up to him, saying, "Teacher, what good deed must I do to have eternal life?" And he said to him, "Why do you ask me about what is good? There is only one who is good. If you would enter life, keep the commandments." He said to him, "Which ones?" And Jesus said, "You shall not murder, You shall not commit adultery, You shall not steal, You shall not bear false witness, Honor your father and mother, and, You shall love your neighbor as yourself." The young man said to him, "All these I have kept. What do I still lack?" Jesus said to him, "If you would be perfect, go, sell what you possess and give to the poor, and you will have treasure in heaven; and come, follow me." When the young man heard this, he went away sorrowful, for he had great possessions" (Matthew 19:16-22 ESV). Greed showed up instantly because his love of this world obstructed his love of God.

The easy life promotes being complacent and self-satisfied; riches are ascribed to one's own efforts instead of acknowledging that all good things come from God. Jesus said, "But seek first the kingdom of God and his righteousness, and all these things will be added to you" (Matthew 6:25-34 ESV).

So, based on the above, it appears that self-centered and narcissistic tendencies are a slippery slope to the gutter where demons reside.

7-Gluttony

Finally, we see where Satan's evil attribute of gluttony is served up as continuously as our appetites dutifully remind us. Look at the stern warnings about the wisdom of controlling food and drink intake. "Be not among drunkards or among gluttonous eaters of meat, for the drunkard and the glutton will come to poverty, and slumber will clothe them with rags" (Proverbs 23:20-21 ESV). Also, "The one who keeps the law is a son with understanding, but a companion of gluttons shames his father" (Proverbs 28:7 ESV). Woefully, ". . . put a knife to your throat if you are given to appetite" (Proverbs 23:2 ESV).

Self-control starts with the widely used phrase, "Just say no!" Here are some additional relevant scriptures to ponder in your favorite version of the Bible, Deuteronomy 21:20, Proverbs 23:2, 2 Peter 1:5-7, 2 Timothy 3:1-9, 2 Corinthians 10:5, and Galatians 5:22.

So, it also appears that being overstuffed with food and/or wine was recognized even in those days as a wrongdoing. Slop chutes with an ample stench of beer, wine, and whiskey (or worse) still abound today.

Know Your Enemy

The Screwtape Letters by C. S. Lewis goes into great detail about the Devil's tactics, all of which should be firmly understood by Christians.[55] To know your enemy is a key principle of war.[56] Sometimes it is us! Christian martyrdom in the Roman coliseum clearly revealed the enemy; however, many times the enemy is a lot less obvious and often comes through temptation and is highly seductive.

Satan is the opponent of God and believers, the archenemy of good. He incites evil, and he is a formidable opponent constantly accusing us falsely and using conniving deception, even as an angel of light promising good. But he is an adversary, exposer, and slanderer. The Bible makes more than fifty references to Satan, the Devil, and Lucifer in more than forty verses.[57]

Satan Is a Created Being

1. Satan has intelligence.

2. Satan was created perfect and beautiful.

3. Satan was given free will and choice, and he sinned.

4. Satan has pride, which was the cause of his downfall.

5. Satan was once in heaven "upon the holy mountain of God."

6. Satan and his angels were cast out of heaven and to the earth.

    a. Isaiah 14:12–15

    b. Ezekiel 28:3, 12–19

    c. Luke 10:18

    d. 2 Thessalonians 2:3–4

    e. Revelation 12:9

7. Satan is the instigator of spiritual warfare that is still taking place between the powers of darkness and light.

    a. Ephesians 6:11–17

8. Satan is the enemy for which the Son of God was manifested so that He might destroy the works of the Devil.

    a. Genesis 3:15

    b. Hebrews 2:14

    c. 1 John 3:8

Satan's Person

1. Satan is a being, not an influence or power.

2. Satan and his demonic angels are spirit beings.

3. Satan was talking to Jesus when He was tempted in the wilderness.

4. Satan has a memory.

    a. Matthew 4:1–10

5. Satan can talk and shout.

6. Satan spoke with the Lord.

7. Satan can travel "to and fro in the earth" and seek rest.

    a. Job 1:6-12; 2:1–2

    b. Zechariah 3:1–2

8. Satan has feelings and emotions (i.e., anger).

9. Satan knows the time is short.

    a. Revelation 12:12, 17

10. Satan can see and discern strengths and weaknesses.

11. Satan recognizes those who are saved.

    a. Matthew 13:39

    b. Mark 4:8, 15

    c. Acts 16:16–17

12. Satan can seek and accept worship.

    a. 2 Thessalonians 2:3–4

    b. Revelation 9:20

    c. Revelation 13:4, 8, 12

13. Satan believes there is one God.

    a. James 2:19

14. Satan can influence man to lie.

15. Satan can incite man to sin and violate God's will.

    a. Acts 5:3

    b. 1 Chronicles 21:1

16. Satan has great strength to overpower man.

    a. Mark 5:2–4

    b. Luke 13:16; 22:3

    c. Acts 10:38; 19:16

Satan's Character

1. Satan has boldness.

2. Satan is devious.

3. Satan is an antagonist.

4. Satan is an accuser.

5. Satan is an adversary.

    a. Job 1:6–12; 2:1–6

    b. Zechariah 3:1–2

    c. 1 John 3:8–10

    d. 2 Corinthians 11:14

6. Satan has subtlety.

7. Satan has cunning and deception.

    a. Genesis 3:1–6

    b. Revelation 20:3–8

8. Satan is self-centered, has self–ambition and strong self-will.

9. Satan himself desired to be like the Most High.

    a. Isaiah 14:12–14

    b. 2 Thessalonians 2:3–4

10. Satan tempted man with ambition.

    a. Genesis 3:4–5

Satan Is Subject to God

1. Satan is not omniscient, but he is knowledgeable of doings on the earth.

2. Satan covets our worship.

3. Satan knows our worship belongs to God alone.

    a. Exodus 20:1–4

    b. Matthew 4:1–10

    c. Revelation 12:12

    d. Revelation 13:4, 8, 12

4. Satan is not omnipotent; his power is limited.

   a. Job 1:12; 2–6

   b. 2 Thessalonians 2:9

   c. Revelation 2:10

5. Satan is subject to God.

   a. Job 1:1–10

6. Satan's works will be destroyed by Jesus.

   a. Colossians 2:15

   b. Hebrews 2:14

   c. 1 John 3:8

7. Satan can perform lying signs and wonders.

   a. Matthew 24:24

   b. 2 Thessalonians 2:9

Satan's End

1. Satan rebelled against God, resulting in a war in heaven.

2. Satan and his angels shall be judged for their rebellion against God.

   a. 2 Peter 2:4

   b. Jude 1:6–7

   c. Revelation 12:7–12

3. Satan's end shall be the eternal lake of fire in hell.

   a. Revelation 20:10

God's Power over Satan

1. Disciples of Jesus Christ were given authority and victory over all the power of the enemy.

2. Believers are given authority to cast out demons in the name of Jesus Christ.

3. Believers must submit to God. If you resist the Devil, he will flee from you.

   a. Matthew 10:1–8

   b. Mark 16:17

   c. Luke 10:19–20

d. Romans 16:20

e. James 4:7

4. God does not want us to be ignorant of Satan's schemes and devices.

5. God does not want Satan to get an advantage over us.

a. 2 Corinthians 2:11

6. God provides us with armor to protect us from the fiery darts of Satan.

7. We must put on the whole armor of God.

a. Ephesians 6:11-17

Table 10. Know Your Enemy

Satan's Plan

From the deception of Adam and Eve to the end of time, Satan is always trying to win our souls as his treasured prizes and achieve a perceived victory over the Lord. Satan wants to be above God. He uses all the tools at his disposal to accomplish his evil ambition.

His Tactic—Exploit Our Every Weaknesses

In his effort to exalt himself above God at every turn, the Devil uses our needs and wants (food, air, water, sex, ego, etc.) against us through temptation, seduction, enticement, inducement, doubt, misgiving, disobedience, rebellion, defiance, waywardness, ignorance, indolence, obliviousness, influence, lust, stimulus, intrigue, conspiracy, diversion, departure, envy, greed, delay, suspicion, defeat, and discouragement to exploit our weaknesses and gain our following. His resources are vast.

Contest God for Our Souls

Satan hates truth and all things good. He is bent on being above God at any cost. He treasures our souls as booty in battle and winnings; however, victory in his war with God is hopeless. Thanks be to God!

Recently the opportunity arose for me to visit with a woman patient in her mid-fifties. It quickly became apparent that she had her share of physical and emotional conditions that warranted hospital care; however, spiritual care was unnecessary in her opinion. She said, "I know I am headed for hell, and I can't wait. I don't believe in your God. He has already dished out plenty of hell in my life. I can't understand how anyone could believe in a God that inflicts so much pain, misery, hurt, grief, heartache, sorrow, sadness, and gloom. I don't want to hear about the God of your Bible. Please just go away and leave me alone."

Wondering why this patient wanted to see a chaplain, I departed her room, but I did pray for this woman privately in the chapel. I prayed for her for the remainder of that day and even now as the Lord brings her to mind. I wish I could have told her that, like Job, God is not the reason for her many problems. The reason for her troubled waters is because Lucifer is still loose. The same reason applies to all of us. There will be no end to the turbulence Satan creates until he is sealed up in the lake of fire. God will restore to His people's peace, security, and comfort just like He did for Job. I also prayed that the next chaplain would have an opportunity to share thoughts on the real source of her problems and not God.

Certainly, when we stray away from God like Jonah, we subject ourselves to His wrath and punishment. But this is His right as a just Father. Any father would do the same to his children. He doesn't want to lose us to His adversary. He loves us so much that He gave up His Son for us so that we might live eternally with Him. He wants us back. Choose Jesus. He chose us before the foundation of the world in writing.

Dimension Three of Five—Portals of Earthly Time

The third and last dimensional part of our mind map, when decomposed, represents seven portals or attributes of temporal, earthly values on a transverse Z-axis (Figure 3). It is everything **ugly** that is in our transitory lives; it is the ultimate battlefield. It will soon wither and fade like grass.

Psalm 90:1–17 says,

> Lord, you have been our dwelling place in all generations. Before the mountains were brought forth, or ever you had formed the earth and the world, from everlasting to everlasting you are God. You return man to dust and say, "Return, O children of man!" For a thousand years in your sight are but as yesterday when it is past, or as a watch in the night. You sweep them away as with a flood; they are like a dream, like grass that is renewed in the morning: in the morning it flourishes and is renewed; in the evening it fades and withers. For we are brought to an end by your anger; by your wrath we are dismayed. You have set our iniquities before you, our secret sins in the light of your presence. For all our days pass away under your wrath; we bring our years to an end like a sigh. The years of our life are seventy, or even by reason of strength eighty; yet their span is but toil and trouble; they are soon gone, and we fly away. Who considers the power of your anger, and your wrath according to the fear of you? So teach us to number our days that we may get a heart of wisdom. Return, O Lord! How long? Have pity on your servants! Satisfy us in the morning with your steadfast love, that we may rejoice and be glad all our days. Make us glad for as many days as you have afflicted us, and for as many years as we have seen evil. Let your work be shown to your servants, and your glorious power to their children. Let the favor of the Lord our God be upon us, and establish the work of our hands upon us; yes, establish the work of our hands!

Earth

For earthly endeavors in life, the signal light is always **amber** for **ugly** when we invest time in worldly or temporary things. Hence, in continuing to study our area of tension on the battlefield, look for the **amber** terrain next. It is all very **ugly** and quickly fading away.

Regarding earth, I sometimes reluctantly and timidly allow myself to think of it as God's universal laboratory and we are categorized as the lab rats. This comes from strongly suspecting that in His quest for His vision of a perfect pure kingdom someday, the design of His lab includes room for our use of our free will, even considering His free grace. Spencer Johnson's book *Who Moved My Cheese?* illustrates how the rats in his maze had free will (within limits) too. When the cheese was moved, they could just sit there in the same empty area of the laboratory maze starving, or they could break out and search for cheese in new areas. We need to search for some unseen, lasting (and eternal) subsistence too. This world will soon melt like snow, and we'd better move in the direction of Jesus, who holds the prize for His followers at His *bema seat*.

Let's see what the Bible says about earth. "Then the King will say to those on his right, 'Come, you who are blessed by my Father, inherit the kingdom prepared for you from the foundation of the world.'" (Matthew 25:34 ESV).

Is your eye on the real eternal prize or just on the worldly temporal cheese that will not last?

Earth Is Temporal

Believe it or not, it is best to focus our minds not on the physical things of this world but on unseen spiritual goals. God is most concerned about what is unseen, not our earthly wealth or possessions. Paul writes,

> So we do not lose heart. Though our outer self is wasting away, our inner self is being renewed day by day. For this light momentary affliction is preparing for us an eternal weight of glory beyond all comparison, as we look not to the things that are seen but to the things that are unseen. For the things that are seen are transient, but the things that are unseen are eternal (2 Corinthians 4:16–18 ESV).

One day we will see clearly, face-to-face with His eternal glory. There is more.

Earth Is Decaying

Paul writes that creation is currently enslaved to rust and decay. It waits frustrated for the children of God to liberate it.

> For the creation was subjected to futility, not willingly, but because of him who subjected it, in hope that the creation itself will be set free from its bondage to corruption and obtain the freedom of the glory of the children of God. For we know that the whole creation has been groaning together in the pains of childbirth until now. And not only the creation, but we ourselves, who have the first fruits of the Spirit, groan inwardly as we wait eagerly for adoption as sons, the redemption of our bodies. For in this hope, we were saved. Now hope that is seen is not hope. For who hopes for what he sees? But if we hope for what we do not see, we wait for it with patience (Romans 8:21–25 ESV).

Liberation time will be a time to celebrate. A day is coming!

Earth Is Replaceable

Once purified and destroyed by fire, the earth will have a new purpose. It will serve as the place where heaven, the New Jerusalem, will reside—but not just yet. God has some planned program activities for this earth before that happens.

We are waiting. "But according to his promise we are waiting for new heavens and a new earth in which righteousness dwells." (2 Peter 3:13 ESV).

We must conquer. "The one who conquers, I will make him a pillar in the temple of my God. Never shall he go out of it, and I will write on him the name of my God, and the name of the city of my

God, the new Jerusalem, which comes down from my God out of heaven, and my own new name." (Revelation 3:12 ESV).

We must watch diligently. "Then I saw a new heaven and a new earth, for the first heaven and the first earth had passed away, and the sea was no more. And I saw the holy city, new Jerusalem, coming down out of heaven from God, prepared as a bride adorned for her husband." (Revelation 21:1–2 ESV).

We must endure.

> Behold, I am sending you out as sheep in the midst of wolves, so be wise as serpents and innocent as doves. Beware of men, for they will deliver you over to courts and flog you in their synagogues, and you will be dragged before governors and kings for my sake, to bear witness before them and the Gentiles. When they deliver you over, do not be anxious how you are to speak or what you are to say, for what you are to say will be given to you in that hour. For it is not you who speak, but the Spirit of your Father speaking through you. Brother will deliver brother over to death, and the father his child, and children will rise against parents and have them put to death, and you will be hated by all for my name's sake. But the one who endures to the end will be saved. When they persecute you in one town, flee to the next, for truly, I say to you, you will not have gone through all the towns of Israel before the Son of Man comes (Matthew 10:16–23).

We must be cautious.

> And Jesus answered them, "See that no one leads you astray. For many will come in my name, saying, 'I am the Christ,' and they will lead many astray. And you will hear of wars and rumors of wars. See that you are not alarmed, for this must take place, but the end is not yet. For nation will rise against nation, and kingdom against kingdom, and there will be famines and earthquakes in various places. All these are but the beginning of the birth pains. Then they will deliver you up to tribulation and put you to death, and you will be hated by all nations for my name's sake. And then many will fall away and betray one another and hate one another. And many false prophets will arise and lead many astray. And because lawlessness will be increased, the love of many will grow cold. But the one who endures to the end will be saved. And this gospel of the kingdom will be proclaimed throughout the whole world as a testimony to all nations, and then the end will come. (Matthew 24:4–14 ESV).

My mind could dwell on the new heaven and new earth at great length, but for now, let's dwell on some of the things we can see in this present earth. After all, they are greatly involved in filling up our tension area of this mortal life.

Attributes of an Earth Focus, Axis Z

There are seven portals or attributes of temporal, earthly values on the transverse Z-axis. They are the ways we spend our time on earth. A good mnemonic for this high-level view is F-I-S-H-E-R-S. Each has its own subset of sub-attributes (Figure 4).

1. Family

2. Interpersonal

3. Specialty

4. Health

5. Education

6. Recreation

7. Spiritual

Earthly temporal life is most often **ugly**. So be cautious. The signal light is always **amber** for temptations on this **earth**. These are the things that get in the way of us lighting our lamp and keeping it on a lampstand.

I find that many hospital patient encounters take me to places where ugly happens a lot. When this becomes apparent, a quick determination must be made on how to provide the most effective pastoral care. Three key roles are repetitively involved many times a day: (1) the good shepherd, (2) the wounded healer, and (3) the court jester. These three pastoral care roles have proven very helpful when I am visiting patients. Sometimes a mixture of these roles needs to be used to meet the total needs of a particular patient.[58]

As a good shepherd, I try to concentrate on finding and reinforcing a patients' basis for faith and lead them to an understanding of the imposing dynamics that are working in God's plan.

As a wounded healer, care not to overly assume anything is of the utmost importance. Some hospital patients I see find it beneficial when I share my similar personal experiences when God was at work in my life, especially when they feel that God is missing in action in their lives. When I detect these moments, I try to carefully share how God worked in my life (or someone else I know) during the toughest times. I relate to them that at the time of the occurrence, these things seemed to present insurmountable odds to overcome. Many people have had many more sever conditions to cope with than I have, and I can't compete with them on their horrific hardships. Although I have had my share of stressful times, I don't risk making an unbalanced comparison as the wounded healer.

As a court jester, I try to meet patients at their levels of acceptable and beneficial humor. Humor does have an element of healing power that may not be attained by other roles if it is not too absurd.

Our "connections" described in the next chapter titled Dimension Four of Five—Portals of Connection Time and our "relationships" described in the chapter titled Dimension Five of Five—Portals of Relationship Time that follows, pertain to the dynamics at work in all three of the roles previously outlined.

Patients also bring a lot of baggage to the hospital that has nothing to do with a particular infirmity. The following seven temporal attributes on the transverse Z axis affect everybody on the battlefield; however, they are amplified in many patients, and they are vital flags in pastoral care environments.

These flags are the same ones noted in the chapter titled Dimension One of Five—Portals of Godly Time under "Seven Prayer Components to Consider." These seven components represent where the tensions in life start, so as they present themselves, pray hard, pray often, and pray continuously. Be in communion with the Lord about everything. Leave no pockets unemptied. Mary, the mother of Jesus, gives us a model of how to leave everything on the field when we are encountering the hand of God as she did in the presence of an angel. Are you holding back something that belongs on the field? Assess the seven earthly attributes that follow and see for yourself. The only white flags allowed on the battlefield are to signal surrender to Jesus.

1-Family

Patients from broken homes deeply move me when they are bruised emotionally and sometimes physically by the effects of shattered family environments. A recent patient encounter involved a young man whose childhood and mine were almost identical. After a lengthy discussion we prayed for physical, emotional, and spiritual healing, focusing on eternal versus meritless temporal values. He seemed like he benefited from hearing from this old, wounded healer as much as I did from him. It makes me wonder if God does not bring about meetings like that by design.

When the need arises—and if it appears helpful to be the wounded healer as it was during this patient visit—I willingly share my personal story of growing up by summarizing and explaining that it was almost at my birth when I was given to an aunt and uncle as substitutes for my disaffected real parents. I have been told as a relatively undernourished newborn baby meagerly subsisting on Carnation canned milk, I needed a stable home fast. Thankfully, my patriarchal grandmother made a command decision and I was placed in a good home with one of her daughters and her husband. My new family could not have children of their own, so they literally raised me as if I was their own child, even with their own name. They did a fine job until substance abuse separated them. Then I was informed that they were not my real parents at the age of nine. I was vehemently removed by my real father from that shattered setting and returned to his home, where I learned he had remarried for a third time. I also discovered that I had two half-sisters and one half-brother from his first marriage and that he was partially disabled by an accidental fire while he was working in an oil field environment. He was a real roughneck, prize fighter, and grindstone kind of character. Fortunately, he had a soft spot for the Lord, and he often spent time in God's Word and singing his favorite hymns while playing a guitar. It was there he found his greatest peace and hope.

My mother's sister, Aunt Beulah, helped with my support briefly during the seventh grade when all other family support had collapsed. She was a woman who knew God's Word, and she taught Sunday school to young children for more than thirty years, while suffering quietly over the loss of her son in combat during the Korean War.

During my time with Aunt B, I learned my real mother was fully disabled when I was born because of an aneurism and blood clots that affected her brain. She was treated eleven years before her wounds healed, and the clot was finally properly diagnosed and dissolved with medication. She soon returned to a normal lifestyle. At age thirteen I was able to spend part of my freshman year in high school with her and her second husband. While I was there, I observed her reading her Bible daily, and she painted an indelible image in my mind that studying God's Word was imperative for real comfort and joy.

Eventually I graduated from high school while I was enrolled in a Christian children's home. It was a very solid and dependable platform where I could get a solid footing so that I could make it on my own. I also found the Lord while I was there. By the time I left the strict regimen at the children's home, introduction to the U.S. Marines after college seemed almost like basic training was a piece of cake and somewhat enjoyable. It seems now that all three structured regimens offered the kind of discipline I needed.

My life's story casts a shadow that is almost identical with the young patient in the visit noted earlier. I never had a clue that two individuals could travel down such parallel paths. My prayer with him included thanks for a special reinforcing relationship among the two of us; but, more so with Jesus as we trust in Him along the way.

2-Interpersonal

Patients who are treated for injury because of conflict with others tug at my heart as well. I see way too much powerlessness to take their noses off the grindstone when things like lust, anger, pride, envy, or greed get in the way. One such patient seemed to be hunting for and engaging with grindstones to destroy them before they destroyed him. So I traded a few notes with him to test the waters and see how much he cared about people and to see if he could care enough to let the grindstones go and think about the needs of others before his own. I shared the following story with him.

I recently made a trip to the post office to mail a box containing some clothing for my youngest daughter's baby shower. I parked in a stall facing a curb on the sidewalk and went inside to mail the package. When I departed the post office to get into my car, I noticed that someone parked in a stall adjacent to my car so close that I could not get into my vehicle. The right front tire of that car was over the line and protruding into my parking stall. I have a hump in the front seat that eliminated the option of getting into my vehicle on the passenger side and sliding across. I was too tall to crawl in through the tailgate and over the back seat, so I thought about other options and concluded that I would just have to wait until the other driver returned. I leaned on the bumper and started watching for a driver to return. A man came out rather quickly but went to another car. A woman came out real slowly, but she went to another car too. Another man came out, but that turned out to be the driver of another car. After about fifteen minutes a man came out and headed for the car next to mine. He looked at me and said, "Can't you get in?"

I said, "Nope, you are too close."

He said, "Well, a car next to me was way over in my stall."

I said, "Let's just go."

As I drove home and thought about what had just happened, I thought how the other driver could have chosen another stall or parked inside his stall leaving me ample access to my car. However, the other driver was quick to blame the condition on another driver, and there was no apology. As we went in our own directions, I patted myself on the back and said to myself, "Hey, you are finally getting it. Not bad, kiddo! Keep it up! Keep that scarred nose of yours off those grindstones!"

This brief traffic story pales in comparison with many interpersonal encounters that take place in every instance where the grindstone takes its toll and things do not go so smoothly, where there is no forgiveness, no patience, no harmony, no discernment, and no love. I continued to toss out some other ideas to the patient seeking more of his reactions. He seemed to thrive on seeking out grindstones. So, I decided to enlarge the domain by floating a larger balloon. On the international and national scale, we face far more severe consequences and negative impact on our lives and loved ones. I lead with, the thought that man has been at war with man since almost the beginning of time. Sadly, not much has changed except for the tactics and grindstones employed, and many conflicts are now also rooted in cleverly conceived evil ideologies. Yet there are only three kinds of war—classic combat, coup d'état, and terrorism. However, in each kind the principles of war have not changed.[59] The attributes of Satan discussed in the chapter titled Dimension Two of Five—Portals of Sinful Time are still at work throughout the globe regardless of the kind of warfare employed. While it seemed like I was getting nowhere with this approach with this patient, I thought I would try one more idea by further expanding the scope of atmosphere.

Without dwelling on global conflict any further, I drifted into problem areas concerned with globalization, the economy, and world trade. Those conflicts are not going to be reversed any time soon either. Since the world tilts on its axis, agricultural harvests occur at opposite times of the year in each hemisphere, but many food demands across the globe remain the same all year long. Accordingly, three advances in globalization come to mind; (1) dependency on intermodal containerized/bulk shipping (i.e., air, rail, ship/barge, truck, pipeline, etc.); (2) impact on attaining better delivery of the supply of food products; and (3) ever-increasing reliance on advanced data systems. These three advances now make transporting annual crops to where the demand exists mostly routine. However, this new normal takes us into uncharted waters where people do not play by common economic rules and values. Surprise! This presents a new challenge if we are going to find peace and harmony with such diverse players in the global economy. It appears that we need to practice fair ethical standards to level the world trade playing field. For example, Steve Forbes, chairman of Forbes Media, recently stated that returning the US dollar and the world to the monetary gold standard would be a good place to start. Although I personally think that is a wonderful idea, not much response from this patient was provoked by this starter example either. So I deliberately went into my listening mode with this patient.

After what seemed like endless talk of this patient's personal grindstone environments, we prayed for the ability for him to recognize grindstones and make conscious decisions about gracefully detaching from them quickly and permanently. Ultimately, he came to see the benefit of thinking outside of his tension box and focus on the larger picture (Figure 3). He came to Christ that day and became born again. Come to Christ with him.

3-Specialty

A hospital patient with signs of abnormal professional stress opened our pastoral care visit by him urging me to give advice on threats to his job security. The desire to have a discussion on that far outweighed the desire to talk about any infirmity he had or anything else. So I felt compelled to share some of my experience and allow him to draw his own conclusion.

This is what I shared. I found out strong leadership at work is essential for success. You must stay above the line of blame, denial, justification, surrender, impeding, and evil-centered behavior to succeed and not violate your self-worth and ethical values. Authenticity, credibility, professionalism, and enthusiasm are the marks of a true leader (Figure 6).

Within the context of the word *enthusiasm*, we have to know that it is an attribute indicating that God is in us. His Spirit lives in us. Paul tells us in 1 Corinthians 3:16, "Do you not know that you are God's temple and that God's Spirit dwells in you?" We are His temple, and if we talk the talk, we must walk the walk in all walks of life.

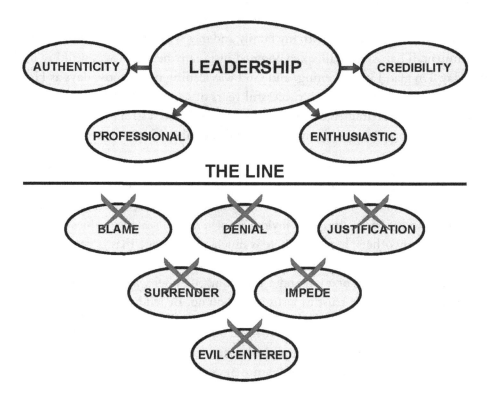

Figure 6. Staying Above the Line

Failure to stay above the line usually means you must move on or suffer the consequences of the unfriendly and always present grindstone. Sometimes the environment can also dictate a physical move, so be prepared if necessary. I eventually grew accustomed to a three- to four-year cycle as the norm for navigating through organizational channels. Year one was spent thoroughly learning a new job. During year two, I learned to manage the job, and during year three or four, I could train others to take over the job.

After proper preparation, I then reviewed my options and quickly ran to a new target job. I learned not to hold on to anything but to stay comfortably in motion until I peaked. It has been said, "A body in motion has a tendency to stay in motion. A body at rest has a tendency to stay at rest." Don't take anything personal and stay moving. Concentrate on the next play(s) or move(s) and do it. As in golf, forget the last shot and concentrate on the next one.

I also shared that one of my biggest physical moves came when I recognized that near the end of my service career, I had a relatively short time to transition to something else outside of the military. I had a daughter in college and a daughter in elementary school, so completely retiring was not an option. One day when I was leaving the gym after a noonday jog, I headed back to my office, and as I passed below a large oak tree, I heard an internal voice in my ear that sounded like it originated from the tree. It said, "Get ready!" That's it, nothing more. Chills passed through my entire body, and the hair on my neck (as short as it was) stood up and bristled. I knew the Lord or one of His messengers was talking to me, and I knew what He meant. There was no time to waste. Reckoning I would need a master's degree to be competitive in a civilian workplace, I enrolled for graduate work in business management courses at night. A year later I had earned an MA in business management and accounting. I then returned to Texas with my family and met with quick success, finding employment in state government. That still, small voice boomed inside my head as I was walking under that old oak tree that day. I'm glad I was listening, and God was leading me in those days as He continues to do today. That move led me to thirteen successful years of service with several state agencies. While I was eligible for a second retirement, even then I knew there was a strong chance that the still, small voice was poised for more changes in my professional specialty. I knew I needed to keep listening.

Many other professionals share their success stories, some more than others. One such professional is Warren Buffet, a wealthy billionaire who recently listed five tips to build wealth and success. He said you should: (1) live below your means, (2) bounce back from defeat, (3) be a self-promoter, (4) have street smarts, and (5) buy cheap.[60] Obviously for temporal earthly values that plan works for him and probably many others; however, there is much, much more that is needed to satisfy eternal values. Don't limit your scope to this world: (1) don't forget to get a spiritual pancake, (2) know the difference between a profession or a job and a vocation, (3) either way, stay above the line, (4) listen for that still small voice, and (5) trust in Jesus in all you do. Be led by the Spirit of God.

This patient and I prayed for him to have a sure hand on the throttle, knowing when to reduce power and when to go full throttle. He picked up on the "tension area" concept box quickly, and he met Jesus at the fork in his lifeline and said yes (Figure 3). He is now born again.

4-Health

A young hospital patient with a concussion from football practice was despondent about the painful headaches that prevented him from getting back on the field. He could not accept that such a thing could happen to him. I asked him if he had time to hear about a wounded healer that had the same kind of experience. He said, "Yes."

I shared with him that my headaches lingered for years after I had received a concussion in high school football practice one afternoon. During tough "bull ring" drills, a teammate is obliged to sound a loud verbal yell after his number is called out before he engages the player in the center of the circle. I was in the center of the circle, and I kept turning to find the approaching player whose number had been called by the coach. Somewhere in the jumble of noise, I never heard a distinguishable alarm. When his helmet struck the side of my helmet as I was turning into his path, I dropped like a rock! For months after it happened, any strain to the shoulders and neck brought back the same debilitating and throbbing painful symptoms. Even years later during strenuous physical training, obstacle or confidence courses, and intense pugil-stick matches in U.S. Marine Corps basic training, the pain would quickly return. As I look back, I think I should have stuck with baseball and track. Finally, after I successfully made it through Marine OCS, I briefly attended flight training, but I had to drop out on my own volition because the same recurring pain interfered with flight safety while I was performing high-G aerobatic maneuvers. On one occasion I could not remember an abnormal loss of altitude after a spin recovery. The bottom of loops presented the same loss of awareness and disorientation. After discussions with medical staff, instructors, and command staff, I voluntarily returned to basic school for additional ground training. Even though the problem persisted during strenuous exercise, I managed to carefully steer safely through rigorous physical training. I encouraged this patient to do some similar introspective personal evaluations like I was forced to do. The decision to change and adjust to other endeavors was the right thing to do on behalf of myself and those around me. It was the right thing to do even though I loved to fly. He agreed.

We prayed for wisdom and discernment that day. We also did a simulated flight through his personal tension area until his lifeline came to the fork in the road at the diamond-shaped symbol <> (Figure 3). He took the "yes" path that day. Now he has a strong partner in his corner that would carry him through life's tough wickets. He was born again. His heart now belongs to the Lord.

Also, it seems many hospital patients are admitted for treatment of heart conditions, often to their complete surprise. While I was visiting one such patient in the observation area, I heard a lot about this disbelief. I shared how I, too, experienced the same disbelief when I had to call EMS early one morning in 2006 to get to a hospital because I was experiencing a very painful heart attack. I was fortunate that it was temporarily resolved with three stents and a pacemaker along with what seemed like every kind of heart pill known to the medical profession. It seems these patients have a willingness to talk about spiritual pancakes more readily than most other patients. So I serve them some of my special pancakes, and the plate is consumed before I know it. This patient appreciated having an opportunity to evaluate his spiritual pancake and we prayed for healing and restoration of his physical and emotional pancakes in light of God's will. This patient happily took in his full serving.

Shortly afterward I responded to a page to visit with a middle-aged female patient with symptoms of prolonged substance abuse (beer, wine, alcohol, smoking, drugs, and even foods like sugar and sweeteners) that resulted in the loss of her teeth, throat cancer, diabetes, skin inflictions, digestive problems, circulatory problems, and respiratory problems. I drew her a little tension box to study, and then I listened for feedback. Amazingly she said, "Chaplain Bill, I need to let go of the **ugly** and unnecessary rubbish that is killing me, don't I?"

I said, "Yup, it appears to me that you just need to keep your nose off those personal grindstones that are wrecking your health and your life. Flee from them as fast as you can. Remember, they will just be fuel in the day of the Lord. Start by finding new acquaintances who will not want to lead you back to those old haunts. And know this—our lifeline may at times be like skiing or waterskiing. One ski is the spiritual ski, and the other is the worldly physical or emotional ski. Although they move along with us together as if they are connected; you may find you need to develop a "fence" between each ski to help you block out the competing temporal earthly attractions on your path. I call it my Jesus fence. We must live in the world, but we don't have to lose our spiritual connection regardless of where we are at any point in time. When you hear that still, small voice inside of you say, 'Get out of here,' do it yesterday. Better yet, lead others out of those same traps the same way we are talking about now. Lean on God's Word for strength." I gave her a Gideon Bible and marked 2 Peter 3 as I turned over the corner of the page. I also suggested that she search the web for "saltwater burns" and then imagine how much fuel there is in the big pond out there off our coasts. All temporal, ugly stuff will go up in smoke in the day of the Lord. Why cling to it now? Let it go before it gets you.

We prayed for discernment, healing, and restoration and for continuous communion with the Spirit of God to fight off distractions and temptations.

5-Education

While I was visiting one young hospital patient that was despondent about how he had allowed himself to begin abusing various substances, I asked what he thought was the reason he had started down that path. He stated that he took to a wide variety of drugs and alcohol as an experiment to get relief from combating a heavy study load in college. He was hopeless about how to refocus.

Deploying the wounded healer again, I shared with him that I quickly experienced similar stress as a young pre-dental student. Further, I shared that I never acquired the high school preparation for the science and math courses required to be admitted to dental school. After I finally completed trigonometry (after the third time), I was really dejected about the direction I was taking. I knew that as a result of making too many moves throughout childhood, it resulted in too many disconnects in my studies from fourth grade through high school making it improbable for me to be highly effective in college. But before I turned to something sinister for relief, I heard a still, small voice saying, "Go back and review your aptitude test results." Fortunately, I kept a copy of my scores from the Kuder and Strong interest inventory exams I took during admission. These results indicated I had high aptitude for: (1) serving among military and police organizations, (2) government management and business administration, and (3) service to others through teaching and preaching. I can't imagine retaking those tests and getting any other results. I knew they were reliable indicators. They also told me that I was in the wrong field of study at that time. If only I had examined those scores more closely before I signed up for all the math and expensive science classes, I could have finished college a year sooner. Looking back over the years I have served in each professional and vocational area, and I have seen the Lord move me during the process. My story gave the young man some ideas. His demeanor improved as I prepared to depart his room.

Before I left, we traveled along his lifeline through his personal tension area as he related it (Figure 3). He knew he needed to decide "yes" in the diamond-shaped symbol <>. He did, and he asked me what to do next. I told him to read God's Word repeatedly, searching for the blood line of Christ from cover to cover, and to find a church home where he could be around other believers. We prayed for spiritual guidance and assistance from pastoral staff at a new church home.

6-Recreation

A visit with a hospital patient who had just fallen off his horse and was sporting a new halo leg cast that would require months of healing and follow-up therapy resulted in a special dose of empathy. Sports and hobbies can provide a very high level of satisfaction and joy; however, many of them also expose us to high levels of risk of injury or even death.

I shared with the patient that I owned a boat that I had to sell recently because of old age and my inability to withstand heat and motion after my heart attack. I told him that my heart medications probably factored into the equation as well. I remember thinking that if I became incapacitated while out on the water, I could be in real trouble and potentially expose family or friends to unnecessary emergency conditions. After a couple of falls in the heat of the day, I finally decided to let the boat go to a younger angler. I'm glad I did.

Understanding came quickly for this patient. We prayed for wisdom and discernment that day. I also encouraged him to trace his lifeline through his personal tension area and, to my joy, I found that he had already decided yes at the diamond-shaped symbol <> (Figure 3) long ago; however, like me, he too, was guilty of having too much on his platter, which was interfering with him strengthening his relationship with God. I demonstrated how he could build his own personalized inventory by using the 343 mini cubes in his Theo-metric cube (Figure 4). Then I encouraged him to use the results to eliminate or combine activities to cut out unnecessary stress and multitask wherever possible. He was well on his way when we finished a prayer together.

7-Spiritual

It is always a joy to visit a hospital patient who is filled with spiritual joy; however, there are times when that is not so. One day an elderly woman received my greeting by returning a glob of spit in my direction. Fortunately, she missed. I quickly left, stating that I would lift her up in prayer in the chapel and that she could let the nurses know to page me if she felt like she needed a visit later. Two days later, she again hurled another spitball in my direction, but again her aim was off. I'm glad she wasn't armed with a peashooter and poison darts.

This patient encounter reminded me that I had times in my life when I resisted the Lord, going after earthly treasures as long as I could. But thankfully the Lord did not give up on me. When He wants you, He is going to get you. I lifted this patient up in prayer that day for peace and comfort while I was in the chapel. The third time I visited her, she tolerated my presence without any visible hostility, and the last time I visited with her, she was even graceful.

That day we prayed together with joy for the peace that surpasses all understanding. Grace is the crossroads where God and humankind meet. The cornerstone of Christian living is grace. God met human beings in a condition of sin and oppression with good news and offered salvation.[61]

But for all the personal trials experienced by hospital patients like those referenced previously in this chapter, I usually find the healing words of the old hymn "There Is a Balm in Gilead" still healing more than physical wounds. It is the "balm that makes the wounded whole. It heals the sin-sick soul."[62]

Dimension Four of Five—Portals of Connection Time

The fourth part of our mind map is **connectional** rather than dimensional. It connects each of the three axes described previously by connecting to form a personal tension cube that represents our space we occupy as air-breathers; it also contains our individual lifeline (Figure 3).

Job 38:4 says, "Where were you when I laid the foundation of the earth? Tell me, if you have understanding."

Ecclesiastes 3:2 says, there is ". . . a time to be born, and a time to die; a time to plant, and a time to pluck up what is planted."

Matthew 10:39 says, "Whoever finds his life will lose it, and whoever loses his life for my sake will find it."

Romans 5:12 says, "Therefore, just as sin came into the world through one man, and death through sin, and so death spread to all men because all sinned."

James 1:15 says, "Then desire when it has conceived gives birth to sin, and sin when it is fully grown brings forth death."

Revelation 13:8 says, ". . . and all who dwell on earth will worship it, everyone whose name has not been written before the foundation of the world in the book of life of the Lamb who was slain."

Revelation 17:8 says, "The beast that you saw was, and is not, and is about to rise from the bottomless pit and go to destruction. And the dwellers on earth whose names have not been written in the book of life from the foundation of the world will marvel to see the beast, because it was and is not and is to come."

Our Tension Area of Life

The tension cube depicts this dimension of our time using six surface planes in the positive quadrant of the 3-D model. This dimension is the tension area wherever we live out our mortal lives along our lifeline from the time we are conceived until the moment we die—no more, no less (Figure 3). We each have a personal tension area and a personal lifeline that is influenced by the dynamics of the external pressures that originate along the X, Y, and Z three-dimensional axes. How our lifeline moves within the cube is dependent on the dynamic pressures (i.e., who, what, where, when, why, and how) levied on us from each directional dimension and our corresponding responses.

Connection with Christ

So, **connection** is the key fourth relational dimension that delineates our tension area which encases our lifeline. This dimension facilitates helping us determine what kind of relationship is desirable now and the kind of relationship that is waiting for us in eternity. Because the two smaller **connection** components (tension area and lifeline) are inseparable in life, they are also critical in safely leading us to a right relationship with Christ.

Relationship with Christ

The two larger relational dimensions (**connection** and **relationship**) are also inseparable for Christians. Together they remind me of the wheels on a roller coaster and the support of the tracks. The wheels and the tracks operate in tandem to maintain connection. If they get separated, the wheels will really come off, and they can lead down a path to destruction and the lake of fire with Satan. The chapter titled Dimension Five of Five—Portals of Relationship Time will address the attributes of the fifth and last relationship dimension to complete our Theo-metric mathematical 3-D array. At that point, the emerging issue will be where is your relationship going to be? Will it be with Jesus or Satan? Come to Jesus yesterday and find comfort and peace.

Attributes of Connection Time

For now, observe how our personal tension area of life encloses our lifeline. Think of the cube as the time we live out our individual lives as people who breathe air. Pictorially, our lifeline bends like the tracks of a modern roller coaster mentioned previously as it passes through our tension area. The bends in the tracks conform to the dynamics exerted on our lifeline from the three directional tensions placed on us as we travel through life. But be aware, our lifeline has a hidden switch at a fork in the tracks. When we come to that switching point, we are forced to decide *for* Jesus Christ or *not* before we go any further (Figure 3). Keep in mind this decision point becomes the basis for developing our eternal relationships (detail discussion is included in the chapter titled Dimension Five of Five—Portals of Relationship Time). Jesus says, "Whoever finds his life will lose it, and whoever loses his life for my sake will find it" (Matthew 10:39 ESV).

So when does that happen? It happens at a point along our lifeline when we are either born again or lost forever to eternal death. Our lifeline actually begins long before birth and continues far beyond the grave all the way to heaven if we believe and abide in Jesus Christ. Otherwise, we will end up in hell. Our soul is with Christ or Satan immediately upon the termination of our physical air and blood flow. We know our tension area is filled with works, sin, and grace that demand our conscious awareness and deliberate assessment all along our lifeline. Therefore, we must continuously drill deep along our vertical, horizontal, and transverse directional axes to determine how these powers or tensions may influence not only our lives, but also our destination. Now put on your hard hat because this is the toughest, most gut-wrenching, and personally demanding part of making your personal Theo-metric assessment. Connection time has seven high level attributes that follow:

1-Lifeline Focus

How long is our lifeline? Overall, it is unlimited; however, that is in the larger context outside our personal tension area. Since our names were placed in the Lamb's Book of Life before the foundation of the world, it goes a long way back. Since we will spend eternity with the sheep or the goats, it goes way out ahead of us too. There we have it. Where do you want to spend eternity? With the sheep? With the goats?

2-Time-Line Critical

Before we get to our final destination, we first have to assess what is going on before our personal lifeline reaches the end of its earthly timeline and bursts out of our tension area. And we must assess not only who we need to connect with but also who we need to relate to before that point is reached. With Satan? With Jesus?

3-Desire-Driven

Upon God's delivery of His free grace, the Spirit of God enables us to act on our free will desire to solidify our choice as to how we will spend eternity. Just like a person searching the classified ads for employment is driven by a desire to be financially secure, we must "want to" find a relationship through faith with Jesus leading to eternal security.

4-Relation Desire

We need the aspiration to fully "relate to" Jesus so much and so closely that we can be confident if we ever must tell Him He has spinach on His teeth, He will thank us for the tip. He understands that we would do something like that because we love Him. I once served as a general's aide, and I was put in a position where it was my job to address anything out of the ordinary; however, I also desired to relate to the man himself professionally to help further the success of our mutual mission. Are you that close to our Lord? He wants to be that close to us.

5-Free Grace

Free grace is one of the two halves of God's two edge sword of faith. In Matthew 19:13–15, Jesus said, "Let the little children come to me and do not hinder them, for to such belongs the kingdom of Heaven." God's free grace is taken willingly by little children. We should too. Just trust and obey. There is no other way.

6-Free Will

Free will is the other half of God's two-edge sword of faith. Between free grace and free will, the desire to connect and relate makes us unstoppable. Paul writes,

> No, in all these things we are more than conquerors through him who loved us. For I am sure that neither death nor life, nor angels nor rulers, nor things present nor things to come, nor powers, nor height nor depth, nor anything else in all creation, will be able to separate us from the love of God in Christ Jesus our Lord (Romans 8:37–39 ESV).

7-Free Choice

Our free choice is permanent. The Bible says in Luke 9:26 that Jesus said, "For whoever is ashamed of me and of my words, of him will the Son of Man be ashamed when he comes in his glory and the glory of the Father and of the holy angels." Make the right choice. It's permanent.

Dimension Five of Five—Portals of Relationship Time

The fifth, and last, part of our mind map is **relational** rather than dimensional. While it accounts for how we respond to the dynamics in our tension area limited by our personal tension cube, it includes the time spent during our lifeline as well. This fifth dimension is the most important because it mandates pinpointing your relationship with Jesus or Satan (Figure 3).

This fifth dimension consummates an accounting of all critical dimensions God might utilize in His plan to restore His pure kingdom; it is the basis for the recovery of His saints. These elect who are the predestined chosen ones marked for His New Jerusalem are the ones whose names were written into the Lamb's Book of Life by God before the foundation of the world. This relational dimension is the "truth teller" for determining where you will be when you get where you are going.

This relational dimension operates with both elements of God's two-edge sword, where God's unmerited free grace is on one edge and our God-given and enabled free will is on the other edge. By grasping the handle of faith, the razor-sharp edges will enable us to cut through all that is **ugly** and all that is **bad** while securing for us all that is **good** and what is reserved for us in His New Jerusalem. His mighty sword is like a two-edge sickle that cuts down both the wheat and the tares at the God-initiated great harvest, enabling the final separation of the wheat from the chaff on the grinding room floor (Matthew 13:24-30). Now that is a grindstone I look forward to seeing with great anticipation. So, get ready, put on your full armor of God; you will find God's double-edged sword in your combat load. Keep your hand firmly on the handle of faith!

Attributes of Relationship Time

I was shocked some years ago when I met a young college man for the first time. During the first couple of minutes together he stated, "I don't care anything about people." Dazed by the cold, harsh comment, I could not gather myself sufficiently for a coherent reply. But I tucked it away for posterity. While thinking to myself, I hold high caring for people as everything in life; and caring for God is equally important, that lasts beyond this temporal life. Since then, I have often wondered how much the young man may now allow people and God to weigh on his conscience. My prayer for him is that he will begin to observe the words of Jesus when He said to the Pharisees, "You shall love the Lord your God with all your heart and with all your soul and with all your mind. This is the great and first commandment. And a second is like it: You shall love your neighbor as yourself. On these two commandments depend all the Law and the Prophets" (Matthew 22:37–40 ESV).

In the case of the first meeting with the young man previously mentioned, it was obvious that there was plenty of self-love on display for the remainder of the time I was with him. I still lift up prayers as the Lord brings him to mind for him to soften his heart for both people and God. A look at the seven attributes of our relationship time shows why that is a good idea.

The following seven attributes of relationship time pertain to God and people.

1-Dependency

Our dependency on God and others is quickly revealed in the Lord's Prayer. We are taught to recognize God in His holy, highest, hallowed post and plead with Him for Him to do His will in heaven and on earth. Come, Lord Jesus, please come! Our lament for bread today and tomorrow reveals how we are dependent on not only a full crop of grain but also the collective labor resources to shape the harvest into serving portions for our table. We desperately need God and people. We must ask for forgiveness, and we must also grant forgiveness. We especially need God and people to protect us from the Evil One. Finally, we again acknowledge God and His almighty kingdom, unmatched power, and glory throughout all eternity. Jesus taught His prayer while simultaneously revealing His plan. It starts with a pure kingdom and ends with a pure kingdom, and in between, evil will be crushed to ruins. We are dependent on Him for all of our needs, and we are dependent on others like we are dependent on ourselves. The recognition of the role of dependency is vital to a strong relationship.

2-Alliance

Building alliances with the right group and the right stuff is also a critical element in a relationship. There must be a foundation of trust built on integrity, authenticity, and credibility. Try to approach other people without this type of foundation, and you will soon meet with disharmony. Don't try it with God because He already knows what is in your heart before you start. The bottom line is that you must work together to achieve a bond in a quality alliance. Additionally, there is no such thing as a successful unholy alliance because the foundation is on sand to start. To the contrary, a holy alliance is built on the rock of righteousness.

3-Affinity

Affinity happens when there is closeness between people, mutual understanding, and similar qualities or interests. Affinity also happens when there is closeness between God and people under the same conditions. How close are you to God and others? Have you worshipped Him lately? Have you read His Word? Are you doing what He says and giving Him praise, honor, and glory? Are you giving Him thanks and supporting His flock with your tithes? Are you sharing His Word?

4-Kinship

Kinship includes ties and obligations. It is binding through birth, marriage, or other feelings shared jointly. Kinship should be between people and with God. Jesus brought kinship when He came to earth to experience what we experience. He came into this special kinship to lead us out of harm's way much like when He said, "Greater love has no one than this, that someone lay down his life for his friends" (John 15:13 ESV).

Examples of this love abound as we see tragedy and hardship around us daily. Special relationships are forged with adversity staring us in the face. Often, the courageous are nearby to lend a helpful hand.

5-Consanguinity

Since we all share common blood with one mother, we will forego the blood part in this setting; however, the quality, state, or closeness in a relationship is similar and highly desirable. We need to be washed in His blood. Jesus has our back. Do you have His? If you believe He is who He says He is and do what He says to do, you do! Keep it up.

6-Mutuality

When we are close enough to share sentiments, we achieve mutual success. If we study God's Word to know and share His sentiments and His precepts, we arrive at mutuality with God. We achieve mutuality best when we love His Son, Jesus Christ, and do what He says. Know His Word. Read it over and over.

7-Involvement

Including God and others as part of you through evidence of your activity proves your relationship is one of enthusiasm. Leadership dictates that involvement can and should be done in every activity of our lives (see above section on "FISHERS" titled: **Attributes of an Earth Focus, Axis Z**).

Dynamic Demonstration

A demonstration is in order at this point. Only by retrieving all four sets of attributes previously discussed can we deliver a working relational model. Beginning with the **ugly** first, recall those temporal attributes, then follow that by the **bad** attributes. Save the best for last and recall the **good** attributes.

Works and Our Tension Area of Life

Drill transversely to identify how works play a role in stirring our lifelines. See where the mnemonic FISHERS starts the drill bit turning along the Z-axis.

Second Peter 3:1–18 says,

> This is now the second letter that I am writing to you, beloved. In both of them I am stirring up your sincere mind by way of reminder, that you should remember the predictions of the holy prophets and the commandment of the Lord and Savior through your apostles, knowing this first of all, that scoffers will come in the last days with scoffing, following their own sinful desires. They will say, "Where is the promise of his coming? For ever since the fathers fell asleep, all things are continuing as they were from the beginning of creation." For they deliberately overlook this fact, that the heavens existed long ago, and the earth was formed out of water and through water by the word of God, and that by means of these the world that then existed was deluged with water and perished. But by the same word the heavens and earth that now exist are stored up for fire, being kept until the Day of Judgment and destruction of the ungodly. But do not overlook this one fact, beloved, that with the Lord one day is as a thousand years, and a thousand years as one day. The Lord is not slow to fulfill his promise as some count slowness, but is patient toward you, not wishing that any should perish, but that all should reach repentance. But the day of the Lord will come like a thief, and then the heavens will pass away with a roar, and the heavenly bodies will be burned up and dissolved, and the earth and the works that are done on it will be exposed. Since all these things are thus to be dissolved, what sort of people ought you to be in lives of holiness and godliness, waiting for and

hastening the coming of the day of God, because of which the heavens will be set on fire and dissolved, and the heavenly bodies will melt as they burn! But according to his promise we are waiting for new heavens and a new earth in which righteousness dwells. Therefore, beloved, since you are waiting for these, be diligent to be found by him without spot or blemish, and at peace. And count the patience of our Lord as salvation, just as our beloved brother Paul also wrote to you according to the wisdom given him, as he does in all his letters when he speaks in them of these matters. There are some things in them that are hard to understand, which the ignorant and unstable twist to their own destruction, as they do the other Scriptures. You therefore, beloved, knowing this beforehand, take care that you are not carried away with the error of lawless people and lose your own stability. But grow in the grace and knowledge of our Lord and Savior Jesus Christ. To him be the glory both now and to the day of eternity. Amen.

Not surprisingly, a close examination of the attributes listed in the transverse Z-axis (FISHERS) reveals that the things that are closest to us have the greatest potential for creating tension on our lifeline (Figure 3). These attributes also bring direct daily tension to us. The most vital thing to recognize about these attributes is that all but one of them, Spiritual, is temporal. The rest will be destroyed by fire on the day of the Lord.

When the attributes along the Z-axis and the attributes along both other 3-D axes collide, our lifeline has to be altered to some degree. Some of the situations in the patient visitation examples depicted in earlier chapters are good illustrations where the alteration was significant. There are millions more like them. While God has a hand in the turbulence that is created by temptations from Satan and competing temporal values, He has no respect for the choices we make except for one, our decision for Jesus Christ. All our other works are like filthy rags to God, worthless save those following our conversion to Christ. "We have all become like one who is unclean, and all our righteous deeds are like a polluted garment. We all fade like a leaf, and our iniquities, like the wind, take us away" (Isaiah 64:6 ESV).

Sin and Our Tension Area of Life

In continuing to build on the attributes along each axis that affect our lifeline, let's now drill horizontally to review the attributes listed on the X-axis (SLAPEGG). See the callout for the things that can horrify us (Figure 4). Clearly, they can bring exceedingly abundant tension to our lifeline. One must only watch the nightly news to see this kind of evil activity all around us. Recent cowardly "knockout games" reported on national news media and other equally and exceedingly greater depraved evils come to mind.

Exodus 20:1–17 lists the Ten Commandments.

And God spoke all these words, saying, "I am the LORD your God, who brought you out of the land of Egypt, out of the house of slavery. You shall have no other gods before me. You shall not make for yourself a carved image, or any likeness of anything that is in heaven above, or that is in the earth beneath, or that is in the water under the earth. You shall not bow down to them or serve them, for I the LORD your God am a jealous God, visiting the iniquity of the fathers on the children to the third and the fourth generation of those who hate me, but showing steadfast love to thousands of those who love me and keep my commandments. You shall not take the name of the LORD your God in vain, for the LORD will not hold him guiltless who takes his name in vain. Remember the Sabbath day, to keep it holy. Six days you shall labor, and do all your work, but the seventh day is a Sabbath to the LORD your God. On it you shall not do any work, you, or your son, or your daughter, your male servant, or your female servant, or your livestock, or the sojourner who is within your gates. For in six days the LORD made heaven and earth, the sea, and all that is in them, and rested on the seventh day. Therefore the LORD blessed the Sabbath day and made it holy. Honor your father and your mother, that your days may be long in the land that the LORD your God is giving you. You shall not murder. You shall not commit adultery. You shall not steal. You shall not bear false witness against your neighbor. You shall not covet your neighbor's house; you shall not covet your neighbor's wife, or his male servant, or his female servant, or his ox, or his donkey, or anything that is your neighbor's.

Even observance of Halloween by Christians can bring tension in a carnal way. Our family toiled over whether to participate in the neighborhood "trick or treat" activities by dressing up ghoulishly and handing out candy or attending the harvest festival hosted by our local church as a more favorable alternative. Ultimately a very deliberate, carefully considered decision was made about partaking in that spooky practice by choosing to hand out flashlights with our church's name on it and a bookmark inviting all the little goblins and their families to attend our services. A bag of candy was added in to sweeten the deal. Interestingly it was sad that a pop test given at the door to older children on their understanding of All Saints' Day (the day following Halloween) did not produce a single correct response. Recalling from the chapter titled Dimension One of Five—Portals of Godly Time where Paul says, "we are to put on a new self." (Ephesians 4:24 ESV).

Grace and Our Tension Area of Life

Lastly, let's drill vertically along the Y-axis (LHFTPHJ) for some good attributes. Here we find within the third set of attributes that our lifelines encounter the best part. See the tension callout box for the things that come with God's grace (Figure 3). The Word of God delivered by the Spirit of God in the presence of Jesus Christ must command our attention! We are to be confidant that salvation comes through redemption of the whole man. It is offered freely to all who accept Jesus Christ as Lord and Savior, and there is no salvation apart from personal faith in Jesus Christ as Lord. "For by grace you have been saved through faith. And this is not your own doing; it is the gift of God, not a result of works, so that no one may boast" (Ephesians 2:8–9 ESV).

First Corinthians 13:13 says, "So now faith, hope, and love abide, these three; but the greatest of these is love."

Philippians 4:8 says, "Finally, brothers, whatever is true, whatever is honorable, whatever is just, whatever is pure, whatever is lovely, whatever is commendable, if there is any excellence, if there is anything worthy of praise, think about these things."

I venture to say that we can easily assess ourselves with the previously outlined Theo-metrics; however, the next and last step will either undo you or make you whole. Don't stop now. See which direction your lifeline will take into eternity.

Dynamics of the Five Dimensions of Life in Motion

We will be where we want to be when we get where we are going by developing a personal continuous faith-based relationship to trust and obey God the Father, Jesus Christ, His Son, and the Spirit of God as written in God's Word. "We are saved by grace through faith" (Eph. 2:7-8). And, we need communion[63] with God, Jesus Christ, and the Spirit of God constantly.

The Full Theo-Metric Model

Now, may I please have a "drum roll?" With the completion of the fifth and last set of attributes, it is time to unfold the full Theo-Metric model that points to the graphic truth about where you will be when you get where you are going. The graphic truth depicted above in (Figure 3) and (Figure 4) reveals your answer. I hope and pray you said "yes" at the diamond shaped symbol <>.

Jeremiah 1:1–5 says,

The words of Jeremiah, the son of Hilkiah, one of the priests who were in Anathoth in the land of Benjamin, to whom the word of the LORD came in the days of Josiah the son of Amon, king of Judah, in the thirteenth year of his reign. It came also in the days of Jehoiakim the son of Josiah, king of Judah, and until the end of the eleventh year of Zedekiah, the son of Josiah, king of Judah, until the captivity of Jerusalem in the fifth month.

Matthew 24:31 says, "And he will send out his angels with a loud trumpet call, and they will gather his elect from the four winds, from one end of heaven to the other."

Matthew 25:34 says, "Then the King will say to those on his right, 'Come, you who are blessed by my Father, inherit the kingdom prepared for you from the foundation of the world."

Mark 3:29 says, "But whoever blasphemes against the Holy Spirit never has forgiveness, but is guilty of an eternal sin."

Luke 12:10 says, "And everyone who speaks a word against the Son of Man will be forgiven, but the one who blasphemes against the Holy Spirit will not be forgiven."

John 3:3 says, "Jesus answered him, 'Truly, truly, I say to you, unless one is born again he cannot see the kingdom of God.'"

John 3:16–18 says,

For God so loved the world, that he gave his only Son, that whoever believes in him should not perish but have eternal life. For God did not send his Son into the world to condemn the world, but in order that the world might be saved through him. Whoever believes in him is not condemned, but whoever does not believe is condemned already, because he has not believed in the name of the only Son of God.

John 3:36 says, "Whoever believes in the Son has eternal life; whoever does not obey the Son shall not see life, but the wrath of God remains on him."

Romans 1:1 says, "Paul, a servant of Christ Jesus, called to be an apostle, set apart for the gospel of God."

Second Timothy 2:21 says, "Therefore, if anyone cleanses himself from what is dishonorable, he will be a vessel for honorable use, set apart as holy, useful to the master of the house, ready for every good work."

Philemon 1:14 says, "But I preferred to do nothing without your consent in order that your goodness might not be by compulsion but of your own accord."

Hebrews 12:1 says, "Therefore, since we are surrounded by so great a cloud of witnesses, let us also lay aside every weight, and sin which clings so closely, and let us run with endurance the race that is set before us."

Second Peter 2:4 says, "For if God did not spare angels when they sinned, but cast them into hell and committed them to chains of gloomy darkness to be kept until the judgment."

Revelation 13:1–18 says,

And I saw a beast rising out of the sea, with ten horns and seven heads, with ten diadems on its horns and blasphemous names on its heads. And the beast that I saw was like a leopard; its feet were like a bear's, and its mouth was like a lion's mouth. And to it the dragon gave his power and his throne and great authority. One of its heads seemed to have a mortal wound, but its mortal wound was healed, and the whole earth marveled as they followed the beast. And they worshiped the dragon, for he had given his authority to the beast, and they worshiped the beast, saying, "Who is like the beast, and who can fight against it?" And the beast was given a mouth uttering haughty and blasphemous words, and it was allowed to exercise authority for forty-two months. It opened its mouth to utter blasphemies against God, blaspheming his name and his dwelling, that is, those who dwell in heaven. Also it was allowed to make war on the saints and to conquer them. And authority was given it over every tribe and people and language and nation, and all who dwell on earth will worship it, everyone whose name has not been written before the foundation of the world in the book of life of the Lamb who was slain. If anyone has an ear, let him hear: If anyone is to be taken captive, to captivity he goes; if anyone is to be slain with the sword, with the sword must he be slain. Here is a call for the endurance and faith of the saints. Then I saw another beast rising out of the earth. It had two horns like a lamb and it spoke like a dragon. It exercises all the authority of the first beast in its presence, and makes the earth and its inhabitants worship the first beast, whose mortal wound was healed. It performs great signs, even making fire come down from heaven to earth in front of people, and by the signs that it is allowed to work in the presence of the beast it deceives those who dwell on earth, telling them to make an image for the beast that was wounded by the sword and yet lived. And it was allowed to give breath to the image of the beast, so that the image of the beast might even speak and might cause those who would not worship the image of the beast to be slain. Also it causes all, both small and great, both rich and poor, both free and slave, to be marked on the right hand or the forehead, so that no one can buy or sell unless he has the mark, that is, the name of the beast or the number of its name. This calls for wisdom: let the one who has understanding calculate the number of the beast, for it is the number of a man, and his number is 666.

Revelation 22:4 says, "They will see his face, and his name will be on their foreheads."

The bottom line is, did you say "yes" at the <> symbol on your lifeline? If not then see below.

Ever Repent?

Let those who have eyes see their sins. Let those who have ears hear the still small voice of conviction. Let those who repent fall on their knees and beg forgiveness to the Lord Jesus Christ repetitively.

Born Again

God, Jesus, and the Spirit of God intercede somewhere along our lifeline when we become contrite, remorseful, and ashamed in our heart. We are bent back toward God by His mighty and terrible swift double-edge sword, and we claim His Son, Jesus Christ, as our Lord and Savior. Although salvation cannot be earned by man's own effort, once the hand has been laid to the plow, we can't look back. We will spend eternal life in heaven. Are *you* really born again? The grace of God brings us this new birth. It is a change of heart wrought by the Holy Spirit. He makes us see our sins. He makes us hear his voice when He plants remorsefulness in us and convicts us of our sins. As sinners, we respond in repentance with contrite hearts toward God. Our faith is placed in our Lord, Jesus Christ. Repentance and faith are inseparable experiences of God's grace. Although a paradox and a mystery, *God works, and we repent and believe.*[64] It is there that we get regenerated like a camping lantern or field stove by God pumping up our fuel tank with more air pressure. It resumes working brighter and better! Get pumped by the Spirit of God. Get regenerated.

When we accept Jesus Christ by professing Him as our Lord and Savior, acknowledging He alone is the author of our belief and faith, we are born again. The only unforgivable sin is for us to blaspheme the Spirit of God, who delivers God's grace to our hearts. Say no, and you will spend eternity in hell with the goats. Say yes, and you will spend eternity in heaven with the sheep. John tells us that there is only one sheepfold and one Shepherd in heaven. There are no goats. Paul says for us to be sealed by the Spirit.

> Blessed be the God and Father of our Lord Jesus Christ, who has blessed us in Christ with every spiritual blessing in the heavenly places, even as he chose us in him before the foundation of the world, that we should be holy and blameless before him. In love he predestined us for adoption as sons through Jesus Christ, according to the purpose of his will, to the praise of his glorious grace, with which he has blessed us in the Beloved. In him we have redemption through his blood, the forgiveness of our trespasses, according to the riches of his grace, which he lavished upon us, in all wisdom and insight making known to us the mystery of his will, according to his purpose, which he set forth in Christ as a plan for the fullness of time, to unite all things in him, things in heaven and things on earth.

In him we have obtained an inheritance, having been predestined according to the purpose of him who works all things according to the counsel of his will, so that we who were the first to hope in Christ might be to the praise of his glory. In him you also, when you heard the word of truth, the gospel of your salvation, and believed in him, were sealed with the promised Holy Spirit, who is the guarantee of our inheritance until we acquire possession of it, to the praise of his glory. (Ephesians 1:3–14 ESV)

Jesus Christ is where the covenant of law and grace meet.

Likewise, my brothers, you also have died to the law through the body of Christ, so that you may belong to another, to him who has been raised from the dead, in order that we may bear fruit for God. For while we were living in the flesh, our sinful passions, aroused by the law, were at work in our members to bear fruit for death. But now we are released from the law, having died to that which held us captive, so that we serve in the new way of the Spirit and not in the old way of the written code. What then shall we say? That the law is sin? By no means! Yet if it had not been for the law, I would not have known sin. For I would not have known what it is to covet if the law had not said, "You shall not covet." But sin, seizing an opportunity through the commandment, produced in me all kinds of covetousness. For apart from the law, sin lies dead. I was once alive apart from the law, but when the commandment came, sin came alive and I died. The very commandment that promised life proved to be death to me. For sin, seizing an opportunity through the commandment, deceived me and through it killed me. So the law is holy, and the commandment is holy and righteous and good (Romans 7:4–12 ESV).

Blessed are those whose faith is reckoned to Him as righteousness.

What then shall we say was gained by Abraham, our forefather according to the flesh? For if Abraham was justified by works, he has something to boast about, but not before God. For what does the Scripture say? "Abraham believed God, and it was counted to him as righteousness." Now to the one who works, his wages are not counted as a gift but as his due. And to the one who does not work but believes in him who justifies the ungodly, his faith is counted as righteousness, just as David also speaks of the blessing of the one to whom God counts righteousness apart from works: "Blessed are those whose lawless deeds are forgiven, and whose sins are covered; blessed is the man against whom the Lord will not count his sin."

Is this blessing then only for the circumcised, or also for the uncircumcised? For we say that faith was counted to Abraham as righteousness. How then was it counted to him? Was it before or after he had been circumcised? It was not after, but before he was circumcised. He received the sign of circumcision as a seal of the righteousness that he had by faith while he was still uncircumcised. The purpose was to make him the father of all who believe without being circumcised, so that righteousness would be counted to them as well, and to make him the father of the circumcised who are not merely circumcised but who also walk in the footsteps of the faith that our father Abraham had before he was circumcised.

For the promise to Abraham and his offspring that he would be heir of the world did not come through the law but through the righteousness of faith. For if it is the adherents of the law who are to be the heirs, faith is null and the promise is void. For the law brings wrath, but where there is no law there is no transgression.

That is why it depends on faith, in order that the promise may rest on grace and be guaranteed to all his offspring—not only to the adherent of the law but also to the one who shares the faith of Abraham, who is the father of us all, as it is written, "I have made you the father of many nations"—in the presence of the God in whom he believed, who gives life to the dead and calls into existence the things that do not exist. In hope he believed against hope, that he should become the father of many nations, as he had been told, "So shall your offspring be." He did not weaken in faith when he considered his own body, which was as good as dead (since he was about a hundred years old), or when he considered the barrenness of Sarah's womb. No unbelief made him waver concerning the promise of God, but he grew strong in his faith as he gave glory to God, fully convinced that God was able to do what he had promised. That is why his faith was "counted to him as righteousness." But the words "it was counted to him" were not written for his sake alone, but for ours also. It will be counted to us who believe in him who raised from the dead Jesus our Lord, who was delivered up for our trespasses and raised for our justification. (Romans 4:1-25 ESV).

Knowing all this requires regeneration to let grace happen to you, and you must know you are set apart for a purpose by God. At that point you become empowered to progress by faith toward moral and spiritual perfection. Through the presence and power of the Holy Spirit dwelling in you, a change of heart and growth in grace should continue throughout life and lead to holiness. This goal of complete sanctification is never fully realized in this lifetime. It is completed when we meet Jesus Christ face-to-face.[65, 66] Yet, we are tasked to try. James said, "Faith without works is dead."

What good is it, my brothers, if someone says he has faith but does not have works? Can that faith save him? If a brother or sister is poorly clothed and lacking in daily food, and one of you says to them, "Go in peace, be warmed and filled," without giving them the things needed for the body, what good is that? So also faith by itself, if it does not have works, is dead. But someone will say, "You have faith and I have works." Show me your faith apart from your works, and I will show you my faith by my works. You believe that God is one; you do well. Even the demons believe—and shudder! Do you want to be shown, you foolish person, that faith apart from works is useless? Was not Abraham our father justified by works when he offered up his son Isaac on the altar? You see that faith was active along with his works, and faith was completed by his works; and the Scripture was fulfilled that says, "Abraham believed God, and it was counted to him as righteousness"—and he was called a friend of God. You see that a person is justified by works and not by faith alone. And in the same way was not also Rahab the prostitute justified by works when she received the messengers and sent them out by another way? For as the body apart from the spirit is dead, so also faith apart from works is dead" (James 2:14–26 ESV).

On the other side of this life lies full glorification and the culmination of salvation. That is where you will find a final blessed and abiding state where all who are there are the redeemed. Has God convicted you of your sins? Has He revealed Jesus to you as your Savior? Can you feel the work of the Holy Spirit in your life? Can you say, "I know it is so because when it is so, it is so—so be it," and mean it? If you have daily communion with Jesus, you don't have any doubts.

Turn or Burn

If we experience remorse and truly repent, then we will change our outward conduct and our inner attitudes. We will turn from sin and do the works of faith gladly. We must have a hatred of sin. That is the evidence and the proof that we are born again.

The Rev. C. H. Spurgeon in his classic sermon "Turn or Burn" quotes Psalm 7:12 (ESV), which says, "If a man does not repent, God will whet his sword; he has bent and readied his bow."

> We cannot suppose the God of the Bible could suffer sin to be unpunished. To suppose Him all love and no justice would be to strip him of His deity status and make Him no longer God, not capable of ruling this world. Is it not written that there is reserved for the Devil and his angels fearful torment? And do you not know that our Master said? "Then he will say to those on his left, 'Depart from me, you cursed, into the eternal fire prepared for the devil and his angels. And these will go away into eternal punishment, but the righteous into eternal life'" (Matthew 25:41, 46 ESV).

> Do you feel that you are a fit subject for heaven now? If not, don't delay. Find and then feel your remorse and come to Jesus to confess, repent, and abide there at His feet, prostrate with your face in the mud made from your tears.

> But the cry of this age is that God is merciful, that God is love, that He is all-forgiving. Yes, who would deny that? But remember, it is equally true that God is severely and inflexibly just.

> How few there are who will earnestly tell us of the judgment to come. They preach of God's love and mercy as they should and as God has commanded them, but why preach mercy unless they also preach the doom of the wicked?

> For repentance to be true and to be evangelical, there must be a repentance, which really affects our outward conduct. *We must stop!* It must be a hatred of sin. There is a *necessity* that God should sharpen His sword and punish men if they will not turn. What are the *means* of repentance? I do not believe any man can repent with evangelical repentance of himself. We are so desperately set on sin that we have no hope of ever turning from it of ourselves. But listen! He who died on Calvary is exalted on high "to give repentance and remission of sin." Do you this day feel that you are a sinner? If so, ask of Christ to give you repentance, for He can work repentance in our heart by His Spirit, though you cannot work it there yourself. Is your heart like iron? He can put it into the furnace of His love and make it melt. He can make us repent, though we cannot make ourselves repent. If you feel your need for repentance, I will *not* say, "Repent," for I believe there are certain acts that must precede a sense of repentance. I should advise you to go to your houses, and if you feel that you have sinned and yet cannot sufficiently repent of your transgressions, bow your knees before God and confess your sins. Tell Him you cannot repent as you would. Tell Him your heart is hard. Tell Him it is as cold as ice. You can do that if God has made you feel your need of a Savior. Then if it should be laid to your heart to try to seek after repentance, I will tell you the best way to find it. Spend an hour first in

trying to remember your sins, and when conviction has gotten a firm hold on you, then spend another hour at Calvary at the feet of that old, rugged cross. An old divine adage says, "If you feel you do not love God, love Him till you feel you do. If you think you cannot believe, believe till you feel you believe." Many men say they cannot repent while they are repenting. Keep on with that repentance till you feel you have repented. Acknowledge your transgressions, confess your guiltiness, and own that He was just about to destroy you.[67]

To summarize Spurgeon, it appears that Boolean nested logic from modern math and other math studies and teaching can help you along with the words from Jeremiah 38. They were strong then, and they still apply today.

If *(admit)*

Then *(repent)*

Else *(punishment)*

Or *(blessings)*

And *(reunion)*

Regardless of how you get there, it is still all about a decision you must make before you die that causes you to stop sinning and begin hating that sin as you are set apart to run the race for Jesus until you die. Travel along your lifeline in your personal Theo-metric model and see where you will go if you make a "yes" response at the diamond-shaped decision symbol <>. This "fork" in the road results in having a segment of our lifeline that goes up (continues toward heaven), not down (defaulting toward hell). Figure 3 pertains.

I can actually remember the specific time in my lifeline when I made my decision for Christ. You should too. I was about fourteen. I was in high school while I was living at a Christian children's home, and I was responsible for milking two dozen cows along with two other boys early one winter morning at about 5:00 a.m. I was assigned to the pit with the milking machines where the cows were fed a mixture of oats mixed with honey while they were milked. After I filled the first three of the four feed bins in the four elevated stalls, I went to fill the fourth feed bin with the final bucket of grain, but before I could dump the grain into the bin in that stall, a big black snake came out of the bucket so fast I didn't even have time to move. It crawled up my arm, behind my head, down my other arm, and out the door before I could even react. I didn't even know that snakes were that fast. I remember feeling the weight and the movement of that snake as it used my body as a bridge to escape the confines of the dimly lit milk barn. I've been told that they are still looking for that old bucket today. I'm inclined to think that it may be the first man-made object on the moon.

On the way back to our cottage after I completed the milking chore, I had to walk past the little chapel on the campus. It had a steeple with a cross on top, and I remember thinking, *Lord, You don't have to do that again. I'm Yours from now on.* I changed that day. I suddenly became certain that Christmas had a more important meaning than just Santa Claus bringing toys and that Easter had more important significance than just a big bunny hiding colored eggs. I began searching for the unseen that early winter morning. I found it in Jesus! He found me when I wasn't even looking and was not fully awake! Grace abounds!

Writing Your Personal Audit Finding

So, a personal Theo-metric graphical assessment and a deliverable audit report of your current status of faith should be forthcoming. Your findings should include the following essential elements and conclusions:

1. FINDING—I am a sinner.

2. CRITERIA—Jesus is the only Way.

3. CONDITION—I can't save myself. I can't even approach God in my sinful state. It is He against whom I have sinned. I can only reconcile with God by His grace through my faith in Jesus Christ and His blood, which was shed for me on the cross.

4. CAUSE—I fell away from God along with everybody else.

5. EFFECT—Without Jesus, I am doomed to spend eternity in hell.

6. RECOMMENDATIONS—

   a. I should believe, recognize my sins, feel contrite and remorse in my heart, repent, confess, undergo daily baptism, and obey.

   b. I should exercise my faith through my free will as empowered by the free grace from the Spirit of God to trust and obey Jesus Christ for my salvation; I know they are the two critical operative elements of God's two-edge sword, and they work together according to the council of His will.

   c. I will not reject the Spirit of God; that is unforgivable.

This audit finding of mine is highly personal, and it is only you who can create one like it for yourself. Nobody can perform it for you. You must write it by yourself. No parent can take the steps for you. You alone are accountable. No sect, denominational faith group, or religion can socially intervene as a public entity on your behalf. You must meet the Lord face-to-face at mortal death or the rapture/resurrection, whichever comes first, privately and personally. Are you ready?

For aviators, these internal control steps are like keeping the ball centered in the ball and needle gauge on the instrument panel as you control your rudder to maintain balanced flight until you get where you are going. Pilots will remember being taught the phrase "Step on the ball." about controlling the direction of the rudder pedals. They also know the consequences of unbalanced flight, especially during an approach turn. There is no room for more than one set of feet on the rudder pedals. There is no room for error. So now is the time for all of us to individually step on the ball! Nobody can do it for you. Do not stall out, spin, or burn. Spurgeon would say, "Turn or burn."

If you decided yes and believe that Jesus is who He says He is and God is who He says He is and you accept true salvation is totally a work of God by the power of the Holy Spirit, you are now justified to act just as if you had always done right. God's gracious and full acquittal for sinners is now yours. For sinners who repent and believe in Jesus Christ, you now have a proper relationship of peace and favor with God. You may be wondering if your faith nullifies the law. No, the law is our gauge to maintain balanced flight! Paul writes, "Or is God the God of Jews only? Is he not the God of Gentiles also? Yes, of Gentiles also, since God is one—who will justify the circumcised by faith and the uncircumcised through faith. Do we then overthrow the law by this faith? By no means! On the contrary, we uphold the law" (Romans 3:29–31 ESV).

Paul Says for Us to Live as Those Made Alive in Christ.

The first three dimensions of all five dimensions of life are conveyed by Paul in his letter to the Colossians where he provides three of those dimensions that are *directional* in nature as: (1) things **above**, (2) things **earthly**, and (3) things **evil**.

> If then you have been raised with Christ, seek the things that are **above**, where Christ is, seated at the right hand of God. Set your minds on things that are above, not on things that are on **earth**. For you have died, and your life is hidden with Christ in God. When Christ who is your life appears, then you also will appear with him in glory.
>
> Put to death therefore what is earthly in you: sexual immorality, impurity, passion, **evil** desire, and covetousness, which is idolatry. On account of these the wrath of God is coming. In these you too once walked, when you were living in them. But now you must put them all away: anger, wrath, malice, slander, and obscene talk from your mouth. Do not lie to one another, seeing that you have put off the old self with its practices and have put on the new self, which is being renewed in knowledge after the image of its creator. Here there is not Greek and Jew, circumcised and uncircumcised, barbarian, Scythian, slave, free; but Christ is all, and in all.
>
> Put on then, as God's chosen ones, holy and beloved, compassionate hearts, kindness, humility, meekness, and patience, bearing with one another and, if one has a complaint against another, forgiving each other; as the Lord has forgiven you, so you also must forgive. And above all these put on love, which binds everything together in perfect harmony. And let the peace of Christ rule in your hearts, to which indeed you were called in one body. And be thankful. Let the word of Christ dwell in you richly, teaching and admonishing one another in all wisdom, singing psalms and hymns and spiritual songs, with thankfulness in your hearts to God. And whatever you do, in word or deed, do everything in the name of the Lord Jesus, giving thanks to God the Father through him. (Colossians 3:1–17 ESV)

First, We Are to Set Our Hearts on Things Above (Good).
We are to love God and others as we love ourselves.

Second, We Are Not to Set Our Minds on Earthly Things (Ugly).
We are not to let the things of this earth become idols that get in our way of loving God and others.

Third, We Are to Put to Death Whatever Belongs to Our Earthly Nature (Bad).
We are to hate sin and all that is evil.

Ezekiel Says for Us to Know that God is Sovereign; Daniel Fortifies

The last two dimensions of life are *relational* and are graphically described by Ezekiel as the magnitude of God's **connections** and by Daniel as our **relationship** with the presence of God. Ezekiel and Daniel describe these dimensions in visions. Note how Ezekiel's vision says, "And I will give you a new heart, and a new spirit I will put within you. And I will remove the heart of stone from your flesh and give you a heart of flesh. And I will put my Spirit within you, and cause you to walk in my statutes and be careful to obey my rules" (Ezekiel 36:26–27 ESV). And, how Daniel's vision says "His body was like beryl, his face like the appearance of lightning, his eyes like flaming torches, his arms and legs like the gleam of burnished bronze, and the sound of his words like the sound of a multitude. And I, Daniel, alone saw the vision, for the men who were with me did not see the vision, but a great trembling fell upon them, and they fled to hide themselves." (Daniel 10:6-7 ESV)

So, these last two *relational* dimensions (connection and relationship) are vital to our dynamic personal assessment of our individual souls. Here is how I drill down to the primitive level for the fourth and fifth dimensions for my own spiritual assessment. The visions of these two prophets are where I start.

Fourth, We Are to Recognize the Unlimited Power of God (Connection).

We are to give up on understanding God and His power. God does what He wants without human understanding by using, for one example, a *Kairos* multi-linear format for time. He is not limited to human limitations regarding motion or the boundaries of a *Chronos* linear clock. He is in command of all **connections** in our lives and all the dynamics at work in all its tension areas. Nothing escapes the power of God. He knows all about the dynamics of everything and everybody all at the same time since before the foundation of the world and before He spoke it into being. Think about the magnitude of God's mighty connectivity in this vision from Ezekiel:

> Now as I looked at the living creatures, I saw a wheel on the earth beside the living creatures, one for each of the four of them. As for the appearance of the wheels and their construction: their appearance was like the gleaming of beryl. And the four had the same likeness, their appearance and construction being as it were a wheel within a wheel. When they went, they went in any of their four directions without turning as they went. And their rims were tall and awesome, and the rims of all four were full of eyes all around. And when the living creatures went, the wheels went beside them; and when the living creatures rose from the earth, the wheels rose. Wherever the spirit wanted to go, they went, and the wheels rose along with them, for the spirit of the living creatures was in the wheels. When those went, these went; and when those stood, these stood; and when those rose from the earth, the wheels rose along with them, for the spirit of the living creatures was in the wheels. (Ezekiel 1:15-21 ESV)

But there is more,

> And I looked, and behold, there were four wheels beside the cherubim, one beside each cherub, and the appearance of the wheels was like sparkling beryl. And as for their appearance, the four had the same likeness, as if a wheel were within a wheel. When they went, they went in any of their four directions without turning as they went, but in whatever direction the front wheel faced, the others followed without turning as they went. And their whole body, their rims, and

their spokes, their wings, and the wheels were full of eyes all around—the wheels that the four of them had. As for the wheels, they were called in my hearing "the whirling wheels." And every one had four faces: the first face was the face of the cherub, and the second face was a human face, and the third the face of a lion, and the fourth the face of an eagle. (Ezekiel 10:9-14 ESV)

God's wheels go where God wants them to go. No path is impossible for God! Just read about Jonah and God's big fish. No human has wheels like God! We can't even comprehend the connections involved.

Fifth, We Are to Recognize that God Is Present in Our Lives on His Terms (Relationship).

We also need to be very humbly aware that our **relationship** with God is determined by God. God enters our lives whenever God wants. He commands relationships over and over as a critical dimension with all of us. Daniel states,

I lifted up my eyes and looked, and behold, a man clothed in linen, with a belt of fine gold from Uphaz around his waist. His body was like beryl, his face like the appearance of lightning, his eyes like flaming torches, his arms and legs like the gleam of burnished bronze, and the sound of his words like the sound of a multitude. And I, Daniel, alone saw the vision, for the men who were with me did not see the vision, but a great trembling fell upon them, and they fled to hide themselves. So I was left alone and saw this great vision, and no strength was left in me. My radiant appearance was fearfully changed, and I retained no strength. Then I heard the sound of his words, and as I heard the sound of his words, I fell on my face in deep sleep with my face to the ground. And behold, a hand touched me and set me trembling on my hands and knees. And he said to me, "O Daniel, man greatly loved, understand the words that I speak to you, and stand upright, for now I have been sent to you." And when he had spoken this word to me, I stood up trembling. Then he said to me, "Fear not, Daniel, for from the first day that you set your heart to understand and humbled yourself before your God, your words have been heard, and I have come because of your words. (Daniel 10:5-12 ESV)

Considering the above visions of Ezekiel and Daniel, all the dynamics needed are now supplied to proceed with your personal spiritual assessment. And as we do, thanksgiving such as depicted by Psalm 100 must constantly come from our contrite hearts and preferably facedown pleading in the mud made by our tears.

Make a joyful noise to the LORD, all the earth! Serve the LORD with gladness! Come into his presence with singing! Know that the LORD, he is God! It is he who made us, and we are his; we are his people, and the sheep of his pasture. Enter his gates with thanksgiving, and his courts with praise! Give thanks to him; bless his name! For the LORD is good; his steadfast love endures forever, and his faithfulness to all generations. (Psalm 100:1–5 ESV).

God's Call

Sometimes God's call is dramatic, although a lot less dramatic and harrowing than some. I know exactly when I got the **green** light to go forward with a response.

Preacher? Who? Me?

I wrestled with God's call since high school. I was picked to be the preacher of the 1962 class; I hope chaplain is close enough. I had just about put the thought aside permanently until after the death of my first wife, Judy, to breast cancer in June 2003. I was leaving the office late one evening that winter, and I remember saying silently, "God, just give me a sign that shows me what you want me to do. My kids are grown and gone, and my wife of thirty-three years is with You." I had no sooner finished that thought than I looked over to the edge of the nearly empty parking lot and saw a medium-aged live oak tree blowing in the cold wind. The leaves had formed a silhouette of a single lone dove in flight against Austin's gray winter sky. Something urged me to think, *Okay, Lord, is that You?* Next, thinking that it was a coincidence, and everything was all over, I started the car and began to back out of the stall, but before I drove away, I thought that I better look at that tree one more time for good measure. When my eyes landed on that same tree, the silhouette of a dove was still there, painted with the backdrop of the same gray winter sky and shaped by the rustling leaves blowing in the cold wind as before; however, this time the dove was flying in the opposite direction. Chills covered my entire body and the hair on the back of my neck bristled to a standing position of attention. I then said to the Lord, "Okay, I get it, Lord. It is time for me to do a 180-degree turn in my life, right?" There was no answer, not even after a significant pause. So I gathered my wits, and I began to drive away; however, before the tires even began to roll on the asphalt, I turned my head in the direction of the live oak tree to clear any traffic, and lo and behold, a lone white-winged dove flew out of that oak tree and went directly over the top of my car by about ten feet. It was headed in the direction of Fort Worth, where I knew some seminaries were located. I said, "Okay, that's it. I can hear You clearly now." Incidentally the white-winged doves had departed Austin weeks before to their southern migration home in the Rio Grande valley. What was this one single lonesome dove still doing in Austin? Why was it headed north? What? Am I senseless? It didn't take a prophet to interpret these events. Not even a still small voice was uttered. But I could feel the Spirit of God in the "wind" speaking to me like it never has before. Thanks Lord.

The next day my typed resignation was on the desks of the appropriate people at human resources and those immediate supervisors in my department. I have never looked back. I entered seminary in Fort Worth in January of 2004 for the spring semester. What a blessing it was to feel the hand of the Lord at work on me personally. I'm just glad He didn't knock me out of a camel's saddle and blind me like He did with Paul. With that event over, even with the grief of my wife being gone and now residing with the Lord, I found nothing but a sense of joy in the days ahead. I remember reflecting on my wife's final question, "What will you do when I am gone?" and the response I gave her, "I guess I'll go back to seminary." Her strong confirming reply of "That's good!" that she stated that day is unforgettable. That voice stayed in my ear daily as I worked on class assignments, especially late at night. It is still there even now as I revised this manuscript nineteen years later. Seminary demands were a team project with her at my side, pushing and nudging me as only a few could do along the way. Thank you, Judy. Thank you. I will always love you.

From a Snake to a Dove

Sometimes God's voice comes in different ways, even though an experience with a big black snake in a milk barn like it did for me. The best way to make sure that you don't miss it is to stay connected

117

and have a constant relationship with Jesus Christ. Seek Him, commune with Him continuously. Think YHWH as you breathe in YH, and out WH.

Being mindful that a heavy price may be exacted as a delivery boy for the gospel of Jesus Christ, I am reminded by Matthew 10:16–17 where Jesus is on record when He said, "Behold, I am sending you out as sheep in the midst of wolves, so be wise as serpents and innocent as doves. Beware of men, for they will deliver you over to courts and flog you in their synagogues."

Considerations for Gaining Understanding

Religion v. Spirituality

Consider that the word *religion* is an overarching infinite social term, while the word *spiritual* is narrower and personal. Both compliment the other but in different ways.

In making a Theo-metric assessment, label religion at an "element-level" under the "Interpersonal" high-level "attribute" of the temporal Z-axis. We all know this element can often get ugly with many conflicting boundaries and doctrinal tangents which will eventually run out of temporal time.

Notice that religion also demands another label at the "component-level" to set it apart from other equal level components like aesthetics and ethics, all of which have their own unique roots.

Now label spiritual at a "root-level" under the component-level labeled religion. All is fine until we recognize that this spiritual root possesses the unique power to transcend the temporal limits of our "area of tension" (or tension box) that sets boundaries for our life. Without accounting for this connection and relationship to the Y-axis (or X-axis), nothing about spiritual computes. Because this root runs deep where a personal connection and relationship with God is possible for eternity, its endurance on the Z-axis would be only as good as the Z-axis itself.

Simply put, spirituality will outlast us, whereas religion will not. So, when examining the overarching social sphere of the religion component, recognize that its spiritual root exists, and it is only that part that has any eternal value. Otherwise, religion is totally temporal. Spirituality is eternal because it provides the resource (tunnel) for us to connect and relate to the eternal godly Y-axis (or the evil X-axis). Bingo! Theo-metrics at work.

So, it is inadequate to address the two words religion and spiritual in matrices without pinpointing their complete address in the matrix along the Z-axis. Here we see where the religion element has three component levels that have underlying roots which are:

Z Axis Address	Attribute Level	Element Level	Component Level	Root Level
Z=1	INTERPERSONAL ATTRIBUTE			
Z=I.1		RELIGION ELEMENT		
Z=I.1.1			Aesthetic Component	
Z=I.1.1.1				*Physical Root*
Z=I.1.2			Ethical Component	
Z=I.1.2.1				*Emotional Root*
Z=I.1.3			Religion Component *(has unique "tunneling" capacity *)*	
Z=I.1.3.1				*Spiritual Root (has unique "tunneling" capacity *)*
Z=S	SPIRITUAL ATTRIBUTE			
Z=S.1		TRINITARIAN GOD ELEMENT		T U N N E L
Z=S.1.1			God, the Father Component	
Z=S.1.1.1				I AM; YHWH Root (*)
Z=S.1.2			Jesus, the Son Component	
Z=S.1.2.1				King of Kings; Lord of Lords Root (*)
Z=S.1.3			God, the Holy Spirit Component	
Z=S.1.3.1				Not to be rejected/ blasphemy Root (*)
Z=S.2		WORD OF GOD ELEMENT		
Z=S.2.1			God's Total Truth Component	
Z=S.2.1.1				One Holy Bible of God's Holy Scriptures Root (*)

Figure 7. Two Theo-metric Examples of Drilling from Attribute to Root Level on the Z-Axis

Now, by focusing solely on the underlying root-level of the religion component, we realize there is a clear path "tunnel (*) to eternity" for us to bring our personal connections and relationship to fruition. Knowing that this "tunnel to eternity (*)" exists, I am compelled to owe Him my constant allegiance and loyalty; marked by duty and responsibility to Him and to others (without the demand of religious elements within interpersonal constraints). So, spiritually, I can then strive for a determined and hopeful heart that is trustworthy, reliable, devoted, dependable, steadfast, dedicated, and conscientious yet deliberately contrite. Insist on your "Jesus Tunnel (*)."

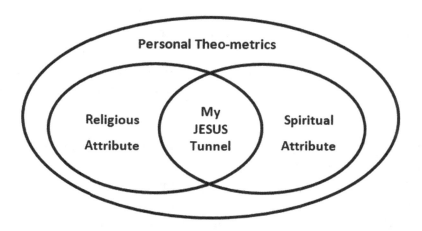

Figure 8. Personal Theo-metrics

Religious (Spiritual) Elements are Useless to Aesthetic (Physical) and Ethical (Emotional) Components

Being determined spiritually, though, goes even deeper and broader. It surpasses being faithful in the physical or emotional spheres of our life. The figure below clearly suggests that we can, and do, sometimes allow components of religion to obscure our spiritual vision from within that overarching element.[68] By following Jesus, we can faithfully and easily tunnel past that bubble (perhaps using our understanding of Theo-metrics as an aid) with the power of the Holy Spirit to get to the eternal Y-axis.

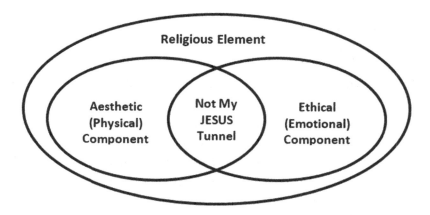

Figure 9. Religious Element

Martin Luther comes to mind. He knew how to "tunnel." What determined courage in the face of what must have appeared to him as daunting and insurmountable fire. His spiritual determination would not allow him to give up his quest to reform religion in the Roman Catholic Church and elsewhere.

Similarly, the determination of Sir Winston Churchill was on display during a visit to Harrow School following the blitz in 1941. He is reported to have said, "Never give in. Never give in. Never, never, never, never—in nothing, great or small, large or petty—never give in, except to convictions of honour and good sense. Never yield to force. Never yield to the apparently overwhelming might of the enemy."[69] His determination echoes in our hearts even today. We should be so determined in our quest for communion with God. We should never give up! We should look in the smallest and largest of places to connect and relate to Him, while always listening as well. Nurture your determination for spiritual truth, the enemy is powerfully deceptive even in religious social realms and our deepest spiritual roots.

Spiritual Demarcations Surpass Religion with a Two-Edge Sword

We can study *religion* to determine what works we need to **do** for salvation until the cows come home, but what we really need is the personal spiritual determination and enthusiasm to help us attain personal communion with the Spirit of God. God's Spirit enables us to believe that our salvation is secure through **God's free grace** and **our free will** to have **faith in His Son, Jesus Christ.** That kind of two edge sword will lead us home when our hand is tightly gripping the handle of faith! Through that enthusiasm and faith, we will then be able to obey His commandments and abide in His love. If we fall, we are promised that He will be there to pick us up and forgive us when we recognize, confess and repent for our sins.

Let Holy Spirit-led determination, the Word of God, prayer and God fearing enthusiasm direct you personally and spiritually. Peel away nonessential social and religious components like layers on an onion. Spiritual determination while reading Scripture yields stronger vision and insight. I also find that when using a personal Theo-metric assessment of all thirty-five attributes of life's five dimensions, I discover many unmet needs associated with developing a stronger relationship with God and others. This is particularly true during hospital patient encounters. If you sharpen your sword with a comprehensive study of each attribute with God's Word and prayer, I believe you will find a stronger relationship too.

Personal Theo-metrics Can Help

My most rewarding approach to building a relationship with God is through daily, sometimes hourly personal Theo-metric assessments by listening for the Spirit of God and studying the Word of God But even with a dozen cover-to-cover readings so far (and many selective studies), Scripture leaves me unclear about a lot of things. It appears I am not alone. Story has it that, Billy Graham has said, "It is not the things in the Bible that I don't understand that bother me. It is the things in the Bible that I do understand that bother me." It appears Dr. Graham has made a lot of judicious assessments over the span of his life to be wise enough to make that statement. When we consider that we need more understanding, the Spirit of God, our prayers, and our determined study of the Word of God will give us more. Dr. Graham has been clearly blessed by more understanding than many, and he visibly displays that he possesses personal communion with God. "For now we see in a mirror dimly, but then face to face. Now I know in part; then I shall know fully, even as I have been fully known" (1 Corinthians 13:12 ESV).

The following twenty key Scripture passages are a good foundation for seeking personal guidance about what to do in strengthening our relationship with God leading up to and from our second birth until we die. These passages of Scripture shout out, "Born once, die twice. Born twice, die once!" They make for communion with God. They make the water in Baptism more than water; the bread and the wine in Holy Communion more than sustenance. Along with the entirety of God's Word, they bring us **connection** and **relationship** with God the Father and God the Son through the power of the Holy Spirit.

Twenty Scriptures for Building an Eternal Relationship with God

1. **Fear God.**

   a. Ecclesiastes 12:13 says, "The end of the matter; all has been heard. Fear God and keep his commandments, for this is the whole duty of man."

   b. Proverbs 1:7 says, "The fear of the Lord is the beginning of knowledge; fools despise wisdom and instruction."

   c. Matthew 10:28 says, "And do not fear those who kill the body but cannot kill the soul. Rather fear him who can destroy both soul and body in hell."

2. **Go and Teach.**

   a. Matthew 28:19–20 says, "Go therefore and make disciples of all nations, baptizing them in the name of the Father and of the Son and of the Holy Spirit, teaching them to observe all that I have commanded you. And behold, I am with you always, to the end of the age."

   b. Mark 16:15 says, "And he said to them, 'Go into all the world and proclaim the Gospel to the whole creation.'"

   c. Second Timothy 3:16 says, "All Scripture is breathed out by God and profitable for teaching, for reproof, for correction, and for training in righteousness."

3. **Do NOT Blaspheme the Holy Spirit.**

   a. Mark 3:29 says, "But whoever blasphemes against the Holy Spirit never has forgiveness, but is guilty of an eternal sin."

   b. Luke 12:10 says, "And everyone who speaks a word against the Son of Man will be forgiven, but the one who blasphemes against the Holy Spirit will not be forgiven."

4. **Follow and Obey Jesus.**

   a. Luke 9:23 says, "And he said to all, 'If anyone would come after me, let him deny himself and take up his cross daily and follow me.'"

   b. John 10:28 says, "I give them eternal life, and they will never perish, and no one will snatch them out of my hand."

   c. John 15:14 says, "You are my friends if you do what I command you."

   d. Romans 8:36 says, "As it is written, 'For your sake we are being killed all the day long; we are regarded as sheep to be slaughtered.'"

e. Romans 12:1–2 says, "I appeal to you therefore, brothers, by the mercies of God, to present your bodies as a living sacrifice, holy and acceptable to God, which is your spiritual worship. Do not be conformed to this world, but be transformed by the renewal of your mind, that by testing you may discern what is the will of God, what is good and acceptable and perfect."

f. Ephesian 5:8 says, "For at one time you were darkness, but now you are light in the Lord. Walk as children of light."

g. Philippians 1:29 says, "For it has been granted to you that for the sake of Christ you should not only believe in him but also suffer for his sake."

h. Second Timothy 1:8 says, "Therefore do not be ashamed of the testimony about our Lord, nor of me his prisoner, but share in suffering for the gospel by the power of God."

5. **Love God and Others.**

a. John 15:13 says, "Greater love has no one than this, that someone lay down his life for his friends."

b. Ephesian 6:7–8 says, "Rendering service with a good will as to the Lord and not to man, knowing that whatever good anyone does, this he will receive back from the Lord, whether he is a bondservant or is free."

6. **Practice Grace.**

a. Ephesians 2:8–9 says, "For by grace you have been saved through faith. And this is not your own doing; it is the gift of God, not a result of works, so that no one may boast."

b. Philippians 2:15 says, "That you may be blameless and innocent, children of God without blemish in the midst of a crooked and twisted generation, among whom you shine as lights in the world."

Table 11. Twenty Scriptures for Building an Eternal Relationship with God

Spiritual Formation

As seen above, a certain amount of distancing is necessary for doing theological reflection. Only by standing back from things can a growth in understanding come about. Care must be taken, however, to avoid an attendant loss. The sensitivity of an intimate relationship with God may be displaced by an attitude of detachment, and genuine concern for the meaning of faith may give way to mere intellectualizing.[70]

Jesus found a need to stand back from things by going into the wilderness. After His baptism by John, Jesus went into the desert for forty days and was tempted by Satan with offers of vast temporal earthly treasures if He would only bow down and worship him.

Jesus Is Confronted by Satan in the Wilderness

Have you gone into the wilderness like Jesus?

> Then Jesus was led up by the Spirit into the wilderness to be tempted by the devil. And after fasting forty days and forty nights, he was hungry. And the tempter came and said to him, "If you are the Son of God, command these stones to become loaves of bread." But he answered, "It is written, 'Man shall not live by bread alone, but by every word that comes from the mouth of God.'"
>
> Then the devil took him to the holy city and set him on the pinnacle of the temple and said to him, "If you are the Son of God, throw yourself down, for it is written, 'He will command his angels concerning you,' and 'On their hands they will bear you up, lest you strike your foot against a stone.'"
>
> Jesus said to him, "Again it is written, 'You shall not put the Lord your God to the test.'" Again, the devil took him to a very high mountain and showed him all the kingdoms of the world and their glory. And he said to him, "All these I will give you, if you will fall down and worship me." Then Jesus said to him, "Be gone, Satan! For it is written, 'You shall worship the Lord your God and him only shall you serve.'" Then the devil left him, and behold, angels came and were ministering to him. (Matthew 4:1–11 ESV)

When we are tested, follow Jesus' example.

Jesus Tells Us Indicators Show the Way We Practice Our Faith

Jesus makes it clear that we are to keep and teach the Law.

> Do not think that I have come to abolish the Law or the Prophets; I have not come to abolish them but to fulfill them. For truly, I say to you, until heaven and earth pass away, not an iota, not a dot, will pass from the Law until all is accomplished. Therefore whoever relaxes one of the least of these commandments and teaches others to do the same will be called least in the kingdom of heaven, but whoever does them and teaches them will be called great in the kingdom of heaven. (Matthew 5:17–19 ESV)

Have you relaxed a commandment or two or three? What's in your wilderness? Do you know the way out? If you are in a quagmire, look for the Rock, a Living Stone—Jesus Christ.

Need for Works

Serious Christians, just do it! The need is Spirit-motivated, and the good works flow like a steamy hot geyser or a cool bubbling spring in the desert. You just can't turn it off. "They shall hunger no more, neither thirst anymore; the sun shall not strike them, nor any scorching heat. For the Lamb in the midst of the throne will be their shepherd, and he will guide them to springs of living water, and God will wipe away every tear from their eyes" (Revelation 7:16–17 ESV).

We also learn from James, that without works, faith is dead. This may be one reason we have a tendency to think of judgment being some far off decision point. This is one of Satan's favorite tactics. Take a moment to look for the location of the diamond-shaped decision symbol <> in our tension area

(Figure 3). Where is it located? It is *inside* our tension area. It is firmly *fixed* on our lifeline *inside* our tension cube. It *splits* our lifeline into two directions. It *forces* us to decide which path to take *before* we exit our tension cube when we die. Don't let Satan lull you to sleep and dupe you into thinking you have plenty of time to get to that decision point before you start a relationship with God. Act now before it is too late! Remember, the "day of the Lord will come like a thief in the night." (2 Peter 3) Then what would you do? Burn, baby, burn! So, turn or burn!

So, When Is Judgment? It Is Now!

I visited a ninety-six-year-old patient last spring who was restrained to a bed with cloth straps and monitored by a sitter to prevent him from standing and trying to walk as a fall precaution. I kneeled beside his bed while he was angrily rambling on with his eyes closed, and I said, "I am Chaplain Bill. I want you to know that I am here for you, and I have been praying for you. I just left the chapel this morning and you are on my prayer list today, so I lifted you up in prayer."

He instantly opened his eyes, and forthrightly said (to my amazement), "When is the judgment, Chaplain Bill?"

I thought for a moment and said, "You know the line in 'Amazing Grace' that says, 'The hour I first believed.'?"

He said, "Yes, I've given a lot of thought to that line."

"Me too," I said, "and I have actually tied it to John 3:18. You know the words that go, 'He who believes in Him is not judged; he who does not believe has been judged already, because he has not believed in the name of the only begotten Son of God.'"

He said, "Yes, you mean judgment is *now*?"

I said, "Yup. It looks that way to me. I see my judgment like an E-ZPass on the Hardy Toll Road. No stopping, just go. I have a clear lane all the way, say to Galveston from here. I don't have to stop at the tollbooth either. Jesus has already paid the price for my free passage into paradise just like He did with the criminal on the cross who just believed."

"That brings me enormous joy, Chaplain Bill," he said. "Thank you for coming to see me today. I needed that."

I said, "We all need that—to know that judgment is *now*! Can we pray together?"

He said with a tear forming in his eye, "Yup." I wiped the tear away with a tissue as I left.

The hymn "Amazing Grace" reveals that judgment comes "the hour I first believed." Some say that it comes before the foundation of the world when our name was written into the Book of Life. The Spirit of God's delivery truck arrives when God wants it to arrive, not sooner or later but in His own good time, He will ring our bell at our door. His truck always makes it on time for His elect. Not one of His own will be lost.

Digressing for a moment, in product manufacturing terms, the concept and design phase of our life is introduced into the world as a prototype where we are refined, developed, grown, and matured. Ultimately after production begins, we will hit saturation and then decline. Somewhere along the line, we may learn that our product could be flawed and require modifications. This is where the use of prudent judgment is important before we proceed with more production. Many modifications may be needed before we resume assembly and ultimately terminate rollout. What phase are you in? Are you nearing termination rollout?

Sometimes when we finally get the concept of God's judgment in our lives, we go through a similar process before we terminate our time allotted on earth. Prudence dictates that we understand that when we are dealing with our soul and not some temporal consumer product, we must listen for God's input and heed it. The modifications that God wants to see in our lives are based on our belief in His Son, Jesus Christ, as our Lord and Savior and what He did for us on Calvary. When we believe that He was sent to die for our sins, we are issued an E-ZPass, and we travel in His fast lane, unimpeded by the tollbooths until we arrive safely home in His kingdom in heaven. He has already paid our tolls for free passage with His sacrificial blood, which was shed on the cross. It is imperative that we know that we are not judged again when we are judged faithful servants "the hour we first believed." I know it is so because when it is so, it is so—so be it! My tearful heart convicts me. So there! Is your heart crying for conviction and forgiveness or is it stone cold?

Just look very closely at many of the related collective thoughts of John on *believing, judgment*, and *obeying* Jesus from the gospel of John.

> For God so loved the world, that he gave his only Son, that whoever believes in him should not perish but have eternal life. For God did not send his Son into the world to condemn the world, but in order that the world might be saved through him. Whoever believes in him is not condemned, but whoever does not believe is condemned already, because he has not believed in the name of the only Son of God. And this is the judgment: the light has come into the world, and people loved the darkness rather than the light because their works were evil. For everyone who does wicked things hates the light and does not come to the light, lest his works should be exposed. But whoever does what is true comes to the light, so that it may be clearly seen that his works have been carried out in God. (John 3:16–21 ESV).

When is the judgment? We can secure eternal life if we believe *and* obey now! John is not through with the subject of judgment. He tells us not only to believe but also to **obey**. "Whoever believes in the Son has eternal life; whoever does not obey the Son shall not see life, but the wrath of God remains on him" (John 3:36 ESV).

If we do not believe, we cannot obey. If we believe, we can enjoy a foretaste of what is to come in heaven in the fullness of His glory. When is the judgment? We need to hear Jesus and believe in Him **now**. "Truly, truly, I say to you, whoever hears my word and believes him who sent me has eternal life. He does not come into judgment, but has passed from death to life" (John 5:24 ESV).

Hear His voice and believe. It says, "Go straight to go!" Just keep going until you get where you are going. We will be there before we know it. But don't be just a hearer only without understanding. Be a doer of His Word. What is the work of God? By His grace, God works to cause us to believe. "Jesus answered them, 'This is the work of God, that you believe in him whom he has sent'" (John 6:29 ESV).

Jesus is the bread of life. When we believe in Him, we will never be hungry or thirst.

Jesus said to them, "I am the bread of life; whoever comes to me shall not hunger, and whoever believes in me shall never thirst. But I said to you that you have seen me and yet do not believe. All that the Father gives me will come to me, and whoever comes to me I will never cast out. For I have come down from heaven, not to do my own will but the will of him who sent me. And this is the will of him who sent me, that I should lose nothing of all that he has given me, but raise it up on the last day. For this is the will of my Father, that everyone who looks on the Son and believes in him should have eternal life, and I will raise him up on the last day."

So the Jews grumbled about him, because he said, "I am the bread that came down from heaven." They said, "Is not this Jesus, the son of Joseph, whose father and mother we know? How does he now say, 'I have come down from heaven'?" Jesus answered them, "Do not grumble among your selves. No one can come to me unless the Father who sent me draws him. And I will raise him up on the last day." (John 6:35–44 ESV)

Belief in Jesus is the result of being drawn by God to do so. This influence is irresistible, yet we can exercise our free will to refuse and blaspheme the Spirit of God. We don't want to do that because it is the only unforgivable sin, and it will guarantee eternal damnation if we meet death without belief in Jesus Christ. Unbelief, being tempted by Satan to do so, can be overcome by obeying and abiding in the love of Christ Jesus, who said, "If you keep my commandments, you will abide in my love, just as I have kept my Father's commandments and abide in his love" (John 15:10 ESV).

Lastly Luke Embodies All of Salvation

As illustrated in the Introduction chapter, this one passage of Scripture alone embodies the ABCs of salvation—acknowledge, believe, and confess.

One of the criminals who were hanged railed at him, saying, "Are you not the Christ? Save yourself and us!" But the other rebuked him, saying, "Do you not fear God, since you are under the same sentence of condemnation? And we indeed justly, for we are receiving the due reward of our deeds; but this man has done nothing wrong." And he said, "Jesus, remember me when you come into your kingdom." And he said to him, "Truly, I say to you, today you will be with me in Paradise." (Luke 23:39–43 ESV)

Like four leaves in a clover, quatrefoil, or the vertices of a quadrilateral, we can use Scripture, tradition, reason, and experience as collective resources to find a way to fulfill God's work. But remember the most essential thing of all. "The fear of the LORD is the beginning of wisdom, and the knowledge of the Holy One is insight" (Proverbs 9:10 ESV).

Our Dilemma—Born Again by Free Grace or Free Will?

Let there be no doubt that we have the free will to choose in life *who* we will seek and/or follow. The following modest illustration shows how the captain of a tugboat may choose to steer his vessel to the port or the starboard side of a sandbar and the bridge piling ahead. But I've got some awesome news for you. God already knows the answer not only to those decisions but to all our decisions. Through His guiding and loving grace, He knows where we are going to dock before we even see the port!

You may think you have a grip on the helm, but God is in command of the rudder, the throttle, the fuel, the compass, the lights, and everything else on that boat (even what is served from the galley).

Suppose you are the captain of that tugboat in the Houston Ship Channel, and it's your task to move a barge to a destination at one of the ports. Our free will works fine along the voyage (i.e., port or starboard side of a sandbar or a bridge piling, etc.). But for those whose names have been placed in the Lamb's Book of Life before the foundation of the world, God already knows the port where we will dock. He knows everything about our journey too.

The Bible says He knows the ways of our hearts before we can form words in our mouth and before they roll off our lips. He knows the number of hairs on our heads. He knows the stars; He calls them all by name. He puts each grain of sand on the seashore in place. He knits us together in our mothers' wombs one piece of DNA and/or laminin protein molecule at a time. God already knows where we (i.e., the saints, the elect, the chosen, the predestined, etc.) will dock! Read and trust His Word from cover to cover, looking closely for the "bloodline" of Christ and God's "strategic plan" for us. Look at some samples.

Forty Scriptures for Trusting God for Our Eternal Relationship

1. Genesis 12:1–3 says, "Now the LORD said to Abram, 'Go from your country and your kindred and your father's house to the land that I will show you. And I will make of you a great nation, and I will bless you and make your name great, so that you will be a blessing. I will bless those who bless you, and him who dishonors you I will curse, and in you all the families of the earth shall be blessed.'"

2. Exodus 19:5–8 says, "Now therefore, if you will indeed obey my voice and keep my covenant, you shall be my treasured possession among all peoples, for all the earth is mine; and you shall be to me a kingdom of priests and a holy nation. These are the words that you shall speak to the people of Israel. So Moses came and called the elders of the people and set before them all these words that the LORD had commanded him. All the people answered together and said, 'All that the LORD has spoken we will do.' And Moses reported the words of the people to the LORD."

3. Jeremiah 31:31 says, "Behold, the days are coming, declares the LORD, when I will make a new covenant with the house of Israel and the house of Judah."

4. Matthew 16:18–19 says, "And I tell you, you are Peter, and on this rock, I will build my church, and the gates of hell shall not prevail against it. I will give you the keys of the kingdom of heaven, and whatever you bind on earth shall be bound in heaven, and whatever you loose on earth shall be loosed in heaven."

5. Matthew 21:28–45 says,

   What do you think? A man had two sons. And he went to the first and said, "Son, go and work in the vineyard today." And he answered, "I will not," but afterward he changed his mind and went. And he went to the other son and said the same. And he answered, "I go, sir," but did not go. "Which of the two did the will of his father?" They said, "The first." Jesus said to them, "Truly, I say to you, the tax collectors and the prostitutes go into the kingdom of God before you." For John came to you in the way of righteousness, and you did not believe him, but the tax collectors and the prostitutes believed him. And even when you saw it, you did not afterward change your minds and believe him.

Hear another parable. There was a master of a house who planted a vineyard and put a fence around it and dug a winepress in it and built a tower and leased it to tenants, and went into another country. When the season for fruit drew near, he sent his servants to the tenants to get his fruit. And the tenants took his servants and beat one, killed another, and stoned another. Again he sent other servants, more than the first. And they did the same to them. Finally he sent his son to them, saying, "They will respect my son." But when the tenants saw the son, they said to themselves, "This is the heir. Come, let us kill him and have his inheritance." And they took him and threw him out of the vineyard and killed him. When therefore the owner of the vineyard comes, what will he do to those tenants? They said to him, "He will put those wretches to a miserable death and let out the vineyard to other tenants who will give him the fruits in their seasons." Jesus said to them, "Have you never read in the Scriptures: 'The stone that the builders rejected has become the cornerstone; this was the Lord's doing, and it is marvelous in our eyes?'

Therefore I tell you, the kingdom of God will be taken away from you and given to a people producing its fruits. And the one who falls on this stone will be broken to pieces; and when it falls on anyone, it will crush him." When the chief priests and the Pharisees heard his parables, they perceived that he was speaking about them.

6. Matthew 24:22 says, "And if those days had not been cut short, no human being would be saved. But for the sake of the elect those days will be cut short."

7. Matthew 24:31 says, "And he will send out his angels with a loud trumpet call, and they will gather his elect from the four winds, from one end of heaven to the other."

8. Matthew 25:34 says, "Then the King will say to those on his right, 'Come, you who are blessed by my Father, inherit the kingdom prepared for you from the foundation of the world.'"

9. Luke 1:68–79 says,

Blessed be the Lord God of Israel, for he has visited and redeemed his people and has raised up a horn of salvation for us in the house of his servant David, as he spoke by the mouth of his holy prophets from of old, that we should be saved from our enemies and from the hand of all who hate us; to show the mercy promised to our fathers and to remember his holy covenant, the oath that he swore to our father Abraham, to grant us that we, being delivered from the hand of our enemies, might serve him without fear, in holiness and righteousness before him all our days. And you, child, will be called the prophet of the Most High; for you will go before the Lord to prepare his ways, to give knowledge of salvation to his people in the forgiveness of their sins, because of the tender mercy of our God, whereby the sunrise shall visit us from on high to give light to those who sit in darkness and in the shadow of death, to guide our feet into the way of peace.

10. Luke 24:44–48 says,

    Then he said to them, "These are my words that I spoke to you while I was still with you, that everything written about me in the Law of Moses and the Prophets and the Psalms must be fulfilled." Then he opened their minds to understand the Scriptures, and said to them, "Thus it is written, that the Christ should suffer and on the third day rise from the dead, and that repentance and forgiveness of sins should be proclaimed in his name to all nations, beginning from Jerusalem. You are witnesses of these things."

11. John 1:12–14 says, "But to all who did receive him, who believed in his name, he gave the right to become children of God, who were born, not of blood nor of the will of the flesh, nor of the will of man, but of God. And the Word became flesh and dwelt among us, and we have seen his glory, glory as of the only Son from the Father, full of grace and truth."

12. John 3:16–21 says, "For God so loved the world, that he gave his only Son, that whoever believes in him should not perish but have eternal life. For God did not send his Son into the world to condemn the world, but in order that the world might be saved through him. Whoever believes in him is not condemned, but whoever does not believe is condemned already, because he has not believed in the name of the only Son of God. And this is the judgment: the light has come into the world, and people loved the darkness rather than the light because their works were evil. For everyone who does wicked things hates the light and does not come to the light, lest his works should be exposed. But whoever does what is true comes to the light, so that it may be clearly seen that his works have been carried out in God."

13. John 5:24 says, "Truly, truly, I say to you, whoever hears my word and believes him who sent me has eternal life. He does not come into judgment, but has passed from death to life."

14. John 6:44–45 says, "No one can come to me unless the Father who sent me draws him. And I will raise him up on the last day. It is written in the Prophets, 'And they will all be taught by God.' Everyone who has heard and learned from the Father comes to me."

15. John 10:27–29 says, "My sheep hear my voice, and I know them, and they follow me. I give them eternal life, and they will never perish, and no one will snatch them out of my hand. My Father, who has given them to me, is greater than all, and no one is able to snatch them out of the Father's hand."

16. John 15:16 says, "You did not choose me, but I chose you and appointed you that you should go and bear fruit and that your fruit should abide, so that whatever you ask the Father in my name, he may give it to you."

17. John 17:6 says, "I have manifested your name to the people whom you gave me out of the world. Yours they were, and you gave them to me, and they have kept your word."

18. John 17:12 says, "While I was with them, I kept them in your name, which you have given me. I have guarded them, and not one of them has been lost except the son of destruction, that the Scripture might be fulfilled."

19. John 17:17–18 says, "Sanctify them in the truth; your word is truth. As you sent me into the world, so I have sent them into the world."

20. Romans 5:9–10 says, "Since, therefore, we have now been justified by his blood, much more shall we be saved by him from the wrath of God. For if while we were enemies we were reconciled to God by the death of his Son, much more, now that we are reconciled, shall we be saved by his life."

21. Romans 8:26–30 says,

Likewise the Spirit helps us in our weakness. For we do not know what to pray for as we ought, but the Spirit himself intercedes for us with groanings too deep for words. And he who searches hearts knows what is the mind of the Spirit, because the Spirit intercedes for the saints according to the will of God. And we know that for those who love God all things work together for good, for those who are called according to his purpose. For those whom he foreknew he also predestined to be conformed to the image of his Son, in order that he might be the firstborn among many brothers. And those whom he predestined he also called, and those whom he called he also justified, and those whom he justified he also glorified.

22. Romans 8:31–39 says,

What then shall we say to these things? If God is for us, who can be against us? He who did not spare his own Son but gave him up for us all, how will he not also with him graciously give us all things? Who shall bring any charge against God's elect? It is God who justifies. Who is to condemn? Christ Jesus is the one who died—more than that, who was raised—who is at the right hand of God, who indeed is interceding for us. Who shall separate us from the love of Christ? Shall tribulation, or distress, or persecution, or famine, or nakedness, or danger, or sword? As it is written, "For your sake we are being killed all the day long; we are regarded as sheep to be slaughtered."

No, in all these things we are more than conquerors through him who loved us. For I am sure that neither death nor life, nor angels nor rulers, nor things present nor things to come, nor powers, nor height nor depth, nor anything else in all creation, will be able to separate us from the love of God in Christ Jesus our Lord.

23. Romans 10:12–15 says,

For there is no distinction between Jew and Greek; for the same Lord is Lord of all, bestowing his riches on all who call on him. For "everyone who calls on the name of the Lord will be saved." How then will they call on him in whom they have not believed? And how are they to believe in him of whom they have never heard? And how are they to hear without someone preaching? And how are they to preach unless they are sent? As it is written, "How beautiful are the feet of those who preach the good news!"

24. Romans 11:5–7 says, "So too at the present time there is a remnant, chosen by grace. But if it is by grace, it is no longer on the basis of works; otherwise grace would no longer be grace. What then? Israel failed to obtain what it was seeking. The elect obtained it, but the rest were hardened.

25. Romans 11:26–36 says,

And in this way all Israel will be saved, as it is written, "The Deliverer will come from Zion, he will banish ungodliness from Jacob"; "and this will be my covenant with them when I take away their sins."

As regards the gospel, they are enemies for your sake. But as regards election, they are beloved for the sake of their forefathers. For the gifts and the calling of God are irrevocable. For just as you were at one time disobedient to God but now have received mercy because of their disobedience, so they too have now been disobedient in order that by the mercy shown to you they also may now receive mercy. For God has consigned all to disobedience, that he may have mercy on all. Oh, the depth of the riches and wisdom and knowledge of God! How unsearchable are his judgments and how inscrutable his ways!

"For who has known the mind of the Lord, or who has been his counselor?" "Or who has given a gift to him that he might be repaid?"

For from him and through him and to him are all things. To him be glory forever. Amen.

26. 1 Corinthians 15:24–28 says,

Then comes the end, when he delivers the kingdom to God the Father after destroying every rule and every authority and power. For he must reign until he has put all his enemies under his feet. The last enemy to be destroyed is death. For "God has put all things in subjection under his feet." But when it says, "all things are put in subjection," it is plain that he is excepted who put all things in subjection under him. When all things are subjected to him, then the Son himself will also be subjected to him who put all things in subjection under him, that God may be all in all.

27. Ephesians 1:4–23 says,

Even as he chose us in him before the foundation of the world, that we should be holy and blameless before him. In love he predestined us for adoption as sons through Jesus Christ, according to the purpose of his will, to the praise of his glorious grace, with which he has blessed us in the Beloved. In him we have redemption through his blood, the forgiveness of our trespasses, according to the riches of his grace, which he lavished upon us, in all wisdom and insight making known to us the mystery of his will, according to his purpose, which he set forth in Christ as a plan for the fullness of time, to unite all things in him, things in heaven and things on earth. In him we have obtained an inheritance, having been predestined according to the purpose of him who works all things according to the counsel of his will, so that we who were the first to hope in Christ might be to the praise of his glory. In him you also, when you heard the word of truth, the gospel of your salvation, and believed in him, were sealed with the promised Holy Spirit, who is the guarantee of our inheritance until we acquire possession of it, to the praise of his glory. For this reason, because I have heard of your faith in the Lord Jesus and your love toward all the saints, I do not cease to give thanks for you, remembering you in my prayers, that the God of our Lord Jesus Christ, the Father of glory, may give you the Spirit of wisdom and of revelation in the knowledge of him, having the eyes of your hearts enlightened, that you may know what is the hope to which he has called you, what are the riches of his glorious inheritance in the saints, and what is the immeasurable greatness of his power toward us who believe, according to the working of his great might that he worked in Christ when he raised him from the dead and seated him at his right hand in the heavenly places, far above all rule and authority and power and dominion, and above every name that is named, not only in this age but also in the one to come. And he put all things under his feet and gave him as head over all things to the church, which is his body, the fullness of him who fills all in all.

28. Ephesians 2:1–10 says,

And you were dead in the trespasses and sins in which you once walked, following the course of this world, following the prince of the power of the air, the spirit that is now at work in the sons of disobedience—among whom we all once lived in the passions of our flesh, carrying out the desires of the body and the mind, and were by nature children of wrath, like the rest of mankind. But God, being rich in mercy, because of the great love with which he loved us, even when we were dead in our trespasses, made us alive together with Christ—by grace you have been saved—and raised us up with him and seated us with him in the heavenly places in Christ Jesus, so that in the coming ages he might show the immeasurable riches of his grace in kindness toward us in Christ Jesus. For by grace you have been saved through faith. And this is not your own doing; it is the gift of God, not a result of works, so that no one may boast. For we are his workmanship, created in Christ Jesus for good works, which God prepared beforehand, that we should walk in them.

29. Colossians 1:12–14 says, "Giving thanks to the Father, who has qualified you to share in the inheritance of the saints in light. He has delivered us from the domain of darkness and transferred us to the kingdom of his beloved Son, in whom we have redemption, the forgiveness of sins."

30. 2 Thessalonians 2:13–14 says, "But we ought always to give thanks to God for you, brothers beloved by the Lord, because God chose you as the firstfruits to be saved, through sanctification by the Spirit and belief in the truth. To this he called you through our gospel, so that you may obtain the glory of our Lord Jesus Christ."

31. 2 Timothy 2:10 says, "Therefore I endure everything for the sake of the elect, that they also may obtain the salvation that is in Christ Jesus with eternal glory."

32. 2 Timothy 2:19 says, "But God's firm foundation stands, bearing this seal: 'The Lord knows those who are his,' and, 'Let everyone who names the name of the Lord depart from iniquity.'"

33. Hebrews 11:39–12:2 says,

And all these, though commended through their faith, did not receive what was promised, since God had provided something better for us, that apart from us they should not be made perfect. Therefore, since we are surrounded by so great a cloud of witnesses, let us also lay aside every weight, and sin which clings so closely, and let us run with endurance the race that is set before us, looking to Jesus, the founder and perfecter of our faith, who for the joy that was set before him endured the cross, despising the shame, and is seated at the right hand of the throne of God.

34. James 1:12 says, "Blessed is the man who remains steadfast under trial, for when he has stood the test he will receive the crown of life, which God has promised to those who love him."

35. 1 Peter 1:2–5 says,

According to the foreknowledge of God the Father, in the sanctification of the Spirit, for obedience to Jesus Christ and for sprinkling with his blood: May grace and peace be multiplied to you. Blessed be the God and Father of our Lord Jesus Christ! According to his great mercy, he has caused us to be born again to a living hope through the resurrection of Jesus Christ from the dead, to an inheritance that is imperishable, undefiled, and unfading, kept in heaven for you, who by God's power are being guarded through faith for a salvation ready to be revealed in the last time.

36. 1 Peter 1:13 says, "Therefore, preparing your minds for action, and being sober-minded, set your hope fully on the grace that will be brought to you at the revelation of Jesus Christ."

37. 1 Peter 2:4–10 says,

As you come to him, a living stone rejected by men but in the sight of God chosen and precious, you yourselves like living stones are being built up as a spiritual house, to be a holy priesthood, to offer spiritual sacrifices acceptable to God through Jesus Christ. For it stands in Scripture: "Behold, I am laying in Zion a stone, a cornerstone chosen and precious, and whoever believes in him will not be put to shame." So the honor is for you who believe, but for those who do not believe, "The stone that the builders rejected has become the cornerstone," and "A stone of stumbling, and a rock of offense." They stumble because they disobey the word, as they were destined to do. But you are a chosen race, a royal priesthood, a holy nation, a people for his own possession, that you may proclaim the excellencies of him who called you out of darkness into his marvelous light. Once you were not a people, but now you are God's people; once you had not received mercy, but now you have received mercy.

38. 1 John 1:2–10 says,

The life was made manifest, and we have seen it, and testify to it and proclaim to you the eternal life, which was with the Father and was made manifest to us—that which we have seen and heard we proclaim also to you, so that you too may have fellowship with us; and indeed our fellowship is with the Father and with his Son Jesus Christ. And we are writing these things so that our joy may be complete. This is the message we have heard from him and proclaim to you, that God is light, and in him is no darkness at all. If we say we have fellowship with him while we walk in darkness, we lie and do not practice the truth. But if we walk in the light, as he is in the light, we have fellowship with one another, and the blood of Jesus his Son cleanses us from all sin. If we say we have no sin, we deceive ourselves, and the truth is not in us. If we confess our sins, he is faithful and just to forgive us our sins and to cleanse us from all unrighteousness. If we say we have not sinned, we make him a liar, and his word is not in us.

39. 1 John 2:15-17 says,

Do not love the world or the things in the world. If anyone loves the world, the love of the Father is not in him. For all that is in the world—the desires of the flesh and desires of the eyes and pride of life—is not from the Father but is from the world. And the world is passing away along with its desires, but whoever does the will of God abides forever.

40. 1 John 3:2 says,

Beloved, we are God's children now, and what we will be has not yet appeared; but we know that when he appears we shall be like him, because we shall see him as he is."

Table 12. Forty Scriptures for Trusting God for Our Eternal Relationship

Of paramount importance is that the only unforgivable sin is to reject the Spirit of God sent by Jesus to convict our heart and make our relationship right with God. In this high-level context it is important to remember some of God's mighty attributes:

1. Consider the *sovereignty* of God. (Nothing is excluded from God, and nothing is higher than God.) Emphasis is important here, for once we have accepted by faith the dictum that in the beginning an all-wise, all-sovereign God created the heavens and the earth and was not responsible to explain to His creature how or why He did it, we have the secret to faith in anything else God may say. Only He is worthy.

2. There is the *omniscience* of God. (God knows everything from beginning to end, including your total life.)

3. God is *omnipotent*. (God is all-powerful. He cannot suffer defeat.)

4. The *omnipresence* of God is real. (God is everywhere present.)

5. The *omni-righteousness* of God is true. (God is just.)[71]

God only needs to be preached, not proven or defended. God will defend and prove His Word. Our commission is to preach (and teach and share) it (to plant the seeds).[72]

Does God Want Me Back?

Since God wanted His Son back, why wouldn't He want all His elect, chosen, and predestined back too? After all, our names were written in the Lamb's Book of Life before the foundation of the world. God wants all his Saints back. Want evidence? See the compelling case presented by Rick Larson on the recent DVD *The Star of Bethlehem*, and the movie's very important trailer as well.[73]

God also wanted Moses and Elijah (John the Baptist) back. They were seen by Peter and James and John at the Mount of Transfiguration, weren't they? Moses was apparently healthy, right? And wasn't Elijah's head properly restored on his shoulders?

> And after six days Jesus took with him Peter and James, and John his brother, and led them up a high mountain by themselves. And he was transfigured before them, and his face shone like the sun, and his clothes became white as light. And behold, there appeared to them Moses and Elijah, talking with him. And Peter said to Jesus, "Lord, it is good that we are here. If you wish, I will make three tents here, one for you and one for Moses and one for Elijah." He was still speaking when, behold, a bright cloud overshadowed them, and a voice from the cloud said, "This is my beloved Son, with whom I am well pleased; listen to him." When the disciples heard this, they fell on their faces and were terrified. But Jesus came and touched them, saying, "Rise, and have no fear." And when they lifted up their eyes, they saw no one but Jesus only. And as they were coming down the mountain, Jesus commanded them, "Tell no one the vision, until the Son of Man is raised from the dead." And the disciples asked him, "Then why do the scribes say that first Elijah must come?" He answered, "Elijah does come, and he will restore all things. But I tell you that Elijah has already come, and they did not recognize him, but did to him whatever they pleased. So also the Son of Man will certainly suffer at their hands." Then the disciples understood that he was speaking to them of John the Baptist. (Matthew 17:1–13 ESV)

Does the poor man not rest today at the side of Abraham? "The poor man died and was carried by the angels to Abraham's side. The rich man also died and was buried, and in Hades, being in torment, he lifted up his eyes and saw Abraham far off and Lazarus at his side" (Luke 16:22–23 ESV).

When God wants us back, we will be with Him in heaven too.

Don't Be Confused with What Was and What Is

The accumulated losses of Jim, my foster cousin; Joe, my foster father; and Judy, my first wife, shook me hard as each one was called home in that order.

Jim's death was a completely unexpected tragedy. He was in the prime of his life and was a U.S. Air Force major and a highly decorated fighter pilot stationed as an envied exchange officer flying with the Royal Air Force in England. Unfortunately, his life came to a tragic end while he was on a well-deserved leave of absence and vacationing with his wife in France. An autobahn collision between the rented recreational vehicle he was in, and a large commercial truck took his life in a near-head-on crash. He is missed. I admired his skill as a distinguished F-4 Phantom pilot and combat veteran with more than a hundred missions over North Vietnam. While in college at Texas A&M University, Jim was commandant of the Corps of Cadets and a member of the Ross Volunteers. Nevertheless, through a very full and demanding life, Jim claimed the Lord as his personal Savior. Regrettably for me and others, he apparently took a shortcut to get where he was going. I miss his careful guidance and concerning nature. Nobody expected God to take him back so soon.

Joe's death was after a full and successful professional life of hard work in his and his two brother's retail hardware business. The three men put long and demanding hours into the care of their business and the care of their customers. A sign inside and just above the front door was testimony to his and his brother's legacy. It stated, "Through these portals pass the finest people on the face of God's earth, our customers! We are proud to serve them, and it is for whom we gladly service what we sell!"

Joe was a solid citizen. He raised me as a foster parent with love as unconditional and unlimited and as real as a natural father. I cherish the cheerful mornings at the kiddie park with him as a preschool child. We enjoyed many ball games, hunting trips, and fishing excursions together. They were some of the best times of life with him. All of them were treasures. His forgiveness for my many dumb mistakes confirmed what few people knew. He was a gracious man. Joe had a lot of pain in his heart from the murder of his father at a very young age and the broken marriages that deeply bruised his heart. Consequently, Joe was very reserved about his spiritual life, but one day I remember how I probed as we were driving from Texas to the North Carolina coast, where I was assigned to active duty. After a while of searching for indications, I just bluntly asked, "Dad, do you believe in Jesus Christ?"

To my great joy, he said, "Yes, remember when I took you to Brother White's Baptist church on Main Avenue when you were a very young little man? Do you remember the Bible I gave you one Easter when you were in junior high? That was all for you. I claimed Jesus long before that. I don't understand some of the things that I read and heard from Scripture, but I know and believe in Him personally."

I reached down deep and pulled up one of my trusted memories and told him, "That's okay. Allegedly, Billy Graham once said, 'It's not the things in the Bible that I don't understand that bother me. It is the things in the Bible that I do understand that bother me.'"

Joe laughed and said, "That business about the virgin birth is one of the toughest parts for me."

I said, "Well, I guess if the Lord can make a frog out of a tadpole and a butterfly out of a worm, He can make Jesus from a virgin mother."

He said, "You slay me, boy. How did you come up with that one?"

We drove on down the highway. My heart was touched by those precious words from him forever. Joe, my favored and highly treasured foster Dad, publicly claimed the Lord Jesus Christ as his personal Savior. Thanks, Joe! Joe always led from the front and continued to love others for a very long time, even some with many flaws like me. The card that was in the Bible that Joe gave me in my youth is still in those same pages for safekeeping. It says, "Happy Easter—to the finest boy in the entire world." What a legacy of love. Likewise, he treasured the little red chair cushion he used in his office at the hardware store. I gave it to him one Father's Day. It said, "This seat is reserved for the finest dad in the entire world." He would proudly show it to customers, salesmen, and anyone else who had the time to visit.

Judy's death followed a four-year battle with breast cancer that met with her earthly departure. She was a loving mother, perfect wife, and highly treasured daughter. Everyone with whom she met easily and instantly recognized her grace, and I was fortunate that God temporarily loaned her to me for thirty-three years. Judy also openly loved the Lord Jesus Christ. She attested to her deep faith at her last earthly Easter service, where, to everyone's amazement, she rose from her wheelchair, and although struggling to stand, she belted out the "Halleluiah Chorus" along with the congregation's singing of that awesome hymn. I can still hear that sweet music from her voice in my ears. At her passing, many memories and events like that deeply grieved me, but fortunately a longtime friend shared with me at her funeral what I referred to earlier as, a profound and a somewhat commanding phrase, "Bill, God wanted her back!" Later that overpowering statement gave me much-needed perspective and comfort to help me press on. With that single poignant thought, I found I could manage to cope with this major loss. The confusion between what was and what is started to become clear. To my old elementary school classmate, thank you, Charles. I needed that. May God bless you, my friend.

The holes in my heart never got any smaller after the losses of these key people in my life like Jim, Joe, and Judy. The grief ebbs and flows on the shore like powerful waves during a storm. It was once told to me by a valued pastoral care staff member, "When the sea billows roll, just ride those waves. They are God's gifts to help change us, like a beach, into what He is shaping us to be." I discovered that it is okay to well up inside when those waves peak. It is good for the soul to let go and not hold back the tears. I discovered the waves will soon subside upon each occasion; the sands may have shifted but "footprints" are still evident.

In letting go, there is also a need to look ahead. I guess I don't want to be like the coyote in the roadrunner cartoons that always makes too many sudden stops yet survives to see it happen again and again. I've been there and done that.

It is much better to keep your eyes on the horizon ahead and just build on what is in the rearview mirror. I've learned that letting go of the past is personally and individually critical in finding out where you will be when you get where you are going. It is okay to visit one of those holes in your heart occasionally, but we have to keep flying (even with holes in our wings) and seek out a safe place to land.

Jesus is preparing a secure runway for us. Hang on and stay alert. Keep the ball and needle centered in the middle of the flight balance gauge with sure pressure on the rudder pedals. Keep steady hands on the throttle and controls. Nurture all fuel from the Spirit of God. Connect to God's frequency (His Word). Stay in balanced flight, trim your tabs when needed, and always know where you are going. No monkey business. You may have to vector around troubling stormy skies in your path but stay in total relationship with God. Like a loving father, He is already there, waiting for you to come home with an open door, open arms, and an open heart. He will never close any of them, never.

Right Relationship with God

The right relationship with God can be viewed as a continuous loop (Figure 10).[74] It must be that way because there must be room for our failures. But those shortcomings don't have to keep us down. Using King David as an example, we can move from our sin, shame, guilt, remorse, regret, and conviction by sincere and remorseful repenting. We can be restored through God's amazing grace. He will still lead us home!

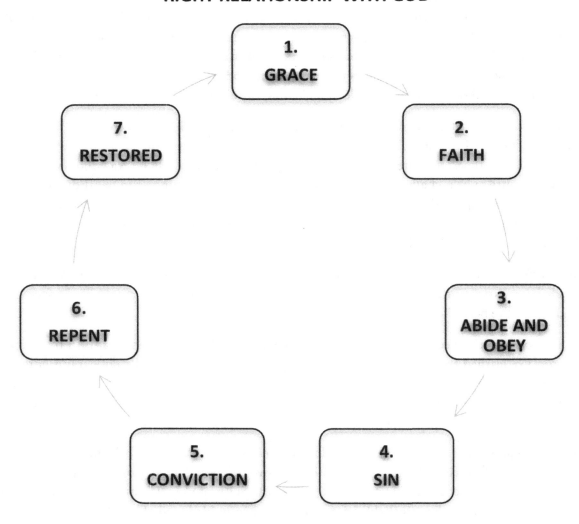

RIGHT RELATIONSHIP WITH GOD

Figure 10. Right Relationship with God

Without getting wrapped around the axle, the previous diagram (Figure 10) contains a critical opening between step 4 and step 5. (Visualize a plumb line attached to step 1, God's grace.) While some religions may espouse a doctrine that asserts that there are eternal reprobates, and some may promote that there is no such thing, we should ask ourselves, "How fast are the steps in the diagram rotating?" As long as step 4 is not the unforgivable sin of perpetual blasphemy, then there is still hope and faith that we will be restored by God's grace when we move to step 5. However, if step 4 is enduring blasphemy, that name will be stripped out of the Lamb's Book of Life, and that soul will be lost and sent into the eternal lake of fire of hell. Go to step 5 every time it comes up on your horizon.

The Journey to Heaven Starts with God's Grace

God's grace is the energy in the above chart, and it drives the flow in the chart back home to God's grace in a full circle like moisture returns to the clouds after it falls to earth in the form of rain. God's grace is equally reliable (Figure 10). "But he said to me, 'My grace is sufficient for you, for my power is made perfect in weakness.' Therefore I will boast all the more gladly of my weaknesses, so that the power of Christ may rest upon me" (2 Corinthians 12:9 ESV).

Now We See in a Mirror Dimly, But Keep the Faith

Oh, what a day that will be when we see Jesus face-to-face. As the Lord strengthens our faith and helps us take the next step when we fall, we must rely on faith, continuously remembering what comes from God. We cannot boast of our own faith. "For by grace you have been saved through faith. And this is not your own doing; it is the gift of God, not a result of works, so that no one may boast" (Ephesians 2:8–9 ESV). And Hebrews 11:1 (ESV) says, "Faith is the assurance of things hoped for, the conviction of things not seen." By the grace of God, faith is the reason we believe Jesus saves.

The Holy Spirit Empowers Us to Abide and Obey

We have to hate sin in order to abide and obey. "Abide in me, and I in you. As the branch cannot bear fruit by itself, unless it abides in the vine, neither can you, unless you abide in me. I am the vine; you are the branches. Whoever abides in me and I in him, he it is that bears much fruit, for apart from me you can do nothing" (John 15:4–5 ESV). Trust, abide, and obey. There is no other way.

Sin Is Part of Us

We cannot escape this truth that we all have sinned and fall short of the glory of God. Even Jesus was tempted, but He prevailed against the fiery darts from that constant adversary, Satan. He prevailed, and through our faith in Him, we can too. It will only be a short time. Difficult historical events come to mind such as the events in ancient Roman arenas where Christians were martyred by being tossed to hungry lions. Little children were likely overheard frantically asking their fathers, "Will the lions hurt us, Daddy?" And the father's assuring response perhaps indicating, "Only for a little while, children. Trust in Jesus to take us safely home to be with Him when they are done with us."

> For I do not understand my own actions. For I do not do what I want, but I do the very thing I hate. Now if I do what I do not want, I agree with the law, that it is good. So now it is no longer I who do it, but sin that dwells within me. For I know that nothing good dwells in me, that is, in my flesh. For I have the desire to do what is right, but not the ability to carry it out. For I do not do the good I want, but the evil I do not want is what I keep on doing. Now if I do what I do not want, it is no longer I who do it, but sin that dwells within me. So I find it to be a law that when I want to do right, evil lies close at hand. For I delight in the law of God, in my inner being, but I see in my members another law waging war against the law of my mind and making me captive to the law of sin that dwells in my members. Wretched man that I am! Who will deliver me from this body of death? Thanks be to God through Jesus Christ our Lord! So then, I myself serve the law of God with my mind, but with my flesh I serve the law of sin. (Romans 7:15–25 ESV)

For I am weak, but Thou art strong. "Likewise the Spirit helps us in our weakness. For we do not know what to pray for as we ought, but the Spirit himself intercedes for us with groanings too deep for words" (Romans 8:26 ESV).

The Holy Spirit Convicts Us of Our Sin

The Holy Spirit brings the full weight of sin on those who are convicted. It melts a cold, hard heart. "Because our gospel came to you not only in word, but also in power and in the Holy Spirit and with full conviction. You know what kind of men we proved to be among you for your sake" (1 Thessalonians 1:5 ESV).

Can you feel the joy beneath the guilt? Think about it. You can recognize God is at work in our lives even when sin is present. Relief is in sight when we begin to recognize them, feel remorse, and repent to God, knowing forgiveness is close at hand.

The Holy Spirit Brings Us to Repent

Repentance completes our joy in knowing that Jesus died for our sins. We were washed white as snow with the blood of the Lamb at Calvary. "From that time Jesus began to preach, saying, '*Repent*, for the kingdom of heaven is at hand'" (Matthew 4:17 ESV).

The vilest of sinners will likely feel the greatest relief upon being led to repent by the Spirit of God. If relief from the quantity of sin is any indicator of relief, those Roman emperors who were led to abolish torturous ancient practices in the arenas, must know that relief firsthand.

Our Relationship Is Restored through Forgiveness by Our Belief in Jesus Christ

Arriving at restoration with God is a good reason to shout to the Lord, knowing that after we have been knocked to our knees by sin and lifted up by His marvelous grace, it is like we have been kept from falling in the first place. "But whoever blasphemes against the Holy Spirit never has forgiveness, but is guilty of an eternal sin" (Mark 3:29 ESV).

Remorse is the first flag of surrender. "And that repentance and forgiveness of sins should be proclaimed in his name to all nations, beginning from Jerusalem" (Luke 24:47 ESV).

Christianity is the only religion that offers forgiveness. "For by grace you have been saved through faith. And this is not your own doing; it is the gift of God, not a result of works, so that no one may boast. For we are his workmanship, created in Christ Jesus for good works, which God prepared beforehand, that we should walk in them" (Ephesians 2:8–10 ESV).

Jesus and the Throne of Grace and Four Christian Millennial Teachings

So, what is the impact of "grace" on where we will be when we get where we are going?. See row #2 below. Because judgment is now, I hold myself out as knowing that I won't be around to observe anything on earth after the rapture of the saints. However, others think a little differently. See the following table to find out what some of the others think.[75] God help those in the tribulation and the millennium after the rapture.

Christian Millennial Teachings	A. Born, Died, Arose	B. Rapture Of The Saints	C. Tribulation	D. Second Coming	E. Millennium	F. Last Judgment
1. **POST-TRIBULATION** **AND** **PRE-MILLENNIALISM**	1st coming of Jesus	?	Tribulation	2nd coming of Jesus	Millennium	Last Judgment
2. **PRE-TRIBULATION (DISPENSATIONAL) AND PRE-MILLENNIALISM**	1st coming of Jesus	2nd coming for the church, the Rapture	Tribulation	2nd coming with the church—The Saints	Millen-nium	Last Judgment, Bema Seat, or the Great White Throne
3. **POST-MILLENNIALISM**	1st coming of Jesus	?	?	?	Millennium	2nd coming, Last Judgment
4. **A-MILLENNIALISM**	1st coming of Jesus	?	?	?	Symbolic Millennium	2nd coming, Last Judgment

Table 13. Jesus' Throne of Grace, and Four Christian Millennial Teachings

Post-Tribulation and Pre-millennialism

Post-tribulation holds that the church will be around to endure a time of suffering during the tribulation period until the return of Jesus at the end of that period. Note also that Daniel splits the 70 week tribulation into two equal periods.

Pre-millennialism holds that Jesus will return to earth prior to a period of one thousand years, during which He will reign.

Pre-tribulation (Dispensational) Pre-millennialism *[Author's Choice]*

Pre-tribulation holds that the church will **not** be around to endure a time of suffering during the tribulation period.

First Coming of Jesus

The first coming of Jesus was completed with His ascension at Mt. Olivet.

Rapture/Resurrection—Second Coming for the Church

Per the above table, our judgment is now (before breath stops). When we believe **now**, we are ready to meet Jesus in the sky with the born-again believers (The dead in Christ will be lifted up first and will reunite with their souls; the living in Christ second, both body and soul). We will receive new bodies. We will be gone before the tribulation begins. We will report to the *bema* seat of Christ for our rewards in heaven. Paul indicates that rewards will be lost or given based on our lives for the Lord

(1 Thessalonians 2:19–20 ESV). "Behold, I am coming soon, bringing my recompense with me, to repay each one for what he has done" (Revelation 22:12 ESV).

In addition to the gift of salvation, rewards for faithfulness in the successful completion of personal objectives toward the accomplishment of the Lord's Great Commission will be bestowed on those Christians with the term "Well done, good and faithful servant!" Loss of rewards for unfaithfulness will be observed in the tribulation.

Tribulation
The tribulation is a time of reign of the Antichrist with one world government, including wars, plagues, famine, earthquakes, and other natural disasters. Daniel 9:27 does indicate the elect may have to endure half of the 70 week period.

Second Coming with Church
The second coming of Christ with the church will be signaled by the sound of Gabriel's horn at the return of Christ with the church to Mt. Olivet (where He ascended to heaven). The battle of Armageddon will occur. The Antichrist will be destroyed, and Satan will be bound for a thousand years.

> Then I saw an angel coming down from heaven, holding in his hand the key to the bottomless pit and a great chain. And he seized the dragon, that ancient serpent, who is the devil and Satan, and bound him for a thousand years, and threw him into the pit, and shut it and sealed it over him, so that he might not deceive the nations any longer, until the thousand years were ended. After that he must be released for a little while.

> Then I saw thrones, and seated on them were those to whom the authority to judge was committed. Also I saw the souls of those who had been beheaded for the testimony of Jesus and for the word of God, and those who had not worshiped the beast or its image and had not received its mark on their foreheads or their hands. They came to life and reigned with Christ for a thousand years. The rest of the dead did not come to life until the thousand years were ended. This is the first resurrection. Blessed and holy is the one who shares in the first resurrection! Over such the second death has no power, but they will be priests of God and of Christ, and they will reign with him for a thousand years. (Revelation 20:1–6 ESV)

Millennium
The millennium begins with Christ reigning for a thousand years with His saints, and the living nations of unbelievers will be judged as well. Satan will be loosed for a second time for a short period. Fire from heaven will consume the armies of Gog (a chief prince) and Magog. A second resurrection will occur for those who were dead at the first resurrection but did not believe in Christ. Heaven and earth will be purged with fire.

Pertaining to unclear prophecy like the armies of Gog and Magog, there is no apparent escape for even that knowledge known only to God. But we do know it is stated that, prophecy against Gog will come! "Son of man, set your face toward Gog, of the land of Magog, the chief prince of Meshech and Tubal, and prophesy against him and say, Thus says the Lord God: Behold, I am against you, O Gog, chief prince of Meshech and Tubal" (Ezekiel 38:2–3 ESV).

The defeat of Satan will come!

> And when the thousand years are ended, Satan will be released from his prison and will come out to deceive the nations that are at the four corners of the earth, Gog and Magog, to gather them for battle; their number is like the sand of the sea. And they marched up over the broad plain of the earth and surrounded the camp of the saints and the beloved city, but fire came down from heaven and consumed them, and the devil who had deceived them was thrown into the lake of fire and sulfur where the beast and the false prophet were, and they will be tormented day and night forever and ever. (Revelation 20:7–10 ESV).

The day of the Lord will come!

> But the day of the Lord will come like a thief, and then the heavens will pass away with a roar, and the heavenly bodies will be burned up and dissolved, and the earth and the works that are done on it will be exposed. Since all these things are thus to be dissolved, what sort of people ought you to be in lives of holiness and godliness, waiting for and hastening the coming of the day of God, because of which the heavens will be set on fire and dissolved, and the heavenly bodies will melt as they burn! But according to his promise we are waiting for new heavens and a new earth in which righteousness dwells. (2 Peter 3:10–13 ESV)

I often reflect on a recent nightly news program that showed a lab demonstration where bowls of salt water were being tested with radio frequencies to determine the results. One bowl ignited when subjected to a particular frequency; the flame was hotter than most previously recorded. I find that sometimes things that we don't know may have potential for enormous impact; the thought of salt water burning gives rise to an eventual ocean on flame.[76]

Last Judgment

The last judgment and final doom of Satan and the unbelieving (second death) will take place. They will be sent to the lake of fire, which never ends. Christ will reign forever and ever in the New Jerusalem with His saints and the new earth for eternity. Behold, all things are new (Figure 11)! "For we must all appear before the judgment seat of Christ, so that each of us may receive what is due us for the things done while in the body, whether good or bad" (Romans 14:10-12; 2 Corinthians 5:10 ESV). The *bema seat* of Christ pertains.[77]

Post-millennialism

Post-millennialism holds that Jesus will return to earth following a period of one thousand years, during which He will reign.

A-millennialism

A-millennialism holds that Jesus is presently reigning through the church and that the one thousand years of Revelation 20:1–6 is a metaphorical reference to the present church age, which will culminate in Christ's return.

So You Say, "Is That All There Is?"

Surely there must be more to salvation than that. No, by God's amazing grace, faith in Jesus Christ will lead us home! Jesus said to His disciples, "Because of the littleness of your faith; for I truly say to you, if you have faith the size of a mustard seed, you will say to this mountain, 'Move from here to there,' and it will move; and nothing will be impossible to you" (Matthew 17:19–20 ESV).

Later Jesus also said, "Let what you say be simply 'Yes' or 'No'; anything more than this comes from evil." (Matthew 5:37 ESV).

Finally it is written, "And I heard a voice from heaven saying, 'Write this: Blessed are the dead who die in the Lord from now on.' 'Blessed indeed,' says the Spirit, 'that they may rest from their labors, for their deeds follow them'" (Revelation 14:13 ESV).

Aha, *deeds* follow us. These are the deeds that follow our born-again experience. Prior to that point, they are counted as nothing. Remember we are also to abide and obey Jesus's teachings all the time following our born-again experience. A believer's slip-ups will be recognized too.[78]

The Bema Seat of Christ

These Scripture passages bring about assurance that our presence at the *bema seat* of Christ will be filled with rewards for our good deeds and service to the Lord here on earth (after our regeneration). For those who have served Christ faithfully, this judgment seat will be a time of commendation and celebration. He will reward us for acts of love that no one else even noticed.[79] What a day that will be. I shudder to think what that other final judgment seat will be like at the end of time for all who denied Christ. I would rather go with the sheep to paradise than with the goats to eternal damnation.

Internal Review Time

Have you reviewed all five dimensions of your life? Have you examined all seven attributes of each? Have you considered all the basic elements surrounding your deeds at this point? These elements are valuable truth tellers regarding the motivation behind those deeds.

1) Meaning

2) Origin

3) Source

4) Nature

5) Working

6) Means

7) Need

8) Essentiality

9) Inclusiveness

10) Purpose

11) Cause

12) Blessings

13) Curse

14) Dangers

15) Fruits

16) Results

17) Foolishness

18) Wisdom

19) Possession

20) Presence (or absence)

21) Dimension

22) Power

23) Impotency

24) Certainty (or uncertainty)

25) Evil

26) Beauty

27) Worth

28) Proof

29) Promise

30) Assurance

31) Basis (or foundation)

32) Way

33) Cost

34) Endurance

35) Judgment

36) Rewards

Also consider the following:

1) What did the deed do?

2) What did it meet or combat?

3) What did it overcome?

4) What was God's remedy for it?

The above elements are only examples that show that all elements of our deeds have origins, natures, characters, workings, influences, purposes, values, and/or accomplishments.[80] The "acid test" question is this: Was the deed done to glorify the Lord Jesus Christ or something else? Phony answers will not hold up to the acid wash. As a minimum, test all 343 mini-tension cubes in your life (Figure 4) using these 36 elements of your deeds while bearing in mind all four special considerations.

Then What? Let's Look and See What We Can Find.

What mortal death does *not* know is that it is not death Christians are fretting. When one is born once, perhaps those folks will certainly sweat mortal death, but when we are born twice, mortal death is the only death. We may not look forward to the event of mortal death, but beyond that, we will not endure any other death. We live on into eternity. We do not stay in the valley of the shadow of death. We move through it. This would be a good time to screen Scripture for many of the indicators for what is to come in eternity. Let's take a quick preliminary look.

What to Expect in Our New Eternal Home in Heaven

For believers, Jesus said that we should not be like Thomas:

> "Let not your hearts be troubled. Believe in God; believe also in me. In my Father's house are many rooms. If it were not so, would I have told you that I go to prepare a place for you? And if I go and prepare a place for you, I will come again and will take you to myself, that where I am you may be also. And you know the way to where I am going." Thomas said to him, "Lord, we do not know where you are going. How can we know the way?" Jesus said to him, "I am the way, and the truth, and the life. No one comes to the Father except through me. If you had known me, you would have known my Father also. From now on you do know him and have seen him."

> Philip said to him, "Lord, show us the Father, and it is enough for us." Jesus said to him, "Have I been with you so long, and you still do not know me, Philip? Whoever has seen me has seen the Father. How can you say, 'Show us the Father'? Do you not believe that I am in the Father and the Father is in me? The words that I say to you I do not speak on my own authority, but the Father who dwells in me does his works. Believe me that I am in the Father and the Father is in me, or else believe on account of the works themselves. Truly, truly, I say to you, whoever believes in me will also do the works that I do; and greater works than these will he do, because I am going to the Father. Whatever you ask in my name, this I will do, that the Father may be glorified in the Son. If you ask me anything in my name, I will do it." (John 14:1–14 ESV)

Furthermore, recent books shed much light on more of the joys that await us in heaven. I commend them to you for help in knowing more answers about where you will be when you get where you are going.

Heaven
Randy Alcorn leads his readers through a Scriptural account of what to expect in heaven that is very compelling, particularly with regard to a physical place when the new heaven and the new earth become one at the end of the age. His book *Heaven* commends Scripture above all else for insights into heaven.[81] I concur.

Heaven Is for Real
Todd Burpo presents a very compelling account in his book *Heaven Is for Real*, telling readers about his son, Colton, being beyond heaven's gates from the eyes of that four-year-old child following his emergency surgery. He shared impossible-to-know details about what he experienced during the time he was in heaven. (For instance, he said, "Hey, Dad, did you know Jesus has a horse?")[82] Your own hope for heaven will creep into your consciousness as the book unfolds.

90 Minutes in Heaven
Don Piper shares a true but tragic story in his book *90 Minutes in Heaven*, which is based on his personal misfortunes from being very seriously injured in a head on automobile crash with a truck. His summation of heaven is this: "Why would anyone want to stay here after experiencing heaven? He asked

God to please take him back."[83] Don's complete message gives great insight as to what is on the other side of the twelve gates of heaven. He wrote in a copy that he autographed for me, "See you at the gate!"

Which Way Is Up?

Mark Peters, author of *Which Way is Up? From Among All This Chaos!* presents a powerful message that will change some things in your life and those around you as well. As you might gather form Mark's title, his scope is forward-looking. It has a strong biblical basis that cuts right through the fog of temporal religious practices with a steady diet of the Word of God. Mark takes dead aim at political correctness and other forms of deviousness by bracketing it with clarity from Scripture. His aim is beyond the gates of heaven too. The feel-good part of the book focuses on time and how you can find happiness when you are using it on things that are truly meaningful as you serve the Lord.[84] You will likely end up reading it twice.

The Knowledge of the Holy

A. W. Tozer, an evangelical author, likewise illuminates some key conclusions that he gleaned from Scripture that are spot on as illustrated in the following excerpt:

> Reducing the whole matter to individual terms, we arrive at some vital and highly personal conclusions. In the moral conflict now raging around us, whoever is on God's side is on the winning side and cannot lose; whoever is on the other side is on the losing side and cannot win. Here there is no chance, no gamble. There is freedom to choose which side we shall be on but no freedom to negotiate the results of the choice once it is made. But, by the mercy of God we may repent a wrong choice and alter the consequences by making a new right choice. Beyond that we cannot go.
>
> The whole matter of moral choice centers on Jesus Christ. Christ stated it plainly: "He that is not with me is against me," and "No man cometh unto the Father, but by me." The gospel message embodies three distinct elements: an announcement, a command, and a call. It announces the good news of redemption accomplished in mercy; it commands all men everywhere to repent and it calls all men to surrender to the terms of grace by believing on Jesus Christ as Lord and Saviour.[85]

Panorama of Our Ultimate Joy—A Holy Communion

Alfred T. Eade, author of *The Expanded Panorama Bible Study Course*, which is available in reprint, similarly gets at the heart of having a personal relationship with God. He states, "Man getting back to God is the living heartbeat of the Christian Faith; the whole sum of substance of Bible revelation. Amazing as it is, the Eternal and Immutable Plan and Purpose of God can be told in the two wondrous words *Holy Communion*."[86] Although Eade leans more toward mortal Armenian works in a few places, overall, he has wonderful graphical insight and emphasis on where we will be when we get where we are going. It is a classic read that I carefully review often. I particularly focus on his awareness and need for accountability by closely following of his bloodline of Christ analogy of Scripture. His cover-to-cover approach from Genesis to Revelation increases credibility of the Biblical Canon.

So, armed with the Word of God, readings like those above, and use of a personal Theo-metric assessment as presented by my efforts here, find out where you will be when you get where you are going. Rush, the judgment is now!

The Place to "Arrive" Is the Kingdom of Heaven, the New Jerusalem

Now pretend for a moment you are observing a family about to embark on a trip together.

The father says, "Okay, kids, it's time to go on a trip."

"Where are we going, Daddy?" they ask.

"We are going to where we will be to spend eternity."

"Oh! Well, what does it look like, Daddy?"

"It looks like a giant cube that has the appearance of frozen lemonade. You can see right through it (Figure 11). Trust me, kids," he says. "It's a beautiful and marvelous place. There is no sorrow, pain, or despair. Let me tell you all about it. Play like we're almost there. It has twelve gates, and it is laid out on twelve foundation stones. The walls are 1,500 miles long. It is called the New Jerusalem. It is where God, Jesus, and the Spirit of God dwell. It is their glorious kingdom."

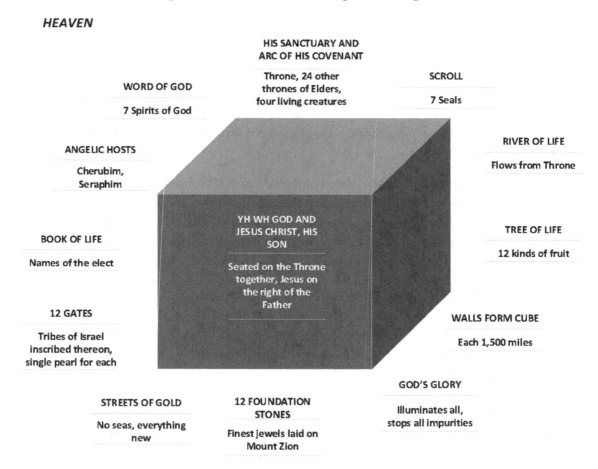

Figure 11. The Kingdom of Heaven—The New Jerusalem is a Cube

"What else will we see, Daddy?" the kids say.

"Well, beginning with this little tourist-like guide map I got from my Bible, it looks like there is so much to see that it will take eternity to see it all. Here are a few of the highlights I found when I peeked in God's Word for clues. I found a few great examples, let's read the little map from the outboard callout boxes first and in a clockwise direction beginning at the top of the cube with the callout box containing His Sanctuary and His Arc of the Covenant."

More Scriptures Leading to Insights into Heaven

- Revelation 9:17 says, "And this is how I saw the horses in my vision and those who rode them: they wore breastplates the color of fire and of sapphire and of sulfur, and the heads of the horses were like lions' heads, and fire and smoke and sulfur came out of their mouths."

- Revelation 4:6 says, "And before the throne there was as it were a sea of glass, like crystal. And around the throne, on each side of the throne, are four living creatures, full of eyes in front and behind."

- Revelation 11:19 says, "Then God's temple in heaven was opened, and the ark of his covenant was seen within his temple. There were flashes of lightning, rumblings, peals of thunder, an earthquake, and heavy hail."

- Revelation 5:8 says, "And when he had taken the scroll, the four living creatures and the twenty-four elders fell down before the Lamb, each holding a harp, and golden bowls full of incense, which are the prayers of the saints."

- Revelation 15:2 says, "And I saw what appeared to be a sea of glass mingled with fire—and also those who had conquered the beast and its image and the number of its name, standing beside the sea of glass with harps of God in their hands."

- Revelation 21:12–14, 21 says,

   It had a great, high wall, with twelve gates, and at the gates twelve angels, and on the gates the names of the twelve tribes of the sons of Israel were inscribed—on the east three gates, on the north three gates, on the south three gates, and on the west three gates. And the wall of the city had twelve foundations, and on them were the twelve names of the twelve apostles of the Lamb … And the twelve gates were twelve pearls, each of the gates made of a single pearl, and the street of the city was pure gold, like transparent glass.

- Revelation 21:22–27 says,

   And I saw no temple in the city, for its temple is the Lord God the Almighty and the Lamb. And the city has no need of sun or moon to shine on it, for the glory of God gives it light, and its lamp is the Lamb. By its light will the nations walk, and the kings of the earth will bring their glory into it, and its gates will never be shut by day—and there will be no night there. They will bring into it the glory and the honor of the nations. But nothing unclean will ever enter it, nor anyone who does what is detestable or false, but only those who are written in the Lamb's book of life.

- Revelation 14:1–5 says,

  > Then I looked, and behold, on Mount Zion stood the Lamb, and with him 144,000 who had his name and his Father's name written on their foreheads. And I heard a voice from heaven like the roar of many waters and like the sound of loud thunder. The voice I heard was like the sound of harpists playing on their harps, and they were singing a new song before the throne and before the four living creatures and before the elders. No one could learn that song except the 144,000 who had been redeemed from the earth. It is these who have not defiled themselves with women, for they are virgins. It is these who follow the Lamb wherever he goes. These have been redeemed from mankind as first fruits for God and the Lamb, and in their mouth no lie was found, for they are blameless.

- Revelation 21:1–4 says,

  > Then I saw a new heaven and a new earth, for the first heaven and the first earth had passed away, and the sea was no more. And I saw the holy city, New Jerusalem, coming down out of heaven from God, prepared as a bride adorned for her husband. And I heard a loud voice from the throne saying, "Behold, the dwelling place of God is with man. He will dwell with them, and they will be his people, and God himself will be with them as their God. He will wipe away every tear from their eyes, and death shall be no more, neither shall there be mourning, nor crying, nor pain anymore, for the former things have passed away."

- Revelation 21:16 says, "The city lies foursquare, its length the same as its width. And he measured the city with his rod, 12,000 stadia. Its length and width and height are equal."

- Revelation 21:19–20 says, "The foundations of the wall of the city were adorned with every kind of jewel. The first was jasper, the second sapphire, the third agate, the fourth emerald, the fifth onyx, the sixth carnelian, the seventh chrysolite, the eighth beryl, the ninth topaz, the tenth chrysoprase, the eleventh jacinth, the twelfth amethyst."

- Revelation 19:13 says, "He is clothed in a robe dipped in blood, and the name by which he is called is The Word of God."

- Revelation 22:1–5 says,

  > Then the angel showed me the river of the water of life, bright as crystal, flowing from the throne of God and of the Lamb through the middle of the street of the city; also, on either side of the river, the tree of life with its twelve kinds of fruit, yielding its fruit each month. The leaves of the tree were for the healing of the nations. No longer will there be anything accursed, but the throne of God and of the Lamb will be in it, and his servants will worship him. They will see his face, and his name will be on their foreheads. And night will be no more. They will need no light of lamp or sun, for the Lord God will be their light, and they will reign forever and ever.

- Revelation 21:18 says, "The wall was built of jasper, while the city was pure gold, like clear glass."

- Isaiah 11:6–9 says,

  > The wolf shall dwell with the lamb, and the leopard shall lie down with the young goat, and the calf and the lion and the fattened calf together; and a little child shall lead them. The cow and the bear shall graze; their young shall lie down together; and the lion shall eat straw like the ox. The nursing child shall play over the hole of the cobra, and the weaned child shall put his hand on the adder's den. They shall not hurt or destroy in all my holy mountain; for the earth shall be full of the knowledge of the Lord as the waters cover the sea.

- Psalm 148:5 says, "Let them praise the name of the Lord! For he commanded and they were created."

- Ezekiel 11:22 says, Then the cherubim lifted up their wings, with the wheels beside them, and the glory of the God of Israel was over them."

- Isaiah 6:2 says, "Above him stood the seraphim. Each had six wings: with two he covered his face, and with two he covered his feet, and with two he flew."

- Revelation 5:1–5 says,

  > Then I saw in the right hand of him who was seated on the throne a scroll written within and on the back, sealed with seven seals. And I saw a mighty angel proclaiming with a loud voice, "Who is worthy to open the scroll and break its seals?" And no one in heaven or on earth or under the earth was able to open the scroll or to look into it, and I began to weep loudly because no one was found worthy to open the scroll or to look into it. And one of the elders said to me, "Weep no more; behold, the Lion of the tribe of Judah, the Root of David, has conquered, so that he can open the scroll and its seven seals.

- Revelation 4:1–8 says,

  > After this I looked, and behold, a door standing open in heaven! And the first voice, which I had heard speaking to me like a trumpet, said, "Come up here, and I will show you what must take place after this." At once I was in the Spirit, and behold, a throne stood in heaven, with one seated on the throne. And he who sat there had the appearance of jasper and carnelian, and around the throne was a rainbow that had the appearance of an emerald. Around the throne were twenty-four thrones, and seated on the thrones were twenty-four elders, clothed in white garments, with golden crowns on their heads. From the throne came flashes of lightning, and rumblings and peals of thunder, and before the throne were burning seven torches of fire, which are the seven spirits of God, and before the throne there was as it were a sea of glass, like crystal. And around the throne, on each side of the throne, are four living creatures, full of eyes in front and behind: the first living creature like a lion, the second living

creature like an ox, the third living creature with the face of a man, and the fourth living creature like an eagle in flight. And the four living creatures, each of them with six wings, are full of eyes all around and within, and day and night they never cease to say, "Holy, holy, holy, is the Lord God Almighty, who was and is and is to come!"

- Revelation 1:10–20 says,

> I was in the Spirit on the Lord's day, and I heard behind me a loud voice like a trumpet saying, "Write what you see in a book and send it to the seven churches, to Ephesus and to Smyrna and to Pergamum and to Thyatira and to Sardis and to Philadelphia and to Laodicea." Then I turned to see the voice that was speaking to me, and on turning I saw seven golden lampstands, and in the midst of the lampstands one like a son of man, clothed with a long robe and with a golden sash around his chest. The hairs of his head were white, like white wool, like snow. His eyes were like a flame of fire, his feet were like burnished bronze, refined in a furnace, and his voice was like the roar of many waters. In his right hand he held seven stars, from his mouth came a sharp two-edged sword, and his face was like the sun shining in full strength. When I saw him, I fell at his feet as though dead. But he laid his right hand on me, saying, "Fear not, I am the first and the last, and the living one. I died, and behold I am alive forevermore, and I have the keys of Death and Hades. Write therefore the things that you have seen, those that are and those that are to take place after this. As for the mystery of the seven stars that you saw in my right hand, and the seven golden lampstands, the seven stars are the angels of the seven churches, and the seven lampstands are the seven churches."

- Revelation 4:9–11 says,

> And whenever the living creatures give glory and honor and thanks to him who is seated on the throne, who lives forever and ever, the twenty-four elders fall down before him who is seated on the throne and worship him who lives forever and ever. They cast their crowns before the throne, saying, "Worthy are you, our Lord and God, to receive glory and honor and power, for you created all things, and by your will they existed and were created."

Table 14. More Scriptures Leading to Insights into Heaven

Then the dad says, "Kids, many more things are revealed about heaven in my Bible that are too numerous to fit on my little tourist-like guide map. Besides I don't want to spoil your jubilant reaction when you see everything for yourself. See if you can find more heavenly things in your Bibles while we go along our way. I made you a list of other topics for you to find. Also, let me know if you find some that I missed. This is kind of like "I spy," isn't it? This is going to be the greatest trip of our lives. We are almost there."

Children of the Elect, Chosen, Predestined—the Saints

We get to go to God's kingdom by His free grace through our Spirit-enabled freewill acceptance and affirmation of faith in Jesus Christ, who elected us, chose us, and predestined us before the foundation of the world when He wrote our names in the Lamb's Book of Life (Table 15). "Who shall bring any charge against God's elect? It is God who justifies" (Romans 8:33 ESV). Jesus has provided for all our needs.

No Memory of Earth

Some folks will be missing even from our memory. Remember King David's laments about his enemies? "May his posterity be cut off; may his name be blotted out in the second generation! May the iniquity of his fathers be remembered before the LORD, and let not the sin of his mother be blotted out! Let them be before the LORD continually, that he may cut off the memory of them from the earth" (Psalm 109:13–15 ESV).

It appears that any negative memories of earth are unwelcome in heaven too since they may generate new hostilities that are not allowed in God's pure kingdom.

Great White Throne of Judgment

Unlike the saints who believe and follow Jesus, all those who reject His salvation will appear before His great white throne of judgment. This is His promise to them. "And then will I declare to them, 'I never knew you; depart from me, you workers of lawlessness'" (Matthew 7:23 ESV).

Believers will not experience the agony of fire.

> And if your hand causes you to sin, cut it off. It is better for you to enter life crippled than with two hands to go to hell, to the unquenchable fire. And if your foot causes you to sin, cut it off. It is better for you to enter life lame than with two feet to be thrown into hell. And if your eye causes you to sin, tear it out. It is better for you to enter the kingdom of God with one eye than with two eyes to be thrown into hell, where their worm does not die and the fire is not quenched. (Mark 9:43–48 ESV)

The Book of Life contains all believers.

> Then I saw a great white throne and him who was seated on it. From his presence earth and sky fled away, and no place was found for them. And I saw the dead, great and small, standing before the throne, and books were opened. Then another book was opened, which is the book of life. And the dead were judged by what was written in the books, according to what they had done. And the sea gave up the dead who were in it, Death and Hades gave up the dead who were in them, and they were judged, each one of them, according to what they had done. Then Death and Hades were thrown into the lake of fire. This is the second death, the lake of fire. And if anyone's name was not found written in the book of life, he was thrown into the lake of fire. (Revelation 20:11–15 ESV)

Christians are assured that we will not see the great white throne of judgment. "There is therefore now no condemnation for those who are in Christ Jesus" (Romans 8:1 ESV). Believe and remain in communion with Christ Jesus.

Heaven Is Huge and Shaped as a Cube

If taken literally, which I do, heaven is 1,500 miles in length, width, and height. It's a really big cube. The distance between Corpus Christi and Philadelphia approximates just one side.

> And the one who spoke with me had a measuring rod of gold to measure the city and its gates and walls. The city lies foursquare, its length the same as its width. And he measured the city with his rod, 12,000 stadia. Its length and width and height are equal. He also measured its wall, 144 cubits by human measurement, which is also an angel's measurement. The wall was built of jasper, while the city was pure gold, like clear glass. The foundations of the wall of the city were adorned with every kind of jewel. The first was jasper, the second sapphire, the third agate, the fourth emerald, the fifth onyx, the sixth carnelian, the seventh chrysolite, the eighth beryl, the ninth topaz, the tenth chrysoprase, the eleventh jacinth, the twelfth amethyst. And the twelve gates were twelve pearls, each of the gates made of a single pearl, and the street of the city was pure gold, like transparent glass. (Revelation 21:15–21 ESV)

Beautiful stones in the walls, gates, and foundation will be seen by all believers.

The Lamb's Book of Life

Our names do not get put into the Lamb's Book of Life by what we do while we are here on earth! It was entered before the foundation of the world! It is blotted out if and whenever we blaspheme the Holy Spirit! Beware! Don't do that! See Exodus 32:32–33.

Ten Scriptures Revealing that Our Names Were Put in the Lamb's Book of Life before the Foundation of the World

1. Proverbs 8:22–31 says,

   > The LORD possessed me at the beginning of his work, the first of his acts of old. Ages ago I was set up, at the first, before the beginning of the earth. When there were no depths I was brought forth, when there were no springs abounding with water. Before the mountains had been shaped, before the hills, I was brought forth, before he had made the earth with its fields, or the first of the dust of the world. When he established the heavens, I was there; when he drew a circle on the face of the deep, when he made firm the skies above, when he established the fountains of the deep, when he assigned to the sea its limit, so that the waters might not transgress his command, when he marked out the foundations of the earth, then I was beside him, like a master workman, and I was daily his delight, rejoicing before him always, rejoicing in his inhabited world and delighting in the children of man.

2. Matthew 25:31–46 says,

   > When the Son of Man comes in his glory, and all the angels with him, then he will sit on his glorious throne. Before him will be gathered all the nations, and he will separate people one from another as a shepherd separates the sheep from the goats. And he will place the sheep on his right, but the goats on the left. Then the King will say to those on his right, "Come, you who are blessed by my Father, inherit the kingdom prepared

for you from the foundation of the world. For I was hungry and you gave me food, I was thirsty and you gave me drink, I was a stranger and you welcomed me, I was naked and you clothed me, I was sick and you visited me, I was in prison and you came to me." Then the righteous will answer him, saying, "Lord, when did we see you hungry and feed you, or thirsty and give you drink? And when did we see you a stranger and welcome you, or naked and clothe you? And when did we see you sick or in prison and visit you?" And the King will answer them, "Truly, I say to you, as you did it to one of the least of these my brothers, you did it to me." Then he will say to those on his left, "Depart from me, you cursed, into the eternal fire prepared for the devil and his angels. For I was hungry and you gave me no food, I was thirsty and you gave me no drink, I was a stranger and you did not welcome me, naked and you did not clothe me, sick and in prison and you did not visit me." Then they also will answer, saying, "Lord, when did we see you hungry or thirsty or a stranger or naked or sick or in prison, and did not minister to you?" Then he will answer them, saying, "Truly, I say to you, as you did not do it to one of the least of these, you did not do it to me." And these will go away into eternal punishment, but the righteous into eternal life.

3. John 10:28–30 says, "I give them eternal life, and they will never perish, and <u>no one will snatch them out of my hand</u>. My Father, who has given them to me, is greater than all, and no one is able to snatch them out of the Father's hand. I and the Father are one."

4. Ephesians 1:4–14 says,

> Even as he <u>chose us in him before the foundation of the world</u>, that we should be holy and blameless before him. In love he predestined us for adoption as sons through Jesus Christ, according to the purpose of his will, to the praise of his glorious grace, with which he has blessed us in the Beloved. In him we have redemption through his blood, the forgiveness of our trespasses, according to the riches of his grace, which he lavished upon us, in all wisdom and insight making known to us the mystery of his will, according to his purpose, which he set forth in Christ as a plan for the fullness of time, to unite all things in him, things in heaven and things on earth. In him we have obtained an inheritance, having been predestined according to the purpose of him who works all things according to the counsel of his will, so that we who were the first to hope in Christ might be to the praise of his glory. In him you also, when you heard the word of truth, the gospel of your salvation, and believed in him, were sealed with the promised Holy Spirit, who is the guarantee of our inheritance until we acquire possession of it, to the praise of his glory.

5. Philippians 4:2–5 says,

> I entreat Euodia and I entreat Syntyche to agree in the Lord. Yes, I ask you also, true companion, help these women, who have labored side by side with me in the gospel together with Clement and the rest of my fellow workers, whose <u>names are in the book of life</u>. Rejoice in the Lord always; again I will say, rejoice. Let your reasonableness be known to everyone. The Lord is at hand.

6. Revelation 3:4–6 says,

> Yet you have still a few names in Sardis, people who have not soiled their garments, and they will walk with me in white, for they are worthy. The one who conquers will be clothed thus in white garments, and I will never <u>blot his name out of the book of life</u>. I will confess his name before my Father and before his angels. He who has an ear, let him hear what the Spirit says to the churches.

7. Revelation 13:7–9 says,

> Also it was allowed to make war on the saints and to conquer them. And authority was given it over every tribe and people and language and nation, and all who dwell on earth will worship it, everyone whose <u>name has not been written before the foundation of the world in the book of life of the Lamb</u> who was slain. If anyone has an ear, let him hear.

8. Revelation 17:7–9 says,

> But the angel said to me, "Why do you marvel? I will tell you the mystery of the woman, and of the beast with seven heads and ten horns that carries her. The beast that you saw was, and is not, and is about to rise from the bottomless pit and go to destruction. And the dwellers on earth whose <u>names have not been written in the book of life from the foundation of the world</u> will marvel to see the beast, because it was and is not and is to come. This calls for a mind with wisdom: the seven heads are seven mountains on which the woman is seated."

9. Revelation 20:11–15 says,

> Then I saw a great white throne and him who was seated on it. From his presence earth and sky fled away, and no place was found for them. And I saw the dead, great and small, standing before the throne, and books were opened. Then another book was opened, which is the <u>book of life</u>. And the dead were judged by what was written in the books, according to what they had done. And the sea gave up the dead who were in it, Death and Hades gave up the dead who were in them, and they were judged, each one of them, according to what they had done. Then Death and Hades were thrown into the lake of fire. This is the second death, the lake of fire. And if anyone's <u>name was not found written in the book of life</u>, he was thrown into the lake of fire.

10. Revelation 22:18–20 says,

> I warn everyone who hears the words of the prophecy of this book: if anyone adds to them, God will add to him the plagues described in this book, and if anyone takes away from the words of the book of this prophecy, God will <u>take away his share in the tree of life</u> and in the holy city, which are described in this book. He who testifies to these things says, "Surely I am coming soon." Amen. Come, Lord Jesus!

Table 15. The Lamb's Book of Life

Good works will not change a thing about the presence of our name in the Lamb's Book of Life. It has been there since before the foundation of the world. Want to keep it there? Don't blaspheme the Holy Spirit. The Lamb's Book of Life is the "Boss File." Through God's grace, cling to your faith in Jesus Christ as your Savior, and when you feel remorse, confess, repent, and seek His forgiveness (2 Peter 2; Hebrews 6; Hebrews 10).

The Marriage of the Lamb Has Come

But our good works in the other journals are counted as righteous deeds of the saints. They are the fine linen, bright and pure.

> Then I heard what seemed to be the voice of a great multitude, like the roar of many waters and like the sound of mighty peals of thunder, crying out, "Hallelujah! For the Lord our God the Almighty reigns. Let us rejoice and exult and give him the glory, for the marriage of the Lamb has come, and his Bride has made herself ready; it was granted her to clothe herself with fine linen, bright and pure—for the fine linen is the righteous deeds of the saints." (Revelation 19:6–8 ESV)

As for our other works before our regeneration, not so much. Cases of these deeds are best seen in the parables like the ten virgins in Matthew 25:1–13 and the rich fool in Luke 12:16–21.

Heavenly Choir for the Lamb on the Throne

And what a choir it is!

> And between the throne and the four living creatures and among the elders I saw a Lamb standing, as though it had been slain, with seven horns and with seven eyes, which are the seven spirits of God sent out into all the earth. And he went and took the scroll from the right hand of him who was seated on the throne. And when he had taken the scroll, the four living creatures and the twenty-four elders fell down before the Lamb, each holding a harp, and golden bowls full of incense, which are the prayers of the saints. And they sang a new song, saying, "Worthy are you to take the scroll and to open its seals, for you were slain, and by your blood you ransomed people for God from every tribe and language and people and nation, and you have made them a kingdom and priests to our God, and they shall reign on the earth."

> Then I looked, and I heard around the throne and the living creatures and the elders the voice of many angels, numbering myriads of myriads and thousands of thousands, saying with a loud voice, "Worthy is the Lamb who was slain, to receive power and wealth and wisdom and might and honor and glory and blessing!"

> And I heard every creature in heaven and on earth and under the earth and in the sea, and all that is in them, saying, "To him who sits on the throne and to the Lamb be blessing and honor and glory and might forever and ever!"

> And the four living creatures said, "Amen!" and the elders fell down and worshiped. (Revelation 5:6–14 ESV)

Green Pastures, Still Waters

What a comforting way to use just two adjectives. "He makes me lie down in green pastures. He leads me beside still waters" (Psalm 23:2 ESV). Green and still are likely to be only a tiny beginning that describes the beauty of where we are going.

Eternal Righteousness

No fangs will be needed. New dentures will certainly be issued to those that need them. "The wolf shall dwell with the lamb, and the leopard shall lie down with the young goat, and the calf and the lion and the fattened calf together; and a little child shall lead them" (Isaiah 11:6 ESV). Similarly, "The wolf and the lamb shall graze together; the lion shall eat straw like the ox, and dust shall be the serpent's food. They shall not hurt or destroy in all my holy mountain." (Isaiah 65:25 ESV).

If fishing is permitted, I'm guessing the policy will be "catch and release." Death has been destroyed, so we will likely eat just fruits and veggies from the orchards that line the banks of the river of life that flows from the throne of God. Think, "Garden of Eden."

No Mountains, No Valleys

The temporal world as we know it will be gone. "And every island fled away, and no mountains were to be found" (Revelation 16:17 ESV).

It appears that lots of changes are in the making. "And the mountains will melt under him, and the valleys will split open, like wax before the fire, like waters poured down a steep place" (Micah 1:4 ESV). Widespread restoration will take place.

Fire Purified Earth

Where will such flames that can destroy the whole earth with fire come from? Well, do you recall from our earlier thoughts that salt water burns? Salt water burns at a level comparable to the hottest flames on record. And there is plenty of fuel out there in the big pond. Many other sources of fire undoubtedly exist that are at God's disposal when He is ready. The Kilauea Cauldron on the Big Island of Hawaii gives us periodic reminders as it erupts molten lava across the landscape and into the sea. (Jude 1:7; Revelation 21:8 ESV).

Authority in Heaven

Jesus is King of Kings, Lord of Lords. "And Jesus came and said to them, 'All authority in heaven and on earth has been given to me.'" (Matthew 28:18 ESV).

And the dad said, "Jesus will win! Game over. We are home kids."

Worried?

In the meantime, maybe you have recently had a pacemaker implanted in your chest along with some new stents, and you are suddenly wondering where you will be when you get where you are going. My pacemaker and stents were implanted in 2006. Needless to say, I have had to curtail my physical activity. I occasionally tell patients that if they make it out of the room before I do, please push the nurses' call button for the chaplain on their way out.

Maybe you have recently been diagnosed with a life-threatening illness like clogged arteries, and you have been told you have to start dieting and exercising. My medications for that were long overdue by the time my chest started to feel like an elephant sat on me. You are thinking, "How did I get to here?" More still, my type two diabetes is on the attack: time for my daily insulin again. Lord, come quickly. Recall, at YH breathe in; at WH breathe out. YHWH, Father God, I love you for every breath I make.

Maybe "Worried?" is the wrong question. Perhaps you should be thinking, *How do I get to there?* For starters, look past current concerns. Time is ticking. Is the Great Physician saying to you, "Take a double dose of this and I will see you in the morning? I'm moving you to a *new room* tomorrow." "And the peace of God, which surpasses all understanding, will guard your hearts and your minds in Christ Jesus" (Philippians 4:7 ESV).

Maybe a loved one is suffering with dementia or Alzheimer's, and you have lost contact with him or her. Remember that hearing is one of the last senses to go and to be careful about what you say. Guard the person's soul and nurture it with your words. I have found that, like some other infirmities, there are periods when patients are more alert than others. I have carried on normal conversations with patients one day when two days before there was only a stare. At times like that I never forget to spend time praying aloud alongside the patient's bed. A chaplain friend of mine once shared with me that he was praying in such a manner and the patient, who was in a coma, sat up and thanked him for praying for her; she then laid back down and returned to her comatose state. He went home early that day.

Maybe a treasured loved one recently died after a long life. What happens to these people? Then you remember, as death was closing in, you asked that person to trust Jesus for all of his or her needs in the days ahead. Then you know the truth when you hear the words like I heard from my former mother-in-law when she answered saying, "I will, Bill. I promise I will." The Lord got them back. He does not miss words like that. Do you know where you will be when you get where you are going? Have you shared your personal conviction about loving Jesus with loved ones to comfort them?

Maybe you are normal, but you haven't even heard that it takes at least three pancakes to make a stack. Go back for "seconds" if necessary to get that spiritual pancake on top, where all the good stuff is—the butter, syrup, nuts, fruit, and whipped cream. The first two pancakes (physical and emotional) will be gone long before the one on top. It never goes away. When you know Jesus Christ on a personal level, you get to keep the good stuff forever.

Heaven and Hell

Jesus himself revealed to us what heaven is like in parables, but He also made it perfectly clear what hell is like by using simple direct terms.

Parables Reveal What Heaven Is Like			Whereas Hell Is Like	
Psalm 109:13–15 Luke 16:19–30	No memory of earth	T	Luke 16:19–30	Memory of earth
Matthew 18:12–14 Luke 15:3–7	The lost sheep	H E	Matthew 25:32–33	Goats on the left
Luke 12:16–21	A landowner, rich fool	E	Matthew 8:12 Luke 16:24	Gnashing of teeth, filth
Matthew 13:31–32 Mark 4:30–32 Luke 13:18–19	A mustard seed	G	2 Samuel 22:5–6 Revelation 14:11 Revelation 20:10 Revelation 21:8	Constant torture, suffering
Matthew 13:47–50	A net	R	Luke 16:23	Excessive torment, no rest
Matthew 13:33 Luke 13:20–21	Leaven/Yeast	E A	Mark 9:43–48 Luke 16:23 James 3:6	Fire and brimstones
Matthew 25:1–12	Ten virgins	T	Revelation 20:13–15	Lake of fire, bottomless pit
Matthew 20:1–16	Owner of a vineyard		2 Thessalonians 1:8–9	Those disobedient to God
Matthew 13:44	A treasure hidden	D	2 Thessalonians 1:8–9	Sorrows and pain at death
Matthew 13:45–46	A merchant looking	I	Mark 9:43–48	Worms that eat the body
Matthew 22:1–14 Luke 14:15–24	A king who prepared	V	Mark 9:43–48 Luke 16:23 James 3:6	Excessive heat, eternal fire
Matthew 13:3–25 Mark 4:1–20 Luke 8:5–15	A man who sowed	D	2 Peter 2:4	Separated from God, Angels and Saints
Luke 16:19–30	A rich man and the beggar, Lazarus	E	Psalm 9:17	Reprobates and wide gates
Mark 4:26–29	The seed growing secretly …		Romans 6:23	Wages of sin is death
Matthew 13:24–30	The wheat and the tares		Numbers 16:33 2 Chronicles 28:1–3 Revelation 19:20	Those that perished alive
Matthew 21:33–46 Mark 12:1–11 Luke 20:9–18	The wicked tenants		Jude 12. 13	Gloom of utter darkness
Matthew 24:32–36 Mark 13:28–32 Luke 21:29–33	Budding fig tree		Luke 16:25 2 Thessalonians 1:5–9	Torment will be mental and spiritual

Table 16. Heaven and Hell

Rope-a-Dope? Yes!

Picture a never-ending rope with a knot in it. It is your rope. We all have our own personal rope. None of us can stay in our knot forever.

- The ALPHA end of our lifeline has one common origin.

- Life is like a knot in our line, it is like a vapor.

- The OMEGA end of our lifeline has two uncommon destinations—Heaven and Hell.

- We must choose our destination while we are still in the knot; it is like claiming a fumble before the whistle blows.

- Claim Jesus; follow the sheep, not the goats.

- Enjoy eternity in paradise.

So, how will you get out of the knot you are now in?

Here is the altar call. Just accept, believe, and claim (ABC) Jesus Christ is Lord and sincerely mean it by confessing to Him that you cannot save yourself. You are totally dependent on His grace and mercy for salvation. Come to Jesus now!

The Ultimate Inappropriate Relationship with God

Satan Makes a Big Mistake

Mess with God like Satan did, and you are in big trouble. Don't mess with God! Satan tries to rise above God, which is the ultimate blasphemy.

We Cannot Make the Same Mistake

If we try to do what Satan did, we commit the only unforgivable sin—blasphemy of the Spirit of God. Blasphemy of the Spirit of God carries the penalty of continued separation from God and eternal death in the lake of fire along with Satan, all of his fallen angels, and others who made the same unforgivable fatal mistake.

Jesus' Last Personal Instruction and Call to Action

The Great Commission

The Great Commission says,

> And Jesus came and said to them, "All authority in heaven and on earth has been given to me. Go therefore and make disciples of all nations, baptizing them in the name of the Father and of the Son and of the Holy Spirit, teaching them to observe all that I have commanded you. And behold, I am with you always, to the end of the age." (Matthew 28:18–20 ESV).

A Promise for Help

Consider the following promise from Jesus for the Father to send us a Paraclete, the Holy Spirit.

> These things I have spoken to you while I am still with you. But the Helper, the Holy Spirit, whom the Father will send in my name, he will teach you all things and bring to your remembrance all that I have said to you. Peace I leave with you; my peace I give to you. Not as the world gives do I give to you. Let not your hearts be troubled, neither let them be afraid. You heard me say to you, "I am going away, and I will come to you." If you loved me, you would have rejoiced, because I am going to the Father, for the Father is greater than I. And now I have told you before it takes place, so that when it does take place you may believe. I will no longer talk much with you, for the ruler of this world is coming. He has no claim on me, but I do as the Father has commanded me, so that the world may know that I love the Father. Rise, let us go from here. (John 14:25–31 ESV)

Do you believe Jesus is who He says He is? Do you do what He says? Then rise, go from here! Go yesterday!

Pastoral Prayer, Benediction, and Blessing.

Pastoral Prayer

Jesus stands at the door and knocks. Let Him into your heart as we pray together.

Our heavenly Father, we love You. We thank You for your incredible gift of salvation through Your Son, Jesus Christ. We praise You for knowing that we can never be lost to your Holy Spirit. We lift up each other in prayer in body, mind, and spirit, both here and afar, both now and always. Bless us all with love, hope, and faith.

As we continue to pray, I invite all of my readers to come to Jesus in your heart. You may never have made a personal commitment to accept Jesus Christ as your Lord and Savior. You may fear coming before Him privately or publicly. Just remember that Jesus died for you publicly. He suffered a cruel death on a rugged cross. But now He sits on His throne in heaven on the right-hand side of almighty God, our Father. If you have never given your heart to Jesus, then allow your heart to melt. Come now. Jesus is tenderly and patiently waiting for you. Come to Jesus!

Lord Jesus, shine Your face upon us that we may be saved by Your blood, which You shed on the cross for us. Come, Lord Jesus, ransom our captive hearts, redeem our sinful hearts, and create in us new hearts. Teach us to live the prayer You taught us, saying,

> Our Father in heaven, hallowed be your name. Your kingdom come, your will be done, on earth as it is in heaven. Give us this day our daily bread, and forgive us our debts, as we also have forgiven our debtors. And lead us not into temptation, but deliver us from evil. For yours is the kingdom and the power and the glory, forever. Amen (Matthew 6:9-13 ESV)

Benediction

Jude's doxology includes the following words of hope:

> Now to him who is able to keep you from stumbling and to present you blameless before the presence of his glory with great joy, to the only God, our Savior, through Jesus Christ our Lord, be glory, majesty, dominion, and authority, before all time and now and forever. Amen (Jude 1:24–25 ESV).

Blessings from the Past

May an old Irish blessing still ring true in our hearts today as we travel on our common road to get where are going.

> May the road rise up to meet you.
>
> May the wind always be at your back.
>
> May the sun shine warm upon your face,
>
> and rains fall soft upon your fields.
>
> Until we meet again,
>
> May God hold you in the palm of His hands.

Go in peace; heaven is waiting. I'll meet you there!

Appendices

Appendix A: Figures

Table of Figures

Appendix B: Tables

Table of Tables

Appendix C: Key Terms

Mission	5, 6, 8, 18, 34, 35, 37, 38, 40, 58, 61, 65, 96, 100, 111, 136, 137, 143, 164, 171, 172, 177
New Jerusalem	21, 49, 50, 87, 88, 101, 150, 152, 167, 172, 179
Objective	5, 6, 42, 46, 60, 144, 172
Omnidirectional	26, 37, 42, 136, 172
Omnipotent	26, 37, 42, 83, 136, 172
Omnipresent	26, 37, 42, 136, 172
Omni-righteous	26, 37, 42, 136, 172
Omniscient	35, 46, 50, 85, 168
Outcomes	5, 6, 55, 172
Outputs	5, 6, 55, 172
Pancakes	11, 12, 13, 16, 20, 95, 161, 172
Perfect kingdom	7, 11, 21, 42, 49, 73, 172
Purified by fire	8, 172
Qualities	5, 6, 28, 102, 172
Rapture	7, 8, 20, 49, 68, 113, 142, 143, 172
Relationship	vii, 2, 10, 12, 13, 14, 15, 16, 18, 21, 22, 24, 25, 26, 27, 28, 30, 31, 33, 36, 37, 41, 44, 50, 55, 56, 63, 77, 89, 91, 97, 98, 99, 100, 101, 102, 106, 113, 115, 116, 118, 119, 120, 122, 124, 126, 129, 136, 139, 140, 142, 149, 163, 167, 168, 173
Remorse	4, 33, 37, 39, 45, 69, 71,72, 108, 111, 113, 139, 142, 159, 173
Repent	vi, 6, 17, 33, 37, 39, 45, 55, 56, 66, 69, 71, 72, 103, 108, 111, 111, 112, 113, 122, 131, 139, 142, 149, 159, 173
Saints	6, 8, 20, 29, 37, 53, 101, 105, 107, 129, 132, 134, 136, 142, 143, 144, 145, 151, 155, 158, 159, 162, 173
Salvation	1, 3, 5, 6, 8, 9, 10, 11, 36, 37, 39, 49, 42, 46, 47, 52, 53, 55, 56, 62, 65, 68, 69, 70, 73, 75, 97, 104, 105, 108, 109, 110, 113, 122, 128, 130, 133, 134, 135, 144, 146, 155, 157, 163, 165, 173, 185
Same god	15, 17, 173
Satan	viii, 3, 6, 7, 9, 12, 16, 21, 22, 24, 25, 26, 31, 44, 48, 63, 65, 70, 72, 73, 74, 75, 77, 78, 79, 80, 81, 82, 83, 84, 85, 92, 99, 100, 101, 104, 125, 126, 128, 141, 143, 144, 145, 163
Separated from God	8, 162, 173
Soul	vii, viii, 1, 3, 4, 5, 6, 7, 12, 13, 14, 16, 21, 22, 26, 37, 38, 40, 43, 45, 47, 49, 54, 57, 60, 61, 62, 67, 75, 76, 84, 97, 99, 101, 115, 123, 127, 139, 140, 143, 144, 161, 173
Spirit of God	v, vii, 1, 5, 11, 13, 15, 19, 27, 29, 35, 39, 40, 44, 45, 46, 49, 72, 94, 100, 105, 106, 108, 113, 117, 122, 126, 128, 136, 139, 142, 150, 163, 173

Table of Key Terms

Appendix D: Table of ESV Scripture Citations

1 Corinthians	10:13; 13:12; 13:4-7; 15:24-28; 2-11; 3:16; 6:9-10	7
1 John	1:2:10; 1:9; 2:15-17; 3:2; 3:20; 5:12	6
1 Peter	1:13; 1:2-5; 2:4-10	3
1 Thessalonians	1:5; 2:19-20	2
1 Timothy	4:4; 6:9-10	2
2 Corinthians	12:9; 4:16-18; 5:10; 6:4-10; 7:10	5
2 Peter	1:3-11; 3:13; 3:8; 3:9-14	4
2 Thessalonians	2:13-14; 3:10	3
2 Timothy	1:8; 2:10; 2:19; 3:16;	4
Acts	16:30; 16:31; 17:30; 2:21; 2:38; 2:47	6
Amos	7:7-8	1
Colossians	1:12-14; 1:13; 1:15-16; 3:1-17; 3:23; 3:3; 3:18-17	7
Daniel	10:5-12; 10:6-7; 9:9;	3
Deuteronomy	32:4; 7:9	1
Ecclesiastes	12:13; 3:2	2
Ephesians	5:8; 6:7-8; 1:3-14; 1:4-14; 1:4-23; 1:7; 2:1-10; 2:8; 2:8-10; 2:8-9; 3:14-19; 4:24; 4:26; 5:5; 6:10-20	15
Exodus	14:13; 19:5-8; 20:1-17; 20:14; 20:17;	5
Ezekiel	1:15-21; 10:9-14; 11:22; 28:17-18; 36:26-27; 38:2-3	6
Galatians	5:16-26; 5:19-20	2
Genesis	12:1-3; 22:13-18	2
Hebrews	11:1; 11:39-12:2; 11:6; 12:1; 13:5; 4:12	6
Isaiah	11:1-5; 14:12-14; 53:6; 55:7; 55:8; 58:9; 6:2; 64:6; 65:25	9
James	1:12; 1:14-15; 1:15: 2:14-26; 5:12; 5:16;	6
Jeremiah	1:1-15; 31:31	2
Job	31:11-12; 38:4	2
Joel	2:32	1
John	1:12; 1:12-14; 1:14; 1:1-5; 1:14; 1:18; 10:16; 10:27-29; 10:28; 10:7-11; 14:1-31; 15:10; 15:13; 15:14; 15:16; 15:4-5; 17:12; 17:1-26; 17:17-18; 17:6; 3:17; 3:18; 3:19; 3:20; 3:21; 3:2-21; 3:27; 3:3; 3:36; 3:8; 5:13; 5:24; 6:29; 6:35-44; 6:44-45; 6:47-54	34
Jude	1:24-25; 1:7	2
Luke	1:68-79: 12:10; 12:15; 12:16-21; 13:29; 13:3; 14:21; 16:19-25; 13:29; 13:3; 14:21; 16:19-25; 13:3; 14:21; 16:19-25; 16:22-23; 23:39-43; 24:44-48; 24:47; 9:23; 9:26;	14
Mark	10:43-45; 16:15; 16:16; 3:29; 6:31; 7:20-23; 8:34; 8:35; 8:36; 8:37; 8:	12

Matthew	10:16-17; 10:16-23; 10:28; 10:39; 11:15; 16:17-19; 16:18-19; 17:1-13; 17:19-20; 18:20; 19:13-15; 19:16-22; 21:28-45; 22:37-40; 24:22; 24:31; 24:4-14; 25:26; 25:41-46; 27:18; 28:16-20; 28:18; 28:19-20; 4:1-11; 4:17; 5:16; 5:17-19; 5:21-26; 5:28; 5:37; 6:13; 6:19-24; 6:25-34; 6:9-13; 7:23;	35
Micah	1:4	1
Philemon	1:14; 1:29; 2:10-11; 2:15; 4:25; 4:7	6
Proverbs	1:7; 13:4; 14:30; 16:18-19; 22:4; 23:2; 23:20-21; 28:7; 6:18-19; 8:22-31; 9:10	11
Psalm	10:4; 100:1-5; 109:13-15; 130:3-4; 139; 147:4-5; 18:31-36; 23:2; 32:3; 46:1-11; 51:1-19; 7:12; 90:1-17; 92:5-9; 95:7; 98:4-9	16
Revelation	1:10-20; 11:19; 12:7-12; 13:1-18; 13:7-9; 14:13; 14:1-5; 15:2; 16:17; 17:7-9; 17:8; 19:13; 19:6-8; 20:11-15; 20:14; 20:1-6; 20:7-10; 21:1-2; 21:12-14: 21:21; 21:1-4; 21:15-21; 21:16; 21:18; 21:19-20; 21:22-27; 21:8; 22:12; 22:1-5; 22:17; 22:18-20; 22:4; 3:20; 3:4-6; 4:1-8; 4:6; 4:9-11; 5:1-5; 5:6-14; 5:8; 7:16-17; 9:17	40
Romans	1:1; 10:10; 10:12-15; 10:17; 10:9; 11:26-36; 11:5-7; 12:1-2; 14:10-12; 16:20; 3:23; 3:28; 3:29-31; 4:1-25; 5:12; 5:8; 5:9-10; 6:23; 7:15-25; 7:4-12; 8:1; 8:21-25; 8:26; 8:21-39; 8:33; 8:36; 8:38-39	27
Total	*Citations*	*310*

Table of ESV Scripture Citations

Appendix E: **About the Author**

Jesse W. "Bill" Addison (January 26, 1945–present) has, until recently, served as a hospital chaplain ordained and commissioned by the Southern Baptist Convention and the North American Mission Board respectively.

After living in multiple broken early childhood homes and a church-sponsored children's home during high school, Bill attended Tyler Junior College in Tyler, Texas, in the fall of 1962. Prior to graduating from Texas State University in 1969 with a degree in business management, Bill taught high school math in San Antonio as a means of working through the remainder of college. Following graduation, he volunteered for service as a U.S. Marine. Bill completed officer candidate school in January of 1969 and went on to perform duties as a logistics and data systems officer. He retired from active duty in October 1991 as a lieutenant colonel, distinguishing himself by his individual professional service in the Marines with one U.S. Navy Commendation Medal and two U.S. Meritorious Service medals.

Bill later served the state of Texas for a total of thirteen years in Austin, conducting multiple audits of agency-wide programs and performing managerial duties within state agencies. Along the way he also completed an accounting degree from Park University, a master's in business management and accounting from National University, and five professional managerial, accounting, and auditing certifications before answering God's long-standing call to ministry.

Following the loss of his first wife, Judy, to breast cancer in 2003, Bill attended seminary at Memphis Theological Seminary, where he graduated in 2007 with a Master of Divinity degree (*magna cum laude*). He has served as a chaplain intern in two VA hospitals and has served as a part-time volunteer hospital chaplain in the Houston area for ten years. Additionally, Bill fulfills pulpit supply opportunities for churches in the greater Houston area and he teaches Bible study a Harris-Montgomery County neighborhood community as the need arises. Bill has two married daughters and three grandchildren. His second wife, Christi, has two children and seven grandchildren.

Bibliography

Addison, Jesse W. 2015. *Where Will You Be When You Get Where You Are Going? Make A Personal Theo-metric Assessment.* 1st. Vol. Original color coordinated text version. Bloomington, IN: WestBow Press.

Alcorn, Randy. 2004. *Heaven.* Carol Stream, IL: Tyndale House Publishers, Inc.

—. 2003. *The Law of Rewards: Giving What You Can't To Gain What You Can't Lose.* Carol Stream, IL: Tyndale House Publishers, Inc.

Assembly, The Westminster. 2018. *The Baptist Confession of Faith 1689.* Carlisle, PA: The Banner of Truth Trust.

Blackaby, Henry T., Claude V. King. 1993. *Fresh Encounter: A Plumb Line for God's People (Member's Book 2).* Nashville: Lifeway Press.

Blanchard, Kenneth, Spencer Johnson. 1981. *The One Minute Manager (1 minute goals, praisings and reprimands).* New York, New York: Harper Collins.

Brown, Francis E. 2006. *Biblical Faith: Growing Strong In The Faith Passing It On To Others.* First. Edited by Francis E. Brown. Conroe, Texas: Francis E. Brown.

Brumley, Albert E. 1932. "I'll Fly Away." *Wonderful Message.*

Burpo, Todd, Sonja Burpo, Lynn Vincent, Colton Burpo. 2010. *Heaven is For Real: A Little Boy's Astounding Story of His Trip to Heaven and Back.* Nashville: Thomas Nelson, Inc.

Carlson, Jason, Ron Carlson. 2005. "Is the Bible the Inspired Word of God?" *Christian Ministries, Inc.* Accessed July 24, 2011. http://www.christianministriesintl.org/articles/05.html.

Carlson, Richard. 1997. *Don't Sweat the Small Stuff . . . and it's all small stuff.* New York: Hyperion.

Churchill, Winston S. 2004. *Never Give In!: The Best of Winston Churchill's Speeches.* November 10, 2004. New York: Hyperion.

Clower, Jerry, The Mississippi Writer's Page. 2008. *http://www.olemiss.edu/mwp/dir/clower_jerry/index.html.* Edited by John B. Padgett. University of Mississippi. November 11. Accessed October 28, 2014. http://www.olemiss.edu/mwp/dir/clower_jerry/index.html.

Crossway Bibles. 2001. *OpenBible.info*. Crossway Bibles. Accessed November 1, 2014. http://www. openbible.info/.

DeHaan, M. R. 1995. *Portraits of Christ in Genesis*. Grand Rapids: Kregel Publications.

Dobson, James. 1998. *Faithful Travelers. A Father. A Daughter. A Fly-Fishing Journey of the Heart*. New York: Bantam Books.

Eade, Alfred Thompson. 1961. *The Expanded Panorama Bible Study Course: From the Creation of the Angels to the New Jerusalem*. Grand Rapids: Fleming H. Revell Co. (A division of Baker Book House Co.).

Edwards, Jonathan. 1856. *"Sinners in the Hands of an Angry God." (Sermon Preached at the Music Hall, Royal Surrey Gardens, Kennington, London)*. Edited by Harry S. Stout. December 7. Accessed July 15, 2011. http://edwards.yale.edu/archive?path=aHR0cDovL2Vkd2FyZHMueWFsZS5lZHU vY2dpLWJpbi9uZXdwaGlsby9nZXRvYmplY3QucGw/Yy4yMTo0Ny53amVVv.

Emmons, D. D. 2003. "Letting Go." *The Upper Room*, June 9, 2003 ed.

Espinosa, Eddie. 1982. *Change My Heart, Oh God*. Baptist Hymnal 2008. Accessed Dec 2012. http:// www.hymnary.org/tune/change_my_heart_espinosa.

Foster, Richard J. 1992. *Prayer: Finding the Heart's True Home*. 1st Edition. San Francisco, CA: Harper Collins Publishers. Accessed November 5, 2013.

Galloway, Bryan. 2008. *bonhoefferblog: Can Dietrich Bonhoeffer make a difference in twenty-first century preachers and preaching?* WordPress.com. February. Accessed March 28, 2014. https:// bonhoefferblog.wordpress.com/tag/prayer-and-intercession/.

Gorsuch, Nancy J. 1999. *Pastoral Visitation*. Minneapolis: Fortress Press.

Graham, Billy. 1981. *Till Armageddon: A Perspective on Suffering*. Minneapolis, MN: Grason.

Handel, George Frideric. 1997. "http://www.hymnary.org/tune/hallelujah_chorus_handel." *http:// www.hymnary.org*. Calvin College. Accessed November 7, 2014. http://www.hymnary.org/tune/ hallelujah_chorus_handel.

Hill, Jim. 1983. *What a Day That Will Be*. #607 Baptist Hymnal 2008. Accessed February 17, 2014. http://www.hymnary.org/hymn/BH2008/607.

Hook, Jr., R. C., Hawaiian Memorial Park Mortuary. 2014. *Dr. Ralph Clifford Hook, Jr.* January 14. Accessed October 28, 2014. http://www.hawaiianmemorialparkmortuary.com/obituaries/Ralph-Hook/?wms_redirected=1#!/Obituary.

Hurco Applications. 2014. *Five Axis Machining.* January 10. Accessed October 31, 2014. http://www. fiveaxismachining.com/.

Johnson, Spencer. 2003. *The Present: The Secret to Enjoying Your Work And Life, Now!* New York: Doubleday (a division of Random House).

—. 2002. *Who Moved My Cheese? An A-Mazing Way To Deal With Change In Your Work And In Your Life.* New York: G. P. Putnam's Sons.

Judge Antonin Scalia, Supreme Court Justice, interview by Tom Krattenmaker. 2013. *What's With All The Talk of the Devil?* McLean, VA: USA Today, A Gannett Company, (November 25). Accessed November 26, 2013.

Kierkengaard, Soren. 1985. *Fear and Trembling.* New York: Penguin Putnam, Inc.

Kirkland, A. J. 1970. *Methods in Sermonizing.* Texarkana, TX: Bogard Press.

Larkin, Clarence. 1918. *Dispensational Truth or God's Plan and Purpose in the Ages.* Mansfield Centre, CT: Martino Publishing.

Larson, Rick. 2011. *The Star of Bethlehem: Unlock the Mystery of the World's Most Famous Star.* MPower Pictures, LLC. Accessed 12 13, 2013. http://www.bethlehemstarmovie.com/.

LaRue, The Rev. Dr. Cleo. n.d. *Day 1 (Formerly "The Protestant Hour").* Princeton, NJ Princeton Theological Seminary. Accessed October 30, 2014. http://day1.org/383-the_rev_dr_cleo_larue.

Lewis, C. S. 1962. *The Screwtape Letters.* New York, New York: The McMillan Company. Accessed November 27, 2013.

Lutzer, Erwin W. 1998. *Your Eternal Reward: Triumph & Tears at the Judgment Seat of Christ.* Chicago: Moody Publishers.

McDonald, Mary. 1997. "Sheet Music Plus, World's Largest Sheet Music Selection." *http://www. sheetmusicplus.com.* Lorenz Publishing Company. Accessed October 26, 2013. http://www. sheetmusicplus.com/title/i-m-goin-up-sheet-music/19581585?ac=1.

Moody, D. L. 1966. *Moody's Anecodotes, Incidents and Illustrations.* Chicago: The Moody Press.

Mote, Edward. 1834. *Timeless Truths Publications A Free Online Library.* Timeless Truths Production Company. Accessed October 31, 2014. http://library.timelesstruths.org/music/The_Solid_Rock/.

Moyer, Harold J. 1956. "Balm in Gilead." *Baptist Hymnal 2008, #119.* Jeremiah 8:22. http://www. hymnary.org/text/sometimes_i_feel_discouraged_spiritual.

Newton, John. 1779. "Amazing Grace." *Baptist Hymnal 2008, #104.*

Peters, Mark. 2010. *Which Way Is Up? (From Amongst All the Chaos!).* Peoria, AZ: Intermedia Publishing Group, Inc.

Philpott, Kent. 2005. *Are You Really Born Again? Understanding True and False Conversion.* Webster, NY and Mill Valley, CA, NY and CA: Evangelical Press and Earthen Vessel Publishing.

Piper, Don. 2004. *Ninety Minutes in Heaven.* Grand Rapids, MI: Revell.

Piper, John. 2009. "Do I Have to Confess My Sin to Another Person In Order to Be Forgiven?" *desiringGod.* desiringGod.org. May 29. Accessed November 6, 2013. http://www.desiringgod.org/resource-library/ask-pastor-john/do-i-have-to-confess-my-sin-to-another-person-in-order-to-be-forgiven.

Presbyterian Church (USA). 2002. *The Book of Confessions, Part 1 of the Constitution of the PCUSA.* Edited by General Assembly PCUSA. Vol. 1. 2 vols. Louisville, KY: Office of the General Assembly. http://oga.pcusa.org/section/mid-council-ministries/constitutional-services/constitution/.

Providence Baptist Ministries. 2014. *Baptist History Throughout the Ages.* Accessed October 30, 2014. http://www.pbministries.org/History/Origin%20and%20Perpetuity/origin_02.htm.

Riddle, Dewight & Sharon. 2013. "Experiencing Worship." *Effective Worship.* Edited by EXW Staff. October 29. Accessed November 5, 2013. http://www.experiencingworship.com/articles/general/2002-1-10-Principles-.html.

Roach, John. 2007. *National Geographic News: Salt Water Can "Burn," Scientist Confirms.* September 14. Accessed October 30, 2014.

Russell, A. J., ed. 1978. *God Calling.* New York: Jove Books.

RW Research, Inc. 2003. "Family Tree of Denominations." *Denominations Comparison Chart.* Torrence, CA: Rose Publishing, Inc.

Smalley, Gary and John Trent. 1991. *The Language of Love.* New York: Pocket Books.

Southern Baptist Convention. 1845. "Baptist Faith and Message 2000." *http://www.sbc.net/.* Agusta, GA: Southern Baptist Convention, May 8-12.

Sproul, R. C., Archie Parrish. 2008. *The Spirit of Revival: Discovering the Wisdom of Jonathan Edwards.* Wheaton, IL: Crossway Books.

Spurgeon, C. H. 1741. *"Turn or Burn." (Sermon Preached at Enfield, Connecticut).* Edited by Phillip R. Johnson. Phillip R. Johnson. July 8. Accessed July 15, 2011. http://www.spurgeon.org/sermons/0106.htm.

—. 2006. *Spurgeon's Sermons on Jesus and the Holy Spirit.* Peabody, MA: Hendrickson Publishers, Inc.

Stachniewski, John, Anita Pacheco. 1998. *John Bunyan Grace Abounding: With Other Spiritual Autobiographies.* New York: Oxford University Press, Inc.

Stanley, Charles F. 2005. *Living in the Power of the Holy Spirit.* Nashville: Thomas Nelson, Inc.

Stephen Ministries. 2013. *Stephen Ministries St. Louis.* Edited by Ph.D. Rev. Kenneth C. Haugk. Accessed October 29, 2014. http://www.stephenministries.org/.

Stone, Howard, James Duke. 1996. *How to Think Theologically.* Minneapolis: Fortress Press.

Strobel, Lee. 2000. *The Case for Faith.* Grand Rapids, Michigan: Zondervan.

Theopedia, an Encyclopedia of Biblical Christianity. n.d. *Five Solas.* Christian Web Foundation. Accessed February 8, 2014. http://www.theopedia.com/Five_Solas.

Thomas, Frank A. 1997. *They Like to Never Quit Praisin' God: The Role of Celebration in Preaching.* Cleveland: The Pilgrim Press.

Tozer, A. W. 2013. *The Knowledge of the Holy: What Every Christian Should Know.* North Charleston, SC: CreateSpace Independent Publishing Platform.

US Department of State. 2014. *About Education.* Outline of the U.S. Economy" by Conte and Carr. Accessed October 29, 2014. http://economics.about.com/od/foreigntrade/a/bretton_woods.htm.

Vedder, Henry C. 1907. *A Short History of the Baptists.* Valley Froge, Pennsylvania: Judson Press. Accessed November 23, 2013.

Vines, Jerry. 2008. ""The Greatest Single Verse in the Bible" preached at the John 3:16 Conference held by Jerry Vines Ministries at FBC Woodstock, GA." *Jerry Vines Ministries, Woodstock, GA.* November 6. Accessed July 24, 2011. http://www.jerryvines.com/.

Vines, Jerry, Jim Shaddix. 1999. *Power in the Pulpit: How to Prepare and Deliver Expository Sermons.* Chicago: Moody Press.

Wikipedia, The Free Encyclopedia. 2011. *3-D Printing.* Wikimedia Foundation. July 8. Accessed February 15, 2014. http://en.wikipedia.org/wiki/3D_printing.

—. 2014. *Helen Keller.* Wikimedia Foundation, Inc. . October 22. Accessed October 29, 2014. http://en.wikipedia.org/wiki/Helen_Keller.

—. 2011. *Millennialism.* Wikimedia Foundation. July 22. Accessed July 22, 2011. http://en.wikipedia.org/wiki/Millennialism.

—. 2011. *Twelve-step Program.* Wikimedia Foundation. July 11. Accessed July 11, 2011. http://en.wikipedia.org/wiki/Twelve-step_program.

Wilson, Jim. 1983. *Principles of War: A Handbook on Strategic Evangelism*. Moscow, Idaho: Community Christian Ministries.

Wilson, Paul S. 2010. *Sistene Chapel Virtual Tour*. Edited by Paul S. Wilson. Connelly Gallery Villanova University. January 28. Accessed October 28, 2014. http://www.paulswilson.net/newsite/.

Wilson, Raymond. 2013. "Jenner of George Street." *Spiritlessons.com*. January 28. Accessed January 28, 2013. http://spiritlessons.com/Documents/Frank_Jenner/Frank_Jenner_of_George_Street.pdf.

Yahoo Finance by Peter Gorenstein and Farnoosh Torabi. 2010. "Financially Fit, Smart Living and Living Well." *Yahoo Inc. Web site*. Yahoo.com. October 2010. Accessed July 23, 2011. http://financiallyfit.yahoo.com/finance/article-110926-6907-5-top-5-tips-to-build-wealth-and-success?ywaad=ad0035&nc.

Endnotes

1   (Hook)
2   (Clower)
3   (DeHaan, 155)
4   (Hill)
5   (Wikipedia: The Free Encyclopedia, "Twelve-step program.")
6   (Edwards)
7   (Wikipedia: The Free Encyclopedia, "3-D printing.")
8   (Hurco)
9   (P. Wilson)
10 (Smalley, 26)
11 (US Department of State)
12 (Wikipedia: The Free Encyclopedia, "Helen Keller.")
13 (Stephen Ministries)
14 (LaRue)
15 (RW Research, Inc.)
16 (Baptist History Throughout the Ages)
17 (Vedder, 3, 69)
18 (R. Wilson)
19 (McDonald)
20 (Brumley 1932)
21 (Peters, 61)
22 (Presbyterian Church (USA), 11)
23 (Presbyterian Church (USA), 52)
24 (Presbyterian Church (USA), 121)
25 (Southern Baptist Convention, BF&M 2000)
26 (Handel)
27 (Brown, 34)
28 (Thomas, 26)
29 (Espinosa)
30 (J. R. Carlson)
31 (Theopedia, an Encyclopedia of Biblical Christianity. Five Solas)
32 (J. Vines)
33 (Riddle)
34 (Presbyterian Church (USA), 185)
35 (Presbyterian Church (USA), 107)
36 (Foster, 191)
37 (Galloway)
38 (J. Piper)
39 (Presbyterian Church (USA), 84)
40 (Mote)
41 (Lewis, v.)
42 (Judge Antonin Scalia)

43 (R. Carlson, 19)
44 (Johnson, The Present: The Secret to Enjoying Your Work and Life, Now!, 61)
45 (Johnson, Who Moved My Cheese? An A-Mazing Way to Deal with Change in Your Work and in Your Life, 74)
46 (Emmons)
47 (Newton)
48 (Thomas, 19)
49 (Verses 16-21 should be read as one complete stream of thought.)
50 (Moody, 28)
51 (Lewis, *vii.*)
52 (Philpott, 26-28; 112-113; 132-133; 140-151)
53 (Larkin, 174)
54 (Spurgeon, "Turn or Burn," sermon preached at Enfield, Connecticut)
55 (Lewis, *vii.*)
56 (J. Wilson, 27)
57 (Crossway—Webpage menu item, "Cross References")
58 (Gorsuch, 16)
59 (J. Wilson, 9)
60 (Yahoo Finance by Peter Gorenstein and Farnoosh Torabi)
61 (Thomas, 26)
62 (Moyer)
63 (Eade, 9, 191-192)
64 (Philpott, 21)
65 (Presbyterian Church (USA), 13)
66 (Southern Baptist Convention, BF&M, Article IV. Salvation).
67 (Spurgeon, "Turn or Burn," sermon preached at Enfield, Connecticut)
68 (Kierkegaard, 23, 95)
69 (Churchill)
70 (Stone, 113)
71 (DeHann, 187)
72 (DeHann, 187)
73 (Larson)
74 (Blackaby, 36)
75 (Wikipedia: The Free Encyclopedia, "Millennialism.")
76 (Roach)
77 (Lutzer, 10)
78 (Lutzer, 10)
79 (Alcorn, 67)
80 (Kirkland, 26)
81 (Alcorn)
82 (Burpo, 73)
83 (D. Piper, 79)
84 (Peters, 176)
85 (Tozer, 244)
86 (Eade, 9)